Created and Directed by Hans Höfer

INSIGHT
GUIDES

PUERTO RICO

Photography by Bill Wassman and others

Edited by Chris Caldwell and Tad Ames

APA PUBLICATIONS

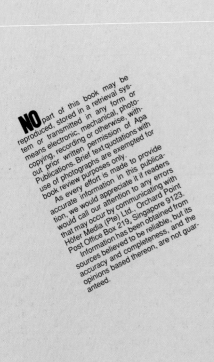
PUERTO RICO

First Edition (3rd Reprint)
© **1991 APA PUBLICATIONS (HK) LTD**
All Rights Reserved
Printed in Singapore by Höfer Press Pte. Ltd

ABOUT THIS BOOK

The resounding success of APA Publications' first Caribbean title, *Jamaica*, published in 1982, and the warm receipt of *Bahamas* (1986) and *Barbados* (1986) by readers and critics alike, were enough to convince founder-publisher **Hans Höfer** that readers were ready for more *Insight Guides* to that region. And *Puerto Rico*, now in your hands, is by no means APA Publications' concluding title on the Caribbean arena, but is regarded as imminent in its efforts to portray leading tourist destinations through its highly acclaimed *Insight Guides* series.

APA Publications' innovative approach to creating travel chronicles has been honored throughout the world. Since Hans Höfer established APA in 1970, the *Insight Guides* series has won worldwide recognition for its sensitive cultural portrayal of leading travel destinations. Höfer has always believed in providing travelers with a new concept type of guide – one that would offer a more insightful look at a country than traditional books did.

APA Publications lost no time in stringing together the perfect team of experts and insiders. While Höfer continues to be the mastermind behind the *Insight Guides* series, 1983 graduate of Harvard University, **Christopher Caldwell**, headed the book's project team. Caldwell worked for three years as a freelance journalist in England and the United States. He was editor of the 1984 edition of *Let's Go: Europe* and has written for such travel guides as *Let's Go: Britain and Ireland* and the popular *Traveller's Survival Kit: USA and Canada*, published at Oxford. Caldwell spent a few months in Puerto Rico, gathering material and contacting local writers and photographers. He traveled all over the island, writing the chapters on San Juan, the Northwest and the Southeast, and selected destinations on the Northeast.

Project co-editor **Tad Ames** pulled the raw material of the book into its final form, seeing to the details needed to ready the book for publication. After graduating from Yale University in 1984, he spent a year reporting police news for a small daily newspaper in Connecticut. Now employed as an editorial writer for the Berkshire *Eagle* in Pittsfield, Massachusets, Ames, a native of Portland, Oregon, has also worked as a writing instructor at Yale.

The principal photographer for this volume was **Bill Wassman**, a resident of New York whose work first attracted international attention in *Insight Guide: Nepal*. Wassman also spent months poking his Leicas into every part of Puerto Rico, gathering literally mountains of pictures despite incurring misfortune upon misfortune during his long expedition through the landscape, greatest of which was the temperamental behavior of his rented bicycle. A graduate of Indiana University in Comparative Literature and Anthropology, Wassman worked as an assistant to photographers Eric Meola and Pete Turner in 1973 and 1974 before establishing his own reputation.

Sarah Ellison Caldwell, whose marriage to Christopher Caldwell temporarily interrupted the book's production, spent long hours in Cambridge libraries shaping her history of Puerto Rico, which opens this volume. She also wrote the article on Rum in the feature of the book. A recent Harvard graduate, Mrs. Caldwell is the author of *Instruments of Conquest*, a comparison of British and Spanish colonial policies in the

Sarah & Chris Caldwell

Wassman

Cherson

American Southeast. The Caldwells live in London.

Webster and **Robert Stone** are San Franciscans who covered the Northeast and Islands. Shortly after Webster's graduation from Harvard, the two coauthored *Zit Wars*, a humorous look at dermatological problems, recently published by Arbor House.

Angelo Lopez, a Texan and another Harvard graduate, spent a number of weeks crossing Puerto Rico in a rented Mitsubishi, capturing the rugged contours of the Cordillera Central in his well-honed prose. A published writer of fiction, Lopez lives in Los Angeles, where he is currently writing screenplays.

San Juan native **Adam Cherson** is an actor and writer living in New York, after graduating from Harvard, Cherson worked as a consultant in arts management. Cherson wrote the language feature, "Let's Hablar Boricua," and delved into his leviathan salsa collection to research "Salsa: Rhythm of the Tropics."

Kathleen O'Connell, author of the "X" feature on life in Puerto Rico, is , in the Puerto Rican lexicon, a part-time Continental. O'Connell is the arts editor of the Middletown (Conneticut) *Press*, but she spends every possible week off on the island with members of her family there. Kathy has roots of her own on the island: she graduated in 1966 from Academia San Ignacio, a primary school.

Hanne-Maria Maijala attributes her taste for the balmier climes to having grown up in Finland and Canada. In 1985, she graduated from Harvard after editing a literary journal, playing rugby, and completing her B.A. in French and English literature. Since then, she has done editorial work for Little, Brown & Co. in Boston, and is currently working as a financial analyst in New York. Her writing has been published in a number of U.S. and Canadian magazines, and broadcast on CBC (Canadian National Radio) on several occasions. She has traveled in Europe, the Caribbean, Australia, New Zealand and French Polynesia.

Eleanora Abreau Jimenez, who wrote the feature on Puerto Rican cuisine , is a native of Guaynabo, Puerto Rico, studying medicine at the University of Puerto Rico at Río Piedras. Abreau attended Tulane University.

Susan Hambleton ("Art"), is an artist from New York who lives and work there. Hambleton passed much of the last two decades in India. While in Puerto Rico, she traveled indefatigably between Old San Juan and Ponce to find the last word on the Puerto Rican art scene.

Finally, without the contributions of Executive Director **Adam Liptak**, the book would have collapsed under its own weight. Liptak served as liaison between the various editors, authors and publisher Höfer, all the while juggling academic responsibility at Yale Law School. Liptak, who has worked with APA since January 1984, is also a former employee of the *New York Times*.

Other contributors and people who deserve special appreciation, having helped in one way or another are, Richard Lamb, Ivan Damyanoff of Arrow Air, Thrifty Rent-a-Car, Irving Greenblatt of Casa del Frances, Jack Becker, Lorenzo Homar, Myrna Baez, Piana Espinosa, John F. Root, Jack Delano, Davey Jones, Sally, Allen and Taddeo of El Batey, Drew J. Guff, Eben W. Keyes, David and Phyllis Caldwell, and LeRoy and Kate Ellison.

The maps were drawn by the cartographic team at Nelles Verlag GmbH, Munich.

—APA Publications

W. Stone

R. Stone

O'Connell

Maijala

Hambleton

History

Places

Features

Maps

PUERTO RICO: A HISTORY

Puerto Rico overflows with vestiges of her past. From the countryside, where ancient Indian farming techniques are still employed, to the cities and towns where buildings from the Spanish colonial days stand juxtaposed to sleek modern edifices, traces of the island's past abound. But the road to the present has been a rocky one for the former Spanish colony. The first inhabitants were conquered by the Spanish. As a Spanish colony, Puerto Rico was barraged by attacks from foreign rivals who recognized the strategic advantages of the island's location — it was first stop on the voyage between Europe and the New World. Falling finally into the hands of the United States, Puerto Rico had to contend with a foreign and culturally alien government. The unique way in which the island has adapted to that challenge and turned it to its advantage is both inspiring and instructive.

The only way to understand the Puerto Rico of today is to know about the Puerto Rico of yesterday. Other Caribbean islands have lush vegetation, long beaches of white sand, fascinating marketplaces. Puerto Rico's history saves it from being another one of those; nowhere will you see such architecture, hear such stories as in the island with the oldest history in the Caribbean.

Preceding pages: Old San Juan doorway; veigante mask dancer; Playa Marchiquita; San Cristóbal Canyon; kiteflying, San Juan; Old San Juan street; surfing at Punta Higuero, Rincón; petroglyphs. Left, Fort El Morro, Old San Juan.

PRE-COLUMBIAN DAYS

Within a year of his triumphant return to Spain with news of his discoveries, Christopher Columbus set sail across the Atlantic on a second voyage to the New World. This time, he traveled under orders of King Ferdinand and Queen Isabella to explore the hemisphere and claim the territories for the Spanish Crown. The "Catholic Monarchs" had already secured the sole rights to the Americas — at least in the eyes of the Roman Catholic Church — by a series of Papal Bulls issued in 1493 which granted Spain "all islands and mainlands, discovered or yet to be discovered, sighted or not yet sighted" in the Western Hemisphere. Not only did Spain claim dominion over all the lands in the New World; the monarchs also appropriated all sovereignty over the Indians who lived there.

When Columbus discovered Puerto Rico on his second voyage in 1493, he found plenty of *Taíno* (also called *Arawak*) Indians already occupying the island. It has not yet been conclusively determined how or when the Taínos arrived, but much has been learned by the discovery at Loíza of a limestone cave containing artifacts of the early people. Carbon-dating reveals that the island has been occupied since the first century AD, and shells fashioned into gouging tools for use in the manufacture of dug-out canoes suggest that the first Indian rowed over from Venezuela, where similar relics have been recovered. There was unquestionably steady communication and trade between the islands. In his journal Columbus describes a Taíno canoe which seated three men abreast and 70 to 80 in all. "A barge could not keep up with them in rowing," he wrote, "because they go with incredible speed, and with these canoes they navigate among these islands . . ."

Part of a well-defined Indian culture that originated in Hispaniola and extended throughout the Antilles, the Taínos in Puerto Rico lived in a highly stratified, semi-advanced society. A great king lived on the island of Hispaniola and district *caciques* — chiefs — governed the districts of Puerto Rico, which the Indians called *Borínquen* — "Island of the Brave Lord." Each district had a centrally located capital village where the *cacique* resided. As in medieval Europe, heredity determined status within society,

which comprised *nitaínos*, or nobles who advised the *caciques* and enjoyed certain privileges; commoners; and *naborías* — slaves — condemned to menial labor for life.

Taíno villages ranged in size from a couple of hundred to a couple of thousand people. Weather clement, the Indians spent most of their time out-of-doors. However, they did build large, campanulate thatch houses in which as many as 40 family members slept. The houses were built around a large open space reserved for public ceremonies and *batey* which the Spanish referred to as *pelota*

— a ball game. The house of the *cacique* was the largest in town and always fronted on this public square. At Tibes, in Ponce, an Indian village has been reconstructed from the ancient ruins.

The Taínos believed in a polytheistic order of creation. *Yocahú* was the Supreme Creator who commanded all the gods, earth and creatures on it. The angry god of the winds, *Juracán*, invoked the eponymous hurricanes which disrupted the routine of island life from time to time. In the central plaza, the Indians observed religious worship and participated in ceremonial dances. Ceramic icons and clay idols displayed in anthropological museums are evidence of the natives' religious past. South of Arecibo, at the thirteen-acre

Preceding page, Lighthouse, Cabo Rojo. Taíno remains are still seen in Puerto Rico today: Indian rock carvings (left), and mask (right).

Caguana Indian Ceremonial Park used as long as eight centuries ago, are preserved stone monoliths, 10 *bateyes*, and other artifacts in a small museum.

Traces of Taíno agriculture remain in Puerto Rico. Their ingenious method of sowing a variety of plants in earthen mounds called *conducos* is still employed by some farmers. The *conduco* system mitigated the problems of water distribution: water intensive crops were placed at the bottom and those requiring good drainage at the top. Cassava bread, the staple of the Taíno diet, was processed from the deadly poisonous root of the yucca. After grating and draining the root, the Indians formed the pulp into loaves and baked them. They also relied heavily upon yams — sweet *batates* and unsweet *ages* — for vegetable calories, and among the plant samples the early settlers sent back to Spain were maize, beans, squash and peanuts. Using *macanas*, stout double broad-swords still used by Puerto Rican farmers, and pointed stocks, the Taínos cleared the thick woods and sowed their fields.

Various sources of animal protein supplemented the starchy Taíno diet. Using nets and lines woven of hemp and hibiscus fiber, the Indians seined and fished in the abundant Caribbean waters. In *canoas* of hollowed-out logs they could row far out to the sea and avail themselves of the schools of fish which passed through the Caribbean currents. With a strong arm, a solid stone and a good eye, a hunter could fell a succulent pigeon or parrot — a tasty accompaniment to a meal of yams and cassava bread.

In the time left over from farming, fishing and bagging small game, the Taínos developed various handicrafts. Early Spanish settlers in the region greatly admired the Indian woodwork: dishes, basins, bowls and boxes. Most prized of all were the ornate *duhos* — carved wooden thrones used by the caciques. The Great Taíno Cacique made a gift of a dozen of these to the Spanish Crown in the 1490s. Indian weavers used cotton and other fibrous plants to make colorfully dyed clothing, belts and hammocks. But the handicraft that aroused greatest excitement among the Spanish was the gold jewelry which the Indians wore as rings in their ears and noses. They neither mined nor panned for gold. When the Spaniards, smitten with desire for the precious metal, coaxed the natives into leading them to their sources, they were taken to beaches where gold nuggets from the ocean floor occasionally washed ashore.

Taíno rock carvings, near Cayey.

GOLDEN OPPORTUNITIES:
THE SETTLEMENT OF PUERTO RICO

Fifteen years passed between the time of Columbus' discovery of Borínquen on Nov. 19, 1493 and serious attempts to settle it. The adventurer to the New World came across the island by chance during his second voyage while he was trying to reach Hispaniola. Renaming it San Juan Bautista, Columbus claimed it for the Spanish Crown and promptly departed. From 1493 until 1508, the approximately thirty-thousand Taínos living on the island enjoyed a period of beneficent neglect: from time to time, Spaniards sailed to San Juan from Hispaniola

maniacal desire for wealth had proved dangerous in the past. Cruel subjection of the Indians on Hispaniola — physical abuse, dissolution of tribes and families, and starvation — had been followed by rebellion and bloodshed. Ponce and Ovando kept the deal quiet, hoping to avoid repetition of that gold rush scene. Moreover, they were both aware that the fewer the people who knew about it, the larger the potential take for those who did.

In July of 1508, Ponce and a band of 50 men — among them Luis de Añasco, the

seeking to barter for food. These encounters were always friendly.

One of the Spaniards who visited the island was Juan Ponce de Leon. The natives' fallals and trinkets of gold caught Ponce's eye. He felt sure that the area was rich in gold and he secretly scouted the southern coast for possible mine locations. In the early summer of 1508 Ponce and the governor of the Caribbean, Nicolas de Ovando, signed a clandestine agreement which granted Ponce rights to mine the island on the condition that he would yield two-thirds of what he uncovered to the king. Secrecy was of utmost importance: through his father Christopher Columbus, Diego Colón had inherited the rights to exploit the island. But his family's mono-

namesake of the river and pueblo — set off for the island of San Juan Bautista. As they sailed eastward along the northern coast, they made friendly contact with the Indians. Agueybaná, the head *cacique* of the island, provided Ponce with an entry which ensured safe passage for him and his crew. Finally, after six weeks of searching, the explorers sighted a suitable site for settlement. In a valley several miles inland on an arm of the Bayamon River, Ponce founded the island's first European town, Caparra (a word that might be translated as "Blossoming"). In official documents, the incipient island capital was referred to as "Ciudad de Puerto Rico."

For the next year relations between the

Indians and the Europeans proceeded swimmingly. Panning the river beds produced enough gold to persuade Ponce that the island merited permanent settlement. He had hoped for a small, strictly controlled group of Spaniards to live and work among the Indians without committing abuses or arousing hostility. However, as soon as King Ferdinand caught wind of Puerto Rico's excellent prospects, he directed a number of family friends there. Meanwhile, Diego Colón also entered the scene. Incensed that Ponce had arrogated the island for himself, he granted titles to two

of his father's supporters — Cristóbal Sotomayor and Miguel Díaz — and subsidized their establishment on the island. San Juan Bautista was now destined to suffer what Ponce had tried to avoid. By a colonial ordinance called a *repartimiento*, one of Colón's men enslaved 5,500 Indians ostensibly in order to convert them to Christianity but in reality to impress them into forced labor.

The enslaved natives were divided and placed "under the protection" of 48 *hidalgos* (from *hijo de algo*, meaning "son of a some-

body"). A combination of feudalism and capitalism, this was the *encomienda* system and it was employed throughout Spain's New World empire in the 16th Century. Across the northern coast the Spanish opened mines and panning operations — all supported by the free labor of the natives. The king appointed Ponce governor in 1510 but did not empower him to relinquish the repartimiento. The mining business proliferated, though there was so much competition for gold that the few who profited were men like Ponce who made their fortunes selling food and supplies to the miners. Moreover, not even Ponce could check the Spanish settlers' abuse of the Indians, especially in the remote western end of the island.

Indigenous Resistance

During the winter of 1511, violence erupted. Near Añasco a group of Indians drowned a Spanish boy to determine empirically whether the rumors about the white men's immortality were true. Discovering that they were not, yet fearing punishment for the murder, they revolted. At the same time a local *cacique* led an attack on the village of Sotomayor in the northwest. Guerrilla warfare spread through the island and small scale attacks and raids continued for weeks.

Ponce responded immediately. Within a few days of the initial outburst he and his captains had captured nearly 200 Indians, whom they subsequently sold into slavery. By June Ponce could write to his sovereign that peace once again reigned and that when possible he had spared the rebel natives' lives and enslaved them, branding them on the face with the King's first initial. As an interesting sidelight to the rebellion of 1511, none of the Indians in Bayamon and Tao, where Ponce's Indian policy was in effect, joined in the revolt.

Unfortunately, the king felt sufficiently threatened by the rancorous Diego Colón that he had perforce to acknowledge his claims. As a result, Ponce lost even more power. Colón's governmental appointments were recognized, and they continued to exploit the Indians according to the *encomienda* system. For a few years, the search for Puerto Rican gold continued at the expense of the Indians' freedom and until 1540, when the island was purged of its last karats, San Juan Bautista remained one of the New World's foremost

Left, modern-day homage to Christopher Columbus; and right, Casa del Libro, San Juan.

suppliers of gold to Spain. To assuage the wounded sensibilities of Juan Ponce de Leon for stripping his office down to little more than a title, King Ferdinand gave him permission to explore the virgin peninsula northwest of the Antilles which the Spanish called "*La Florida.*"

Sugar And Spice

As people continued to immigrate to the island of San Juan Bautista they brought new commercial enterprises. The days when *hidalgos* left their motherland to strike it rich in American gold mines were gone: the supply had simply given out. Gradually, the settlers turned to agriculture as the mainstay of the colonial economy. Land was plentiful

Crown, provided an affordable solution.

Two sorts of farms developed. Some islanders, denied political and social status because they were *mestizos*, the progeny of a white and an Indian or black, were unable to obtain large land grants and credit. They resorted to subsistence farming and on their tiny plots raised cassava, corn, vegetables, fruit, rice and a few cattle. In general, *mestizos* cleared fields in inland regions that would not compete with the large coastal plantations. Over decades, Puerto Rico's large peasant class blossomed from the seeds of these 16th-Century subsistence farmers.

In addition to the subsistence or peasant farmers, there were, of course, owners of large plantations. Usually of purely European ancestry, these immigrants and Creoles (born

and easy to come by. To promote colonization, the king allotted tracts ranging in size from 200 to 1400 acres. Water was plentiful and the climate temperate. Labor posed a problem at first, for the Indians had disappeared quickly after the institution of the repartimiento. Epidemics of European diseases had swept through the communities of enslaved Indians, utterly devastating the population. As in other parts of the New World, imported germs were the most potent means of conquest. Those Indians who escaped enslavement and death fled into the mountainous interior or across the sea to join the tribes of coastal South America. However, West African blacks, imported by Portuguese slavers and supplied by the Spanish

on the island) were chiefly interested in profit. After experimenting with a variety of crops, including ginger and tobacco, they finally settled on sugar as the most dependable and profitable cash crop. Sugar was relatively new to Europeans but their sweet tooth appeared to be insatiable. In 1516 entrepreneurs constructed the island's first *ingenio* — a factory in which raw cane is ground, boiled and reduced to sugar crystals. A decade and a half later, Puerto Rico sent its first sugar exports to Spain. These King Charles found so encouraging that he provided a number of technicians and loans for the industry's growth. Peripheral industries burgeoned as well: demand for timber to fuel the *ingenios* and food to fuel the laborers soared. Where sugar is processed, so inevitably is rum produced. Determined to squeeze all the profit possible out of their sugarcane, the Spanish settlers built distilleries soon after harvesting the first sugar crop. By 1550, there were 10 active *ingenios* on the island. However, the restrictive policies of the mercantilist king led to a crash in the market during the 1580s. Eventually the market recovered, but throughout Puerto Rico's history sugar would be not only one of the island's preeminent products, but also one of its most troubled industries.

After the collapse of the sugar trade in the 1580s, ginger emerged as the most successful product, and by 1598 was the main crop produced. Insistent upon the development of Puerto Rico into a sugar planting colony, the

garrisons with meat for the troops.

As if the mercantilist policies of the Hapsburg monarchy were not enough complication for the Puerto Ricans, the possibility of foreign aggression remained a constant threat to the island. By the 1520s, the economic and strategic promise of the island — now officially called *Puerto Rico* — became apparent. Moreover, the individual with the clearest sense of Puerto Rico's potential and importance was gone. Juan Ponce de Leon died of wounds received in an encounter with Florida Indians in 1521; his remains are interred in the Metropolitan Cathedral of San Juan. Because the colony lacked a leader who enjoyed the king's ear, adequate defensive measures were hard won.

In the year of Ponce's burial, the colonists

obstinate monarch forbade the cultivation of ginger at the turn of the 16th Century. But the colonists considered obedience to the crown secondary to profit, particularly where the consequences of obedience were more severe than the penalty for disobedience. Ginger planting flourished until the market bottomed out as a result of a surplus. Animal husbandry was another lucrative industry. The armies that conquered Peru, Central America and Florida rode Puerto Rican horses. Island *hatos* — cattle ranches — supplied the local

Left, Ponce de Leon; and right, model of an early Spanish galleon.

transferred the capital city from the site chosen by Ponce to a large natural bay to the north and renamed it San Juan. In the old riverbank location, mosquitoes had plagued settlers incessantly. In addition, with the growth of agriculture and industry, the Bayamon site proved too small to support increased water traffic.

Advantageous as the new location was for shipping, it left the citizens vulnerable to foreign invaders. In the 16th and 17th centuries, the French, English and Dutch dedicated themselves to unseating the powerful Hapsburg monarchs both at home and abroad. As part of this campaign, they launched attack after attack on Spanish salients in the New World. Many of these attacks were carried out by privateers.

Encouraged by rumors of impending assault by French war vessels, San Juan officials in 1522 initiated construction of the port's first garrison. The wooden structure had not yet been completed by the time the early San Juaneros realized it would be insufficient in the face of an attack. The island's first real defensive edifice was not completed until 1530, when descendants of Ponce built a house of stone, the 'Casa Blanca,' designed to provide refuge for colonists in the face of foreign aggression. The house still stands in Old San Juan.

Not even the Casa Blanca fulfilled the defensive needs of the settlement, particularly given expectations at the time of large-scale population growth. Two years later, the

residents.

Meanwhile, the southwestern coastal settlement of San Germán fell victim to a series of raids by French corsairs over the next 30 years. Though their resistance could be compared to that of Texans at the Alamo, Spanish settlers were eventually overcome by French depredations. San Germán was relocated 12 miles inland at its present site in "Las Lomas," the hill country.

The French were not the only ones to attack Puerto Rican cities. The celebrated "sea dogs" of Queen Elizabeth, Sir Francis Drake and Captain John Hawkins, forcibly seized dozens of Spanish cargo ships traveling between the Antilles and Spain. In 1585, open war broke out between the two nations. England's well-known defeat of the Spanish

army initiated the construction of La Fortaleza, sometimes known as Santa Catalina, which still stands, and holds the distinction of being the oldest executive mansion in the Western Hemisphere, housing as it does the offices of the governor of Puerto Rico. The Fortaleza did little to supplement the defenses already provided by the Casa Blanca. Before it had been completed, army officers informed the Crown that it had been built in "a poor place" and begged the appropriation of funds for another fortress. El Castillo de San Felipe del Morro, or, simply, *El Morro*, was the product of their entreaties. Placed on the rocky tip of the San Juan Peninsula, the fortification, finished in the 1540s, did much to assuage the fears of the northern capital's

Armada Invincible in 1588 left Spain permanently disabled as a naval power.

Puerto Rico received cursory attention during the 1580s and 1590s. The Council of the Indies, the bureaucracy that oversaw the enforcement and administration of Spanish colonial policy in the Western Hemisphere, conferred upon the governor the title of Captain-General and directed him to better the island's military preparedness. Governor Diego Menéndez de Valdes exercised tremendous initiative during the 1580s. A number of fortresses were constructed during his tenure including El Boquerón and Santa Elena in San Juan. Menéndez ordered the refurbishing of the land bridge known as La Puenta de San Antonio — now La Puenta de

San Gerónimo — and the refortifying of La Fortaleza. In addition, Menéndez beefed up the militia, requisitioning artillery and ammunition and expanding the troop count from 50 to 209 men.

Menéndez stepped in just in the nick of time. A string of English assaults launched with the intention of capturing Puerto Rico was thwarted thanks to the sturdy defenses of Governor Menéndez. A historic confrontation in the autumn of 1594 resulted in an English defeat. During one of these battles, a cannon ball shot through the wall of Francis Drake's ship mortally wounded John Hawkins who was meeting with his cohort in Drake's cabin. Drake was forced to retreat. Yet, the English would not give up. While the king nearly doubled the number of troops at the San Juan

garrison of El Morro up to 409, the veteran sea warrior, George Clifford, third Earl of Cumberland, secretly planned an assault. In 1598 an influenza epidemic wiped out a major proportion of the able-bodied population of San Juan. The city was seriously unprepared for the imminent attack.

In June the onslaught began. From a point 80 miles east of the capital, Cumberland's troops marched toward San Juan, easily taking fortifications as they proceeded. On the first of July, the defenders who had been forced to hole up in El Morro surrendered San

Juan under Cumberland's seige. But the same scourge which had weakened the Puerto Ricans now struck at the English conquerors. More than 400 English soldiers died of influenza within six weeks. The Puerto Ricans availed themselves of the British state of weakness. Refusing to acknowledge Cumberland's authority they engaged relentlessly in skirmishes on the outskirts of town. On August 27, Cumberland withdrew from the island, destroying two plantations in his wake.

Here the Dutch entered the picture. Determined to bring Spanish dominance of the Caribbean to an end, they commissioned Boudewijn Hendrikszoon to take over the island. Hendrikszoon's fleet of eight vessels arrived in San Juan harbor on Sept. 24, 1625.

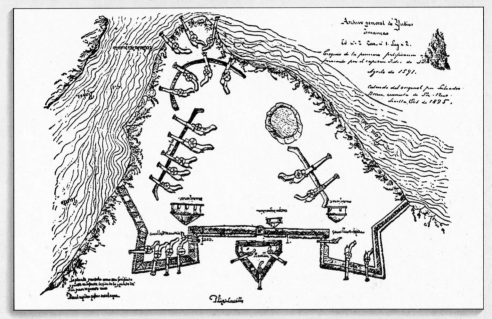

In the course of the next three days, the Dutch slowly advanced, forcing a Spanish retreat into El Morro. The siege of San Juan lasted a month. Finally, the courageous Captains Juan de Amezquita and Andres Botello led surprise attacks on the Dutch trenches on October 22. The next ten days of battle left the Dutch fleet severely damaged — one ship destroyed and the troops depleted.

In the 1630s and 1640s, King Philip IV of Spain realized his plan to fortify the entire city of San Juan: seven fortresses were linked by a line of stone walls that surrounded the city. The natives were inducted into the provincial district militias and Puerto Rico gained fame as the foremost *Presidio* of the Indies.

Casa Blanca, Puerto Rico's oldest fort; and right, 16th-Century plan of El Morro.

Making Ends Meet:
The Consolidation Of Spanish Power

Now relatively safe from foreign invaders, the island leaders turned their attentions to the problem of establishing a strong economic base. As a Spanish colony, Puerto Rico was allowed to keep open only one port — San Juan — and was barred from trading with non-Spanish powers. These strictures seriously limited Puerto Rico's chances for economic growth. In the mid-16th Century, when the influx of African slaves diminished, Britain threatened Spain on the high seas, and when non-Spanish producers in the West Indies developed more efficient means of sugar production, the sugar industry collapsed. Virtually nothing was exported in the 1560s and 1570s — the whole year went by in 1572 without a ship in the harbor and there was a seven-year span in which no European ship docked at San Juan at all! The Spanish Crown, wishing to convert Puerto Rico into a defensive salient, instituted an assistance program called the *situado*. According to this plan, Puerto Rico was to receive from Mexico 2½ million maravedies annually. This was a substantial sum which should have proven sufficient for the colonial government. However, the *situado* was a miserable failure. Privateers repeatedly intercepted the *situado* in transit and there was furthermore no method of ensuring that it had been sent. While the delivery of bullion from Mexico was laughably erratic, it did keep the island limping along until independent economic development occurred.

Ironically, the antidote that turned the flagging island economy around was the circumvention of the Spanish mercantilist policies that were the cause of Puerto Rico's problems to begin with. Refused permanent concessions by the Crown, which continued to impose strict mercantilist policies, the planters and merchants on Puerto Rico engaged increasingly in illicit trade with foreign nations. Local produce — sugar, livestock, tobacco — was exchanged for slaves, staples, tools and other manufactured goods. By the middle of the 17th Century almost everyone, from clerical authorities to soldiers, from friars to peasants, was involved in smuggling. The coastal towns of Aguada, Arecibo, Cabo Rojo and Fajardo grew into busy centers of illicit international trade.

Word of the proliferation of contraband activity and privateering in Puerto Rico eventually got back to Spain. Recognizing that the island's problems were critical, the king sent a commissioner named Alejandro O'Reilly to evaluate the state of Puerto Rico. O'Reilly's report of 1765 was remarkably comprehensive and perspicacious. O'Reilly reckoned the island's population had reached about forty-five thousand: forty thousand freemen and five thousand slaves. Most of the urban inhabitants lived in northeastern coastal

towns and earned their livelihood through smuggling and black market trade. Three-fourths of the Puerto Ricans were younger than 40 years. Though illegal, smuggling was so prevalent that O'Reilly could report extensively on prices, product supply, demand and distribution.

In 1765, a council convened to review O'Reilly's report and to formulate a solution to the Puerto Rican problem. Recognizing the need for a stronger enforcement agent to curb contraband trade, they increased the *situado* more than two-fold and installed as governor Don Miguel de Muesas. He was instructed to get underway the growth of a sturdy domestic economy. By building bridges and roads, by refortifying the island's defenses, and by

Left, the oldest cathedral in San Juan; and right, the patron saint of sailors.

instituting a public education program he hoped to engender agricultural prosperity and domestic self-sufficiency.

Despite the acuity with which O'Reilly pleaded Puerto Rico's case, Spain continued to assign the development of the island's economy a secondary role in juxtaposition to the island's importance as the first naval fortification in her New World empire. Further, a population boom — largely attributable to immigration — had more than tripled the number of residents on the island by the turn of the century. Only San Juan enjoyed official sanction as a port city and trade with non-Spanish nations remained illegal. Meanwhile, Great Britain had her eye on Puerto Rico and was showing a readiness to acquire it. In 1797, after Napoleonic France and Spain had declared war on Great Britain, a British fleet of 60 vessels manned by nine thousand troops under the command of General Abercromby landed at Boca de Cangrejos. On April 17, they took Santurce and quickly laid siege upon the walled capital. Holding them off at the Castile of San Gerónimo, the defenders managed to check the British assault. Militia detachments from around the island arrived and launched a counterattack. Abercromby ordered a retreat on May 1.

Shifting Control

Napoleon's invasion of Spain in 1808 sent shock waves through the empire and led to a complete reorganization of colonial rule. Several countries in the Americas won independence from Spain in this period of weakened control over trans-Atlantic territories. A provisional assembly called the *Cortes* was convened in Spain to rule in the name of the deposed King Ferdinand VII. Fearing that Puerto Rican separatists who sympathized with the rebellious colonists in South and Central America — Mexico and Venezuela particularly — would instigate revolutions at home, the Cortes invited Puerto Rico to send a delegation to Madrid. An island Creole by the name of Ramón Power Giralt went as the colony's emissary and was elected vice president of the assembly. He pushed for reforms designed to ameliorate the social and economic ills of the island. Puerto Ricans gained status as Spanish citizens, tariffs on machinery and tools were dropped, a university was founded, and measures were taken to improve island industry. The Cortes

Early slave marketplace.

disbanded in 1814 when Napoleon retreated and King Ferdinand VII reassumed the throne, but the king, wary of the independence fever pervading the New World colonies, left in place a large fraction of Power's reforms in a *cédula de gracias* (royal decree) granted in 1815.

Shifting Economy

While Puerto Ricans were moving away from the political dominance of Spain, they were establishing strong trading ties with the United States. During the decade beginning in 1795, trade between the United States and the Spanish West Indies grew by a factor of six. Household goods, food and, to a minor extent, slaves were supplied by the United

States in exchange for West Indian staples such as sugar, coffee, rum and spices. In 1803 Puerto Rico sent 263,000 pounds of sugar to the United States and the amount exported grew yearly. Trouble came, however, in 1807. The President of the United States, Thomas Jefferson, placed an embargo on all trade with the Spanish West Indies which cut exports by more than half. After Napoleon's invasion of the monarchic Iberian peninsula, President Jefferson lifted the embargo, and trade with the United States proceeded relatively unhindered. American diplomats in the Caribbean expressed to the colonial governments their country's sentiments: colonies could either try to win independence or remain loyal to Spain, but the

United States could not give approval to a change in colonial rule from Spain to Britian or France.

Not long after the lifting of the Jeffersonian trade embargo, new difficulties floated into Puerto Rican harbors. Trying to respond to the threat Napoleon's armies posed on her borders, Spain called upon her colonies to ship an extraordinary supply of resources which could be used to outfit and maintain her own troops. With most profitable products going to Spain, Puerto Rico's economy suffered. And added to all these woes was the War of 1812 between Great Britain and the United States. The British blockade of the North American coast severely hampered American trade. Puerto Rico, by then one of the major suppliers of sugar to America, had nowhere to turn.

The recovery following this tumultuous period included tremendous growth in the island economy. Ramón Power's economic reforms remained in place and for the first time since their institution began to have a real effect. Trade with the wealthy United States was not only permitted; the tariffs were decreased significantly. The *cédula de gracias* declared by King Ferdinand VII in 1815 ended the mercantilist Spanish trade monopoly in Puerto Rico by permitting trade with other countries. However, according to the dictates of the king only Spanish vessels were allowed to carry on Puerto Rican trade. Once again, the colonial governors took exception to Spanish policy. Disobeying the king's orders, they gave right of entry to ships regardless of their origin. Also, under a civil intendancy plan instituted by Power, an independent official was appointed to oversee financial affairs, rather than leaving them in the hands of the governor. Alejandro Ramírez Blanco filled the post first. During his tenure he opened several ports, abolished superfluous taxes, and increased the export of cattle.

Between 1813 and 1818 Puerto Rican trade grew to eight times its previous level and in 1824 the king finally relinquished the last vestiges of mercantilism, conceding the right of Puerto Rican ports to harbor non-Spanish merchant ships. The future of the Puerto Rican economy was clear to many in the early 19th Century. Spain was neither a reliable nor a tremendously profitable trading partner and the more Puerto Rico moved away from her dependence on the mother country, the faster her economy developed.

Left, strolling in La Fortaleza; and right, view from La Perla.

BREWING STORM: THE HOME RULE DEBATE

In 1820 the population of Puerto Rico was estimated at 150,000. By 1900 the population had mushroomed to almost a million. The character of society drastically changed; for the first time, agitators for Puerto Rican autonomy were vocal and posed a serious threat to the Spanish government. Increasingly, the royally-appointed governor and the colonial army under his command would be identified as an adversary and an impediment to the achievement of Puerto Rican independence. In 1820 Pedro Dubois had scarcely initiated a recruitment program when he was discovered by the government, however. Promptly arresting Dubois, the governor incarcerated him at El Morro and had him executed before a firing squad.

Three years after the Dubois incident, another event in the struggle for autonomy took place. After the restoration of Ferdinand to the throne in 1814, a series of governors with absolute power ruled Puerto Rico. On the first day of 1820, an army commander declared the liberal reformist constitution of 1812 to be still in effect. One by one officials of various districts joined him. The already weak king, hoping to avoid an all-out revolution, had perforce to concede, and called for a meeting of the Cortes for the first time in a decade. Jose María Quiñones went as the representative from Puerto Rico in 1823. He submitted a plan to introduce more autonomy to the island colonies, particularly in the administration of domestic affairs. The Cortes approved the Quiñones proposal, but their intentions fell to pieces before they could see them through. In 1823 the constitutional government of Spain collapsed. The king returned to absolute power and appointed the first of 14 governors of Puerto Rico who exercised unlimited authority over the colony, collectively staging a 42-year reign of oppression and virtual marshal law.

The first of these dictators was Miguel de la Torre. Hanging on to the governorship for 15 years, Torres imposed a ten o'clock curfew and established the *visita* — an islandwide inspection network that allowed him to keep abreast of activity in the colony and maintain tight security. Torres' reign was not only oppressive, however. Taking control of the economy's development, he built roads and bridges and brought in huge numbers of black slaves to foster sugar production. Torres contributed significantly to the lasting development of the local economy.

In 1838 a group of separatist Puerto Ricans led by Buenaventura Quiñones plotted a putsch. Word of the conspiracy leaked out and several of the participants were executed; the others were exiled. Declaring beards subversive, the new governor banned the wearing of facial hair. Subsequent governors passed laws aimed at the suppression of blacks (following the historic slave rebellion on Martinique) and instituted the *libreta* laws which required all inhabitants of Puerto Rico to carry passbooks and restricted unauthorized movement. It was a troubled time for the beautiful island: between 1848 and 1867, seven consecutive military dictators governed the island, taking advantage of the institutions put into place by the Torres administration. To add to the colony's misery, in the 1850s a cholera epidemic swept across the island, claiming the lives of 30,000 people. Ramón Emeterio Betances, a doctor renowned for his efforts against the epidemic, was exiled in 1856 for his criticism of the colonial authorities.

Intimidated by growing separatist fervor in Puerto Rico and Cuba and by the Dominican Revolution in 1862, the Crown of Spain invited Puerto Rico and Cuba in 1865 to draft a colonial constitution in the form of a "Special Law of the Indies." The documents which emerged called for the abolition of slavery, for freedom of the press and speech, and for independence on a Commonwealth basis. While the Crown dragged its feet in granting these concessions, back in Puerto Rico the angry governor, José María Marchessi, exiled several leading reformists, including the recently returned Betances. Fleeing to New York, they joined with other separatist Puerto Ricans and Cubans.

From New York the autonomists directed the independence movement during the 1860s and seventies under the aegis of the Puerto Rican Revolutionary Committee. Covert satellite organizations formed in villages and towns across Puerto Rico, centering around Mayagüez. On Sept. 23, 1863, several hundred men congregated at a farm outside the northwestern mountain town of Lares. Marching under a banner that read *"Libertad o Muerte. Viva Puerto Rico Libre. Año 1868,"* — "Liberty or Death. Long Live Free Puerto Rico. Year 1868" — they took the town and

Left, the Puerto Rican national crest.

arrested its officials. They elected a provisional president and proclaimed the Republic of Puerto Rico. The Republic would be short-lived. Troops sent by the governor met the rebel front at San Sebastián and won an easy victory. Within six weeks the echoes of the Grito de Lares — "the Shout of Lares" — had died completely. However, the Grito de Lares became symbolic in the Puerto Rican independence movement. Today, pro-independence groups still make pilgrimages to Lares in honor of the early fighters for

the skies began to brighten, a dark cloud cast a shadow over the island's future. A coup in Spain undid the new Spanish republican government's reforms in 1875. The colonial governor proscribed meetings and censored the press.

The question of Puerto Rican independence was still largely moot at this stage, and a review of the political camps that formed in this period lend insight into the nature of revolutionary philosophy on a broader level. Hard-core autonomists wanted to cleave completely the colony's ties with mother Spain.

autonomy.

Spain granted Puerto Rico 11 seats on the re-convened Cortes in 1869. Four Liberals and seven Conservatives were elected to the delegation. Over the next two decades, political confusion rained down upon the island. Quickly the Liberals gained the upper hand in Puerto Rico — winning 14 out of 15 seats in 1872 — and the Queen was overthrown by Republicans in Spain. The new Spanish King enacted a program to abolish slavery and ended the libreta system. However, just as

Other separatists inclined toward joining the ambitious Spanish Republicans and remaining a semi-autonomist colony under the new Republic of Spain. And the most moderate of separatists thought that fusion with the Spanish Liberal party would create a viable relationship with Spain, particularly that a monarch installed by the Liberals would grant Puerto Rico independence without the violence and hostility of a revolution. At the other end of the spectrum were the Conservatives who felt that any talk of separatism was treasonous. In general, members of the middle-class and peasants fell in the autonomist camp while the wealthy planters and landowners were Conservative. But many Puerto Ricans were Conservative simply because they feared — not without grounds — that if the colony separated from Spain it would be taken over by the more alien and frighteningly aggressive United States.

When the Puerto Rican Liberals gathered in Ponce to demand autonomy combined with union with Spain, the alarmed Conservatives

of people were tortured to death during the "year of terror."

Puerto Rico did enjoy a brief flash of autonomy in 1897. The Autonomist Party voted to fuse with the monarchic Liberal Party of Spain after forming a pact with their leader Mateo Sagasta which guaranteed Puerto Rican autonomy if the Liberals came to power. On the assassination of the Spanish prime minister, Sagasta became Spain's ruler and he immediately declared Puerto Rico an autonomist state. The former colony acted quickly.

sent a desperate petition to the king begging him to send a new governor general. Soon the new appointee, Romualdo Palacio González, arrived. Moreover, he more than satisfied the Conservatives' demands. Demonstrating an almost paranoid fear of subversive activity, he administered cruel punishment to those he considered threatening to the state. Hundreds

Above, 19th-Century currency, issued by Spain.

Adopting a bicameral constitutional republican form of government, they elected a lower house of assembly and half of the delegates to the upper house. The governor was still appointed by Spain, but his power was carefully restricted. The new government assumed power in July of 1898. Later that month General Nelson A. Miles of the United States landed on the southern coast with an army of 16,000 men. It was the beginning of the Spanish American War and the end of Puerto Rican autonomy.

THE UNITED STATES TAKES CHARGE

'It wasn't much of a war, but it was all the war there was,'' Teddy Roosevelt reflected on the Spanish American War. On August 31, 1898 Spain surrendered. The Puerto Rico campaign had lasted only two weeks; the whole war, less than four months. The United States, at the height of its imperial power under the McKinley administration, suffered four casualties in exchange for the Philippines and Puerto Rico. Unlike Cuba, which gained autonomy in 1898, Puerto Rico did not have the necessary native army to prevent America's arrogation of the island as a protectorate. General Miles tried to assuage the inhabitants' anxiety, however, telling them, "We have come . . . to promote your prosperity and to bestow upon you the immunities and blessing of the liberal institutions of our government.'' His assurances did not pacify everyone. The now aging Betances issued a warning to his fellow Puerto Ricans: "If Puerto Rico does not act fast, it will be an American colony forever.''

On Dec. 10, 1898 the Treaty of Paris which settled the final terms of Spain's surrender was signed. In addition to a large reparations payment, the United States won Puerto Rico and the Philippines from Spain, but Puerto Rico wasn't exactly a grand prize at the time. Her population had reached a million. A third were blacks and mulattoes who generally possessed little capital or land. Only an eighth of the population were literate, and only one out of 14 of the island's 300,000 children was in school. Two percent of the population owned more than two-thirds of the land devoted to agriculture. Yet 60 percent of the land owned was mortgaged at high interest rates.

It Ain't Over Till It's Over

The United States set up a military government as soon as the Treaty of Paris was signed and Puerto Rico was placed under the charge of the War Department. Assuming a hard-headed approach to the problem of underdevelopment and lagging economy, the first three governors-general enjoyed near dictatorial power. They effected the change to American currency, suspended defaulted mortgages, and promoted trade with the United States. They improved public health, reformed tax laws, and overhauled local governments. But the Puerto Rican people were still unhappy.

The autonomy they had fought for and were on the brink of achieving when war erupted was as vital to them now as ever. Yet their new conquerors were reluctant to give any ground to the Puerto Ricans in the struggle for home rule.

Luis Muñoz Rivera

A leading autonomist leader, Luís Muñoz Rivera, organized a new party in an attempt to reach a compromise between the separatists and the United States government. The

BETANCES.

Federal Party and its ally, the new Republican Party, advocated cooperation with the United States, especially in commercial matters, full civil rights, and an autonomous civilian government. But not even the irenic approach Muñoz endorsed satisfied the United States, during the McKinley administration. The colonial Governor General George W. Davis reported to the President that "The people generally have no conception of political rights combined with political responsibilities.'' In contradiction to General Davis' observations the Puerto Ricans did show some awareness of political responsibility in the municipal election of 1899. The election, which went on for a year because of the complicated voting requirements by which only literate men of over 21 years could vote ended in victory for the Federals and the Republicans. They won 66 towns in municipal elections.

Winds of Fortune

As if political turmoil were not enough, Mother Nature put her two bits in as well in the form of Hurricane San Ciriaco in 1899. Three thousand people lost their lives and the damage to property was immense. The hurricane devastated the vital sugar and coffee

recognized the military government's inadequacy. In 1900 he proposed a program for the gradual introduction of autonomy for Puerto Ricans which President McKinley immediately endorsed. However, though Puerto Rico was closer to autonomy than it had been since before the Spanish American War, the path to home rule was not clear yet.

The Following Acts

For the next 48 years, Puerto Rico and the United States were engaged in a historically

crops and left a fourth of the island inhabitants without homes. The U.S. Congress waited months before responding and finally awarded a pittance of two hundred thousand dollars to the island in relief payments.

Puerto Rico faced an unhappy future. The economy on the brink of collapse, the hostilities between Puerto Ricans and often inept American administrators raging, the ostensibly insurmountable difficulties of illiteracy and poverty, the Secretary of War Elihu Root

Left, Ramón Emeterio Betances; and right, American medical officers at Coamo Springs. Smallpox was so prevalent when the Americans came upon the island that the government immediately provided for the vaccination of the entire population.

aberrant colonial-protectorate relationship. While it was widely acknowledged that America possessed enormous wealth from which the colony stood to benefit, Puerto Ricans also feared that Betances' prediction would come true — that Puerto Rico would be "swallowed up" both culturally and economically if her bonds with the United States were to strengthen. The history of the former Spanish salient in the 20th Century has been defined by the struggle to maintain and promote an independent identity under the pressures of American imperialism.

Puerto Rico figures prominently in the history of the United States in the 20th Century. It was the first non-continental U.S. territory and served as the test case for the formation and implementation of colonial policy.

Special interest groups in the United States polarized into two lobbies. The agricultural contingent, fearful of competition from Puerto Rican producers where labor costs ran lower, allied with racists who dreaded the influx of the "Latin race" which would result from granting American citizenship to Puerto Ricans. And as proof of Benjamin Franklin's observation that politics makes strange bedfellows, these opponents of the administration's Puerto Rican colonial plan found themselves under the blankets with liberal Democrats who opposed imperialism of any sort, condemning it as contrary to the ideals of the nation. Ever since the mid-19th Century, Americans had been instructed to heed their

Americans and Puerto Ricans, and a House of Delegates would perform the functions of government.

In addition, a Resident Commissioner chosen by the Puerto Rican people would speak for the colony in the House of Representatives, but would have no vote. An initial 15-percent tariff was imposed on all imports to and exports from the United States and the revenues would be used to benefit Puerto Rico. After two years, free trade was promised. The colonial government would determine its own taxation programs and oversee the insular treasury. Ownership of large estates by American corporations was discouraged, at least in intention, by the prohibition of businesses from carrying on agriculture on more than five hundred acres.

"manifest destiny" and had settled in the west and in Alaska. Before 1900, the seeds of expansionism had blossomed into an imperialism that led some politicians to suggest annexing Mexico and Central America with hopes of eventually spreading out into the whole Hemisphere. The heirs to this tradition, for the most part Republicans, sided with President McKinley on the Puerto Rico question.

The Burgeoning of a Colony

With passage of the Foraker Act, in 1900, Puerto Rico took on a new colonial status. A presidentially-appointed governor, an Executive Council comprising a combination of

However, officials rarely enforced this clause in practice and capital — rich firms from the United States moved in. A sunset clause limited the life span of the Act to 16 years.

Reception of the Foraker Act could have been better. An immediate challenge of its constitutionality brought it before the Supreme Court of the United States where the majority declared that constitutionality was not applicable in an "unincorporated entity" like Puerto Rico. Dissenting Chief Justice Fuller wrote that it left Puerto Rico "a disembodied shade in an intermediate state of ambiguous existence." Puerto Ricans harbored most of the animosity for the Act. Repeatedly the independence factions demanded that Congress hold a insular plebiscite to let the inhabitants determine the island's future. Soon the anti-American politicians held a majority among the elected officials. As a protest against United States' policy, they refused to pass any legislation during 1909. They sent a memorial to the President and Congress in which they claimed that it was "impossible for the people's representatives to pass the laws they desire," under the Foraker Act. The Congress responded by approving the previous year's budget in lieu of a new one. The fight for independence raged on.

The Jones-Shafroth Act

On the eve of the United States' entry into the First World War in 1917, President Wilson approved the Jones-Shafroth Act granting American citizenship to all Puerto Ricans. Under a clause in the new law, those who objected to becoming citizens of the United States could defer it by signing an official document.

The Jones-Shafroth Act was an affront to many Puerto Rican statesmen. For years they had pressed for a break from the United States and now, in blatant contradiction of their demands, Congress was drawing them in even more. Muñoz Rivera, the Resident Commissioner, had beseeched Congress to hold a plebiscite — but to no avail. The "Catch-22" of Puerto Rico's relationship with the United States had emerged full-blown. The more political maturity the colony demonstrated, the more fervently the nationalists agitated for independence. The more hostile to the United States the colony appeared to American lawmakers, the more reluctant they were to give any ground at all. It was an imperialist analog to the classic case of a parent refusing privileges to an adolescent until the youth manifests an acceptance of adult responsibility. As the House Insular Affairs Committee chairman admonished the House of Delegates in 1920, "There is a legitimate ground for a larger measure of self-government, but that has been greatly

injured by independence propaganda." Requests for a plebiscite repeatedly rebuffed, the independence movement leaders needed a new tactic.

Labor Pains

During this period of antagonism between Puerto Rico and the United States, the economy and the population rapidly increased. Efforts to combat poor health care and disease had resulted in a precipitous drop in the death rate. Meanwhile, employment increased, production skyrocketed, and government revenues rose. Big corporations from the United States pocketed most of the profits from this new found growth, and their sway

Left, hijinks at El Morro; and right, U.S. Marine legacy at Guanica Beach.

with Congress assured them of a continued flow of wealth. The average Puerto Rican family earned between $150 and $200 per year; many jíbaros had sold their own little farms to work for American latifundia and factories.

Pablo Iglesias, a disciple of Samuel Gompers — one of the fathers of American trade unions — led the move to organize Puerto Rican laborers. At first the government opposed his efforts and his persistence landed him in jail. An appeal from the American Federation of Labor won his release, but the

under Iglesias' leadership as the Free Federation, identified itself with the labor union movement in the United States. They even assumed the task of Americanizing Puerto Rico. "The labor movement in Porto Rico," Iglesias wrote, "has no doubt been, and is, the most efficient and safest way of conveying the sentiments and feelings of the American people to the hearts of the people of Porto Rico." A cigar strike in 1914 and a cane strike of 1915 brought the movement publicity. Iglesias was elected to the newly-formed Senate of Puerto Rico in 1917.

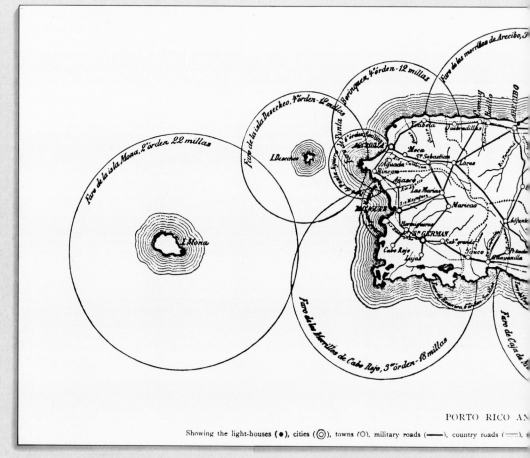

PORTO RICO AN

Showing the light-houses (●), cities (◎), towns (O), military roads (——), country roads (═══),

hostility remained. Ever a believer in compromise and change from within the system, Gompers toured Puerto Rico in 1904 in hopes of pacifying both sides. An inspection of factories and plantations, however, filled him with disgust for his country's policies which would facilitate such drastic social inequities and permit the horrifying working conditions he saw to go unchecked.

By 1909 the labor movement, organized

Trouble Shooting

The Great Depression of the 1930s nearly undid Puerto Rico. Two hurricanes accompanied the collapse of the economy — San Felipe in 1928 and San Cipriano in 1932 — destroying millions of dollars in property and crops. Starvation and disease took a heavy toll on the population during the Depression. Across the island, haggard, demoralized people waited in long queues for government food handouts. Congress, preoccupied by the problems of their constituents, acted sluggishly to provide relief for Puerto Rico. Out of the poverty and deprivation, a new voice emerged.

It belonged to Pedro Albizu Campos, a former American Army officer and a graduate of Harvard Law School. He was of a generation of Puerto Ricans who were children at the time of the United States' takeover. Equipped with a great understanding of the American system, he used it to become a leader of militant revolutionaries.

Feb. 23, 1936. Two of his followers, Hiram Rosado and Elías Beauchamp, shot and killed the chief of police of San Juan. The assassins were arrested and summarily beaten to death, and Albizu and seven key party members were imprisoned in the Federal Prison in Georgia.

A year later, however, the party was still strong. Denied a permit to hold a demonstration in the town of Ponce, a group of Albizu's followers dressed in black shirts assembled to march on March 21, 1937. As the procession moved forward to the tune of *La Borinqueña*

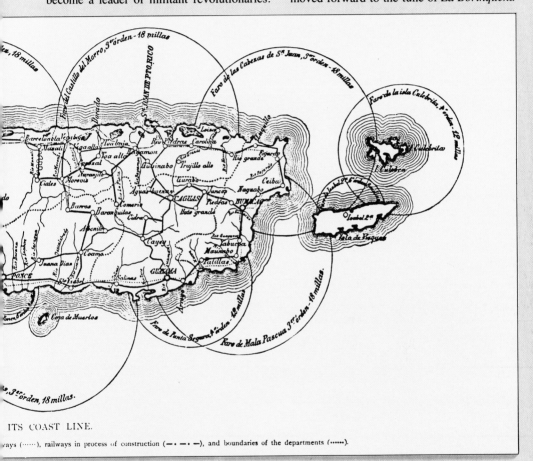

ITS COAST LINE.

...ays (······), railways in process of construction (—·—·—), and boundaries of the departments (·······).

Albizu's accusation was, according to American foreign policy and international law, the United States' claims on Puerto Rico were illegal since Puerto Rico was already autonomous at the time of occupation.

The strength and seriousness of Albizu's Nationalist organization were made clear on

Early Puerto Rico and its coastline.

— the Puerto Rican anthem — a shot rang out. The origin of the gunfire has never been determined, but within moments both the police and the marchers were exchanging bullets. Twenty people were killed and another hundred wounded in the panic-stricken crossfire that ensued. The Governor called the affair ''a riot''; the U.S. Civil Liberties Union, ''a massacre.'' That appelation remains: the event is remembered today as *La Massacre de Ponce.*

The United States began to export Puerto Rico's share of the New Deal in 1933, but it was not a winning hand. President Franklin Roosevelt sent a string of inept appointments to the Governor's Mansion in San Juan, and their attempts to provide relief proved inadequate and aggravating to the Puerto Ricans. Then, from amidst the crumbling political parties and the demoralized masses, a brilliant star in Puerto Rico's history appeared. Luís Muñoz Marín, son of the celebrated stateman Luís Muñoz Rivera, had served in government since 1932 and had used his charm and connections with the American political elite to bring attention to the plight of the colony. In 1938, young Muñoz founded the Popular Democratic Party, running on the slogan "Bread, Land, and Liberty," and adopting the *pava* — the broad-brimmed straw hat worn by jibaros — as the party symbol. In 1940, the Populars took over half the total seats in the upper and lower Houses.

Muñoz, elected leader of the Senate, decided to try to work with the new Governor to achieve recovery. The appointee, Rexford Guy Tugwell, was refreshingly different from his predecessors. Able to speak Spanish and evincing a genuine compassion for the Puerto Ricans, he seemed promising. Muñoz's good faith paid off. By improving the distribution of relief resources and by proposing a plan for long-term economic development contingent upon continued union with the United States, Muñoz convinced Tugwell that Puerto Rico was finally ready to assume the responsibility of electing its own governor. As a first step, President Roosevelt appointed Puerto Rico's Resident Commissioner, Jesús Piñero, to the post. In 1946 Piñero became the first native governor in the island's history. The cautious progress did not placate everyone, however. The *Independentistas* accused Muñoz of needlessly selling out to the United States. They continued to press for a complete break. The year after Piñero's assent to the Governorship, they petitioned the United Nations for help in shaking off their colonial status. Simultaneously, the United States unveiled plans for popular election of Puerto Rico's governor. Muñoz's show of confidence in Tugwell had resulted in an American show of confidence in the colony.

The people elected Muñoz, of course. In 1948 he took office as the first popularly elected governor and put forth his proposal for turning Puerto Rico into an *Estado Libre Asociado* — an associated free state. Taking a lesson from the newly independent Philippines, where instant autonomy had crippled economic and social progress, the United States delayed endorsement of Muñoz's plan. However, on Oct. 30, 1950, President Truman approved Public Law 600, the Puerto Rican Commonwealth Bill. This legislation

PUERTO RICO WANTS YOU

provided for a plebiscite in which voters would decide whether to remain a colony or assume status as a commonwealth. As the latter, Puerto Ricans would draft their own constitution, though the U.S. Congress would retain "paramount power." In June 1951 the voters of Puerto Rico voted three to one in favor of the commonwealth.

Two disturbing events punctuated the otherwise smooth transition to commonwealth status. On the very day President Truman signed Public Law 600, a group of armed Nationalists marched on the Governor's Mansion, La Fortaleza. In a brief skirmish a policeman and four Nationalists were gunned down. Simultaneously, outbursts in five other towns including Ponce and Arecibo left over a

Left, influence of the U.S.-style strip; and right, Uncle Sam wants Puerto Rico.

hundred casualties including 27 dead. What is more, the violence extended beyond Puerto Rican shores. Two Puerto Ricans from New York traveled to Washington and made an attempt on the President's life a month later. In March 1954, four Puerto Rican Nationalists, shouting "¡Viva Puerto Rico Libre!" fired into the House of Representatives from the visitors' gallery and wounded five Congressmen. The Nationalists seemed bent on reminding the United States that alternative political ideologies still existed in Puerto Rico.

Muñoz resigned from political office in 1964. His party kept up the lead in the elections of 1956 and 1960, when the Populars won over 60 percent of the vote. The Republicans also gained strength, claiming 30 percent of the ballots cast in 1960. The Independent Party, on the other hand, diminished into obscurity. Under pressure from Muñoz to evaluate and improve Puerto Rico's position as an "Associated Free State," President Kennedy created a commission of Puerto Ricans and mainlanders to review the island's status. In 1966 the commission determined that commonwealth, statehood and independence all deserved consideration. Seven months later the Popular Party, pushing for a decision, passed a bill mandating a plebiscite. Muñoz re-entered the fray in support of continuing as a commonwealth. He argued that Puerto Rico had placed fourth in the worldwide rate of economic progress only due to its relationship with the United States. Further, he claimed, statehood could easily bring an end to the independent culture of Puerto Rico. His arguments held sway. When the vote came in on July 23, 1967, two-thirds of the ballots were cast for Muñoz's commonwealth.

Over the last three decades, Puerto Rico has continued under commonwealth status. Now there are four political parties: the *Partido Popular Democratico*, the Popular Party Muñoz founded; the pro-autonomy *Partido Independista Puertorriqueno*; the *Partido Nuevo Progresista*, in favor of statehood; and the fledgling communist organization of *Partido Socialista*. At every election Puerto Ricans have a chance to express their opinion on the island's best future.

Puerto Rico pulled itself out of the Depression in the early 1940s. The United States declaration of war spurred the economy forward to its old pace. Aiding it were the new reformist government of Muñoz and a tariff on rum sold in the United States which generated substantial revenues for the Puerto Rican treasury. Muñoz recognized that the key to averting future economic catastrophe lay in avoiding a dependence on agriculture. Relying heavily on one or two crops left Puerto Rico subject to too many risks: weather, foreign production, interest rates. The government established the Puerto Rican Industrial Development Corporation in 1942 to oversee the development of government-sponsored manufacturing. When the state plans floundered, the administration cancelled the program and initiated a new plan, known as Operation Bootstrap.

Aimed at developing an economy based on rum, tourism and industry, the program sent dozens of public relations agents to the mainland on promotional tours. A massive advertising campaign extolled the virtues of the Puerto Rican climate, geography, economy and people in the mass media. During the early years of Operation Bootstrap, jobs in manufacturing quadrupled to over 20,000 and between 1950 and 1954 over one hundred thousand Puerto Ricans moved to the mainland in order to take advantage of the wartime labor market. A slowdown followed the resumption of peace, but the seeds were coming to fruition. In 1955, manufacturing contributed more to the commonwealth economy than agriculture for the first time ever.

By 1960, nearly fifty thousand workers kept more than five hundred plants going. Per capita income remained lower than in the States, but Puerto Rico shone as an example of economic progress among Latin American countries. Puerto Rico's prosperity has continued to grow though at a slower pace than hoped for at the outset of Operation Bootstrap. While the commonwealth leads Latin America in wealth, it still falls well below the poorest state in the United States in income, production and employment. In spite of Congressional attempts to encourage growth, such as the Caribbean Basin Initiative which provides incentives to American firms for operating in Puerto Rico, the commonwealth persistently relies on direct subsidies. In the last few years, entitlements from the Federal government amounted to 25 percent of the commonwealth's gross domestic product. Unemployment runs consistently above 20 percent. These problems, in addition to the question of Puerto Rico's future relationship with the United States, are still to be tackled. In the meantime, Puerto Rico continues to make tremendous strides in education, health care and social equity. Perhaps the island will have to wait for another great leader, like Ponce, Power, or Muñoz, before lasting solutions can be found.

Isabel Segunda, Culebra.

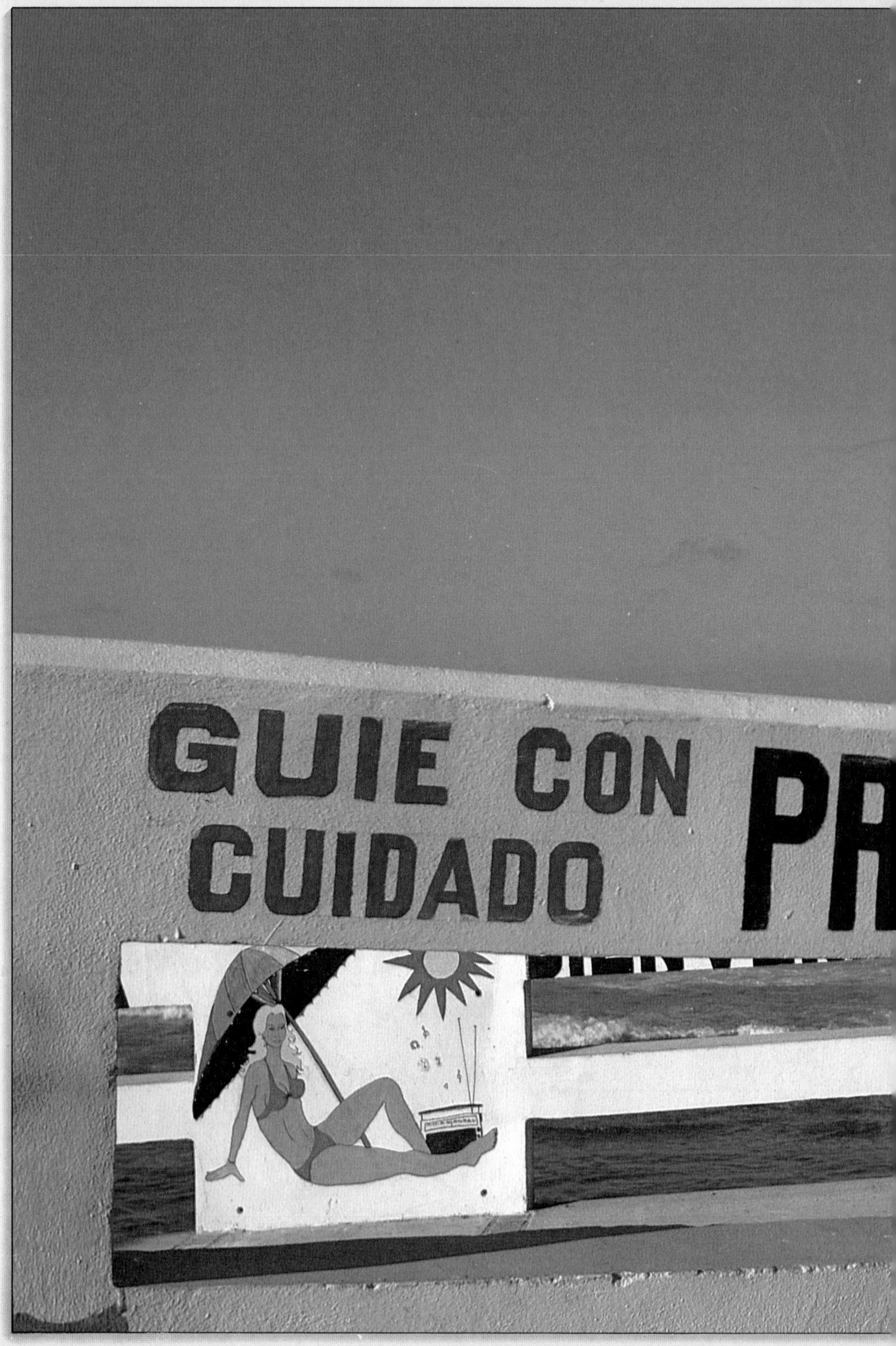
GUIE CON
CUIDADO

LIFE IN PUERTO RICO

There is a song, one among many, which stands as the most evocative of what it means to live in the paradise which is Puerto Rico. If not in fact — there is squalor amid the great natural beauty, a certain sadness amid the promise — this paradise exists in the terrain of the heart.

Written by José Manuel Rivera, "Mi Tierra Borincana" extolls with deceptive simplicity the reasons to endure the *tapones* in San Juan, the ineptitude of certain bureaucracies, and even the preciousness of certain resources — water in particular — Continentals (non-Puerto Ricans from the mainland who come to live there) too often take for granted or with impatience.

"How beautiful it is, to live in this dreamland! And how beautiful it is to be the master of the *coquí's* song!" the song says. "What an advantage it is to reap the coffee of this great gift!"

In a certain sense, the lyrics are themselves an illusion, yet on another they're very real. For while life on the island for natives and emigrants alike is not what it was 20 or even 10 years ago — there is more crime in the bigger cities; its working-class works harder for what seems to be less and less — its lure, for those who truly love Puerto Rico, cannot be silenced.

Living anywhere within the Commonwealth requires a balance of cleverness, common sense, and hard realism for Puerto Ricans and Continentals alike. Opulence is hardly uncommon among those who can afford it — in the wealthier suburbs of San Juan, for example, a modest-looking three-bedroom house with a small yard can cost upwards of $200,000 — but even so the display of wealth isn't encouraged.

What's more important is a sense of belonging, acquired largely through willing readjustment to Puerto Rico's pace. The practice of businesses closing from noon until two or even three in the afternoon isn't as prevalent as it used to be, due mostly to the increasing use of air-conditioning, but it's hardly dead. And the attitude behind it is certainly quite healthy.

It's an attitude which sees work not as an end in itself, but the means by which people can then enjoy themselves. Weekends are

Preceding pages: festival marches, Ponce; relaxing on Culebra Island; La Perla, San Juan. Left, Hato Rey modernity.

taken very seriously, and major holidays, especially Christmas, even more so. In the States, Christmas lasts perhaps a week; on the island the celebrations begin in mid-December and don't stop until Three King's Day, January 6. It's presumed by residents there will be company, people coming from far away to visit or just neighbors stopping by from roughly December 15 (which is also the official start of the tourist season, which runs through April 15 of the following year) until the last *pasteles* are eaten and the last glasses of *coquito* consumed.

It's at times difficult to convince non-residents that day-to-day life in Puerto Rico is hardly the stuff of all those steamy novels about life in a tropical paradise.

Though the University of Puerto Rico's ambitious School of Agriculture continues to experiment with ways of growing kinds of produce which must be imported now, fruits and vegetables almost ubiquitously common in the States are usually hard to find.

And yet, who needs apples when there are still trucks along almost every major road selling native oranges — *chinas* (chee-nas) — at a few dollars for a big bag? Despite the incursion of a horde of mainland products of dubious nutritional repute — the Puerto Rican sweet tooth matches that of the Italians and the Viennese — *comida Criolla* is still the food of the day in most households.

It's heavy food, rich with an invigorating assortment of beans, from *arroz con habichuelas* (rice with either small pink beans or kidney beans) and *arroz con gandules* (pigeon peas) to *lechón asado* (whole roast suckling pig) prepared almost exclusively for holidays and large family gatherings, and its counterpart, *perníl* (fresh picnic ham in most Stateside butcher shops and supermarkets). Both are seasoned with *adóbo*, a thick, fragrant paste of garlic, vinegar, peppercorns, and parsely or oregano.

Strangely, for a place with so much marine bounty — its bluegreen waters are full of grouper, yellowtail, spiny lobster, squid, sea snail, conch and shark — native Puerto Ricans for the most part shun fish, preferring chicken and pork. Saltood — *bacalao* — is, however, a staple as well, which is usually mistranslated as "creole," and that's something else altogether.

Siestas, Cars and Gas

With or without the benefits of a *siesta*, that sort of eating, still mostly done during

Left, nighttime revelry during the Festival San Sebastián.

the lunch hour, tends to make the pace of transacting business a little slower; even, perhaps, more sensible. Only behind the wheels of the island's cars — Puerto Rico ranks sixth in the world for the ratio of motor vehicles to people — is there any indication that anyone's in a hurry.

Cars are bought for either practicality or show, and those who buy for show know they're taking risks. Gas is expensive, since it's brought in, and the island's poverty has been a sad and consistent fact of life. It explains in part the decorative iron grillwork on almost every middle- and upper-class house and why so many cars would seem as at home in rural Maine, well-used, even battered, as they do on the island.

Practicality, however, is yet another given among the island's residents. Its food is practical, and is far less expensive than Stateside delicacies; the *siesta* is practical too, since while Puerto Rico's heat rarely reaches the oppresive levels it can in summer in the States, it's conducive to doing things considerably more slowly.

The island's climate is a meteorologist's dream, since throughout the 100-mile width and 32-mile breadth are at least three entirely different kinds of weather. The north coast is a textbook study in tropical vegetation: palm trees (which are not native to the Caribbean at all; Spanish settlers, who were introduced to them by the Moors, brought them in, banana bushes, hibiscus, jasmine, mimosa.

In the mountains, the greenery is impossibly lush, with orchids and an amazing range of ferns, among other imposing plants. The southern and eastern coasts are drier, even though it rains every day almost everywhere in the island. There are mesquite and cactus along the southern coast, where the arid beauty can be surprisingly deceptive; nestled against a yucca tree there might be a banana plant or mimosa.

The Land of Mountains

Puerto Rico is only technically 32 miles from north to south; if it were to be flattened, it would probably be more than three times that size.

One of the most riveting experiences for commuters is the majesty of the island's mountains. Though the elevations themselves aren't statistically impressive, the effect they generate is.

Mountain's shadow falls upon mountain's shadow; in places such as Barranquitas and

Right, Isabelan unicyclists in festival parade, San Sebastían.

throughout the rest of the island's Cordillera Central — the air is almost too sweet to breathe, and the heat of the lowlands is replaced by an almost silky cool.

The people who live in those mountains — farmers, mostly, still called *jíbaros* in derogation by those who've moved to the cities and the States — treat their surroundings with a mix of love, faith and superstition. Though the island is predominantly Roman Catholic, spiritualism still flourishes. Saints are not only prayed to and celebrated, but relied upon.

It's a fairly common bit of mythology that the island hasn't suffered from the full force of a hurricane since 1932 both because of the special protection given by Our Lady of Providence — usually depicted as the Virgin Mary seated in a chair, holding the Christ child as a little boy with great maternal care — and various waters, allegedly magic, kept in jars in many country houses, as well as more than a few city residences.

The force of the island's beauty, however, can never be underplayed. It's no accident the island has a major observatory at Arecibo; more of the solar system can been seen under a Puerto Rican night sky than just about anywhere else in the Western hemisphere.

There are those who contend weather is born in and around Puerto Rico, and it's not without sound reason. No matter what the weather, the skies over the island are rich with activity. It can rain furiously for 15 minutes, then in another 15, everything will be dry; in El Yunque — the anvil — the island's celebrated rain forest, you can watch it rain on one mountain while the sun shines on another.

The major resorts are clustered around the coast for obvious reasons; there are both calm beaches well-protected by reefs and more open ones favored by surfers.

Much of Puerto Rico's greatest beauty and fascination for the ambitious visitor lies inland. Camping is becoming increasingly popular; there are now five — not counting two others on Culebra and its sister island, Vieques — official campsites with running water, showers and other comforts in relatively out of the way places such as San Germán, which is full of fine, time-weathered Spanish colonial architecture.

Even though camping is beginning to catch on among residents, the traditional pastimes of sailing and holding Sunday picnics at the beach hold sway. Everything in any faint way ritualistic or ceremonial in Puerto Rico is fully a family affair, and this includes seeing

Right, relaxing in Loíza.

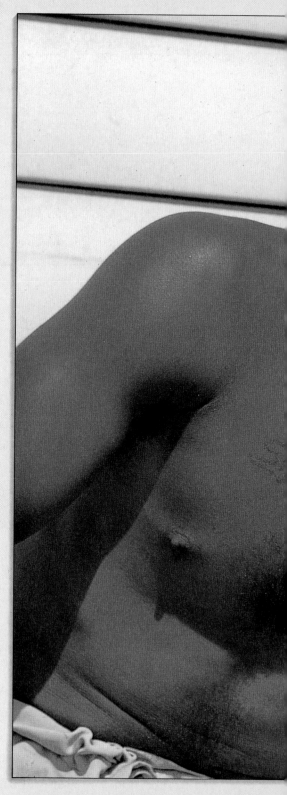

relatives arrive and depart at the San Juan airport.

Brothers, parents, sisters, uncles, aunts and cousins line arrival ramps and immediately surround the appropriate arrivals. The time of year or status of the visitor or returnee doesn't matter at all; it's much more simply a display of both affection and identity. And the visitor comes laden with about as many supplies — clothes for kids, books, records and things which are hard to find on the island, such as mint jelly, inexpensive Christmas tree lights, and real maple syrup — as he or she leaves with, the things someone who becomes homesick for Puerto Rico can't buy unless he or she lives in New York.

The relationship of the island to the mainland has been an enigma since U.S. troops landed at Guanica in 1898. Constitutionally, it exists in a curious limbo; though citizens, Puerto Ricans can't vote for Presidents, and the appointed resident Commissioner to the U.S. House of Representatives has no voting power of his own.

There are three major political parties: the PDP (Partido Democratica Popular), which is the oldest, founded in 1938 and has loose ties to Stateside Democrats. The PDP advocates maintenance of the current system. Although in English Puerto Rico is a Commonwealth like Pennsylvania and Massachusetts, officially it's an ''associated free state,'' which receives federal funding yet pays no federal taxes.

The second, the PNP (Partido Nuevo Progressivo), advocates statehood. Only nominally Republican, its higher-ranking members ignore party lines, mostly, when dealing with Washington. While there has been a configuration of pro-statehood partisans for the last 30 years at least, the party's current structure goes back only to 1968.

The PIP (Partido Independentista Puertoriqueno) was founded in 1946, and favors complete independencé. PIP members are often viewed by pro-statehooders as having decidedly leftist aspirations, but as with everything else of a complex nature on the island, the truth is far more elusive.

A favorite line among drivers of taxicabs and *públicos* (the island's quite legitimate gypsy transportation system, in which rates are highly flexible rather than metered) is that while they think independence is a great idea, they'll never see it in their lifetimes.

Puerto Rico is a place of which it can truly be said everyone comes from somewhere

Right, horseback riding is a popular pastime on an island full of battered automobiles.

else. There are the traces of Taíno and Caribe blood left in the fine, high cheekbones of many of those who've lived on the island for generations and caught in the depth of their deep and beautiful eyes. In the town of Loíza in fact, the evidence of the island's slave-trading days is impossible to ignore; a great many Loízanos are truly black, so the sun shining on their skin gives it a bluish cast.

There are women with skin the color of *café con leche* — the strong coffee with hot milk which is a staple on every breakfast table — whose tightly curly hair is naturally auburn, and children with liquid blue eyes and blond hair whose faces are exotically beautiful, thanks to any number of forebears, traders, pirates, artisans, slaves, colonists.

Despite all varieties of political differences, pride is universal and strong. Though U.S. flags fly alongside all Puerto Rico flags in public places and schoolchildren sing "The Star Spangled Banner" before "La Boriñquena," the island's own hauntingly beautiful anthem, being Puerto Rican always comes first.

And like nearly everything else there, this isn't without its paradoxical side. The people who've chosen to live there, Puerto Ricans and Continentals and others alike, love the island intensely, yet know with conviction that many things are far from perfect. That's where the patience, cleverness and common sense comes in.

The Port Authority (Autoridad de Puertos), for example, is the only municipal agency which consistently makes a profit. Yet those who relay on the ferries it operates between Fajardo, Vieques and Culebra have a well-honed sense of humor towards the less-than-pristine equipment it maintains. It might take two hours. It might take six. *Así es la vida.* That's life.

There is, however, determination under that patience. The attitude of many towards the U.S. Navy, which maintains a major base at Sabana Seca and conducts maneuvers in and around the island's waters ranges from very faint affection to open resentment. This was acute in 1970, when Culebrans were kept off Flamenco — as they had been for decades — during practice bombing runs.

"Enough," said 2,000 people all at once. The red flag went up to keep people off the beach; most of the population headed straight for it, loaded with picnic coolers. They were going to picnic until the Navy stopped their target runs so close to their beach. Three years later, everyone went home when the

Left, taking a break — a forester sits still for a breather in the El Yunque rain forest.

Navy finally agreed to leave Flamenco alone. This tenacity was replayed in 1985 on Vieques with a similar complaint.

Continentals who relocate to the bigger cities and their environs learn very quickly from their neighbors how to be practical. It's unwise, and downright foolish in some places, to flaunt wealth with fancy cars and houses filled with expensive things. To grow too attached to property is almost to court losing it.

As a result, and in no small way a fortunate one, what the island's residents really cherish are the things which have no price tags: family, friends, just the pleasure, challenging as it can sometimes be, of living where they do.

Its anthem says it best, probably. Unlike other nations' songs which speak glowingly of military might and triumph over adversaries, "La Boriñquena" is a celebration of a reality which is at the same time an ideal:

The land of Borinquen,
where I was born
is a flowering garden
of exquisite magic.

A sky, always clear,
serves as its canopy,
and sings calm lullabies
to the waves at its feet.

When Columbus came
to its beaches,
he exclaimed full of admiration
"Oh! Oh! Oh!"

This is the beautiful land
I've been looking for;
it's Borinquen, the daughter,
the daughter of the sea and the sun,
the sea and the sun.

Puerto Rico is a place where beauty co-exists in places with squalor, where politics and poetry very often merge; its most celebrated leaders, among them Llorens Torres and Luís Muñoz Marin, were also poets. It is not accidental.

There is poverty, yes, an ache to those who love their island. But art grows there too, with the craftsworkers, the musicians, the composers, the playwrights and painters and sculptors and actors.

It gives Puerto Rico's beauty a face, one which is proud and at the same time edged in sadness, exotic yet utterly recognizable.

Right, blond hair and blue eyes, a Continental legacy.

PLACES

Puerto Rico? Hmm. That's beaches, right, and *paradors*, and old Spanish forts tossed in around a few frosty rum drinks? Well, yes and no. You won't want to miss tooling around Old San Juan's colorful streets, or standing on El Morro's walls, looking out into the Atlantic at the ghosts of 16th-Century British invaders, and you certainly shouldn't leave the island without chilling your lips with at least one *piña colada*, but there are far more places to see and understand than those fringed with surf and sand.

We've started our travel guide in Puerto Rico's most populous area, San Juan. Old San Juan, an eight-block area on a small peninsula, harkens back to the 16th-Century, but scant miles away in Hato Rey and Río Piedras, modern commerce is being conducted in sleek steel and glass corporate offices.

If metropolitan San Juan is the most humanly populated area of the island, then the Northeast is the most geographically populated. The range of terrain in the region, from beaches to dense rain forest to secluded islands is staggering. The Northeast's natural attractions draw the crowds.

Or head out to the Northwest coast, and you'll be able to traipse around the oddly-scaled karst mountain region. Limestone formations rise above the island's most historic cities — Arecibo, Lares, San Sebastían and Isabela.

Those karstic mountains rise up into the island's spine — the Cordillera Central. The Ruta Panoramica will take the adventurous driver from one end of the range to the other, affording spectacular views all the while.

And if you cross over the mountains to the South and Southwest regions of the island, you'll realize fully the relaxed pace of life on the island. There's Ponce, a pearl of a city, on the coast, but if you're tired of the urban hustle, you'll never be at a loss to find a quiet place to sit in the sun and keep to yourself.

Preceding page, ships lined up at dock in Old San Juan. Left, windsurfing is one of the many ways to enjoy island surf.

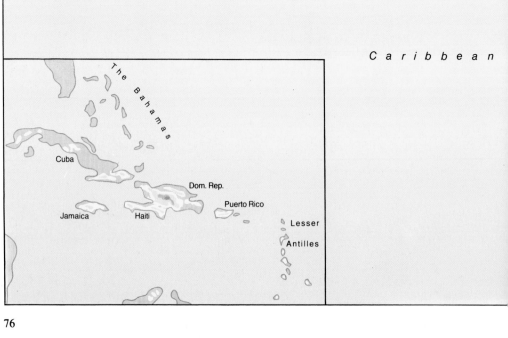

Atlantic

Isabela

Arecibo

Quebradillas
(2)

Cambalanche
Forest Reserve

Laguna
Portuguero

Aguadilla

(2)

Manatí

Pta.
Higüero

(115)

Lago de
Guajataca

Río Grande de Arecibo

Río Grande de Manatí

Rincon

Río

Culebrinas

Camuy
Caves

(2)

San Sebastian

Río Abajo
Forest Reserve

Río Tanamá

(111)

Lares

Arecibo
Observatory ■

(10)

Lago
Dos Bocas

(149)

Río

Grande

de

Añasco

Caguana
Indian Ceremonial
Park

Utuado

Lago
Caonillas

(157)

(119)

Mayagüez

Jayuya

(105)

(128)

Maricao
Fish Hatchery

Monte Guilarte
1205 ▲

Adjuntas

Cerro de Punta
1338 ▲   Toro
Negro

Hormigueros

C E N T R A L

Laguna
Joyuda

(103)

C O R D I L L E R A

(10)

Embalse
Toa Vaca

Cabo Rojo

(102)

San Germán

Canal de

(14)

(2)

Yáuco

Laguna
Cartagena

Tibes Indian
Ceremonial Center

Bahía
de Boquerón

Guayanilla

Bahía de
Guayanilla

Museum
of Fine Arts

Ponce

Bahía
Salinas

Bahía
Sucia

Guanica

Cabo Rojo
Lighthouse

Phosphorescent
Bay

Ensenada
Las Pardas

Caribbean

The Bahamas

Cuba

Dom. Rep.

Puerto Rico

Jamaica

Haiti

Lesser

Antilles

O c e a n

Isla de Cabras

Torrecillas
Lagoon

Vega Baja

Dorado

Cataño

Pta. Miquillo

Cayo
Icacos

Laguna
San José

Carolina

Rio Grande

Luquillo

Isla
Palominos

Bayamon

San Juan

③

Ferry

to Culebra

22

52

El Yunque
National Forest

Fajardo

to Vieques

167

①

Lago
Loíza

Río Fajardo

Ceiba

Isla
Piñeros

Río de Bayamon

Caguas

Juncos

Río

Río Grande

③

Ensenada
Hondo

Comerio

31

Naguabo

San Cristobal
Canyon

156

172

de

Pta. Lima

Aibonito

14

Cayey

Loíza

30

Humacao

Coamo

15

③

Caño de Guayanés

Yabucoa

Coamo
Baths

Lake
Patillas

Maunabo

Pta. Yeguas

52

Patillas

uana Díaz

①

Bahía
de Rincón

Salinas

Guayama

③

Arroyo

Pta.
Figuras

Bahía
de Jobos

Cayos
Caribes

Cayos
de Barca

S e a

Culebra Island

Cabo Northe

Cuelebrita
Isla

Cabo
Luis Peña

Dewey

Vieques Island

Isabel II

Pta. Esta

SAN JUAN

Imagine a city that looks like Paris painted pink, orange, pastel green, and white; a city paved in iron, with streets the color of thunderclouds; a banking center for a dozen island nations; an intellectual hotspot, with a handful of top-notch universities and a vibrant art scene; a tropical city, which has never had a frost.

San Juan is hard to envision until one has seen it, and hard to describe even when one has seen it. Aside from descriptions of stunning scenic beauty, or avowals of a magnificent historical legacy, it is difficult to capture what is so captivating in the city. Perhaps it is the ambiguity of being one of the oldest of Spanish cities in the New World and being subject to the government of an English-speaking power having "two citizenships, two flags, two national anthems."

But, if so, what is it that makes San Juan so special among Puerto Rican cities? Certainly not its size alone. Perhaps again it is the diversity of this city of 1 million which attracts. How can a modern city encompass the quaintness of Old San Juan and the brashness of the Hato Rey business district, the timeless seaside life of Boca de Cangrejos and the modernity of Bayamon? The glitter of the Condado and the austerity of La Perla?

It probably cannot. San Juan is all you have heard it would be. And more. And less. For no one can possibly have the breadth of interest to enjoy all its charms. This makes San Juan a city to captivate any taste. Beauty is in the eye of the creator here; you choose your own San Juan.

Preceding pages: guarding El Morro from invasions; strolling one of Old San Juan's many-hued streets. Left, colonial style in Old San Juan.

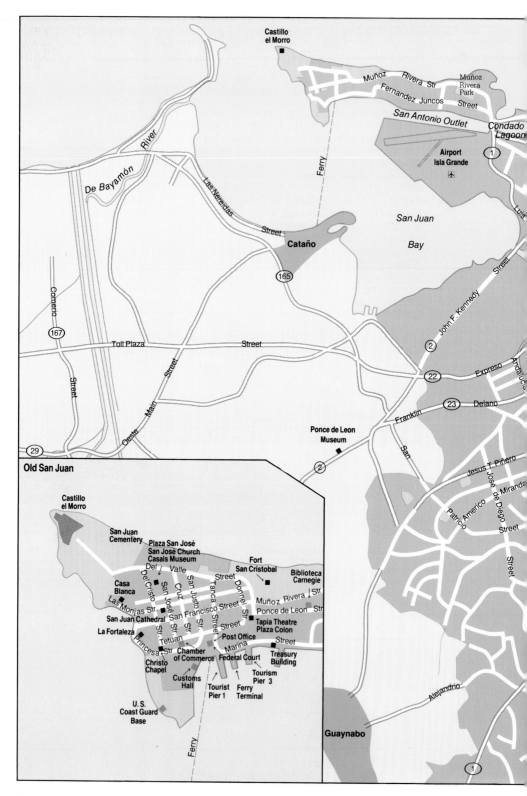

Castillo
el Morro

Muñoz Rivera Str
Muñoz
Rivera Park
Fernandez Juncos Street

San Antonio Outlet
Condado
Lagoon

Airport
Isla Grande

(1)

San Juan

Bay

Luis Muñoz

De Bayamón River

Las Nereidas
Street

Cataño

(165)

John F. Kennedy Street

Comerio

(167)

Toll Plaza   Street

Oeste   Main   Street

Street

(29)

(2)

(22)

(23)   Delano

Expreso

Franklin

Andalucia

San

Ponce de Leon
Museum

(2)

Jesus T. Piñero

José de Diego

Patricio Americo

Street

Street

Street

Old San Juan

Castillo
el Morro

San Juan
Cementery

Plaza San José
San José Church
Casals Museum

Del   Valle
Street

Fort
San Cristobal

Biblioteca
Carnegie

Casa
Blanca

Del Cristo

San José Str

Cruz

San Justo Str

Tanca Street

Donnel Str

Muñoz Rivera Str

Street

Las Monjas Str

San Juan Cathedral

San Francisco Street

Ponce de Leon Str

La Fortaleza

Tetuan   Str

Street

Tapia Theatre
Plaza Colon

Princesa Str

Post Office

Marina

Street

Christo
Chapel

Chamber
of Commerce

Federal Court

Treasury
Building

Customs
Hall

Tourist
Pier 1

Ferry
Terminal

Tourism
Pier 3

U.S.
Coast Guard
Base

Ferry

Guaynabo

(1)

Alejandro

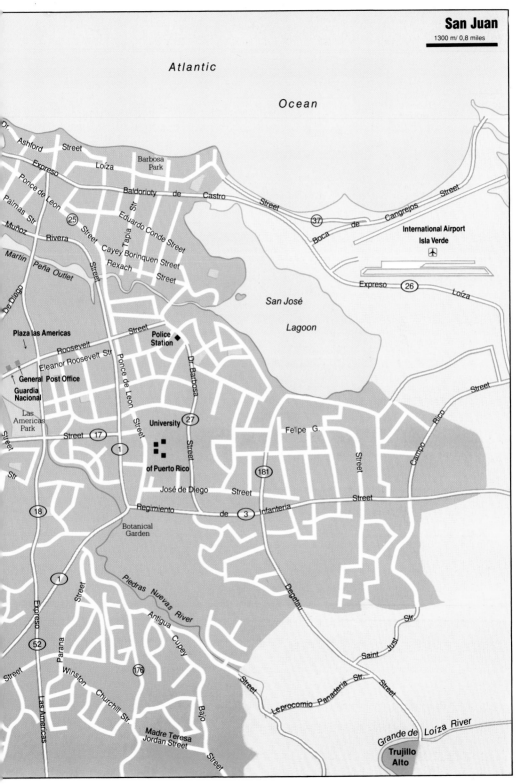

San Juan
1300 m/ 0,8 miles

Atlantic

Ocean

Dr.
Ashford Street
Expreso
Loíza
Barbosa
Park
Ponce de Leon
Baldorioty de Castro Street
37
Boca de Cangrejos Street
Palmas Str
25
Street
Eduardo Conde Street
International Airport
Isla Verde
Muñoz
Rivera
Tapia
Str
Cayey Borinquen Street
Martin
Peña Outlet
Street
Rexach
Street
Expreso
26
Loíza
De Diego
San José

Plaza las Americas
Street
Lagoon
Roosevelt
Police
Station
Eleanor Roosevelt Str
Ponce de Leon
General Post Office
Dr. Barbosa
Guardia
Nacional
Street
Las
Americas
Park
University
27
Felipe G.
Campo Rico Street
Street
17
1
181
Street
of Puerto Rico
Str
José de Diego Street
18
Regimiento de 3 Infanteria Street
Botanical
Garden
Degetau
1
Piedras Nuevas River
Str
Justi
Expreso
Antigua
Cupey
52
Parana
Saint
Street
Winston Churchill Str.
176
Bajo
Leprocomio Panaderia Str. Street
Las Americas
Madre Teresa
Jordan Street
Street
Grande de Loíza River
Trujillo
Alto

OLD SAN JUAN: SOULFUL CITADEL

No matter how much history is crammed into these seven narrow city blocks, no matter how seductive the pastel-and-wrought-iron Spanish colonial houses may seem, no matter how chock-to-the-brim with opportunities for socializing and partying this city may be, it is something altogether more spiritual that attracts Puerto Ricans and foreigners alike to San Juan.

There is something in the place that traps a traveler and forces him to lead his vacation at the pace at which a vacation should be led. If you've rushed through San Juan, you certainly have not been there. Get a good pair of walking shoes and ramble; a car is as much a liability as an asset here, anyway.

This oldest of American cities has iron streets, filled in with *adoquines*, or blocks of slag, from the lowland smelting mills of Spain's 16th Century empire. It has two of the most invulnerable forts ever constructed connected by walls that circle a peninsula. It has some of the finest restaurants and bars in the Caribbean. And the city is full of art galleries.

It is also full of some of the loudest tourists you'll meet anywhere. If you are one of them, best wishes. If not, it might be mentioned that even within its tiny area, Old San Juan has an endless supply of undiscovered attractions. These are what lead second-time visitors to call for a taxi to Old San Juan as soon as they step off the plane at Muñoz Marín Airport.

Into the City

As Puerto Rico's Spanish history begins with Columbus, Old San Juan begins in the **Plaza Colon**, or Columbus Square, a shady quadrangle built around a commemorative statue of the explorer. It is here that the high-speed, heavily trafficked **Avenidas Ponce de Leon** and **Muñoz Rivera** give way to the narrow and scarcely navigable grid that is Old San Juan. If you're unlucky or impecunious enough to be without an automobile in Puerto Rico, Plaza Colon will be your last stop on the municipal bus or *publico*. Those with cars will want to find a place to park them, itself no mean

feat.

Located at the southeastern corner of the Old San Juan quadrant, Plaza Colon is an ideal spot for fanning out on a walking tour of the city. Plaza Colon itself offers a good introductory stroll. On its south side is the **Teatro Tapiay Rivera**, a tasteful, ochre hacienda-like structure dating from 1826 and beautifully restored in the mid-1970s. For all its other cultural achievements, Puerto Rico has produced very little theater of note; Alejandro Tapiay Rivera (1826-1882), after whom the theater is named, is the earliest and perhaps most notable exception. Today the theater premieres plays by Latin America's most exciting contemporary dramatists, among them the Puerto Rican Rene Marques. Across the street from the theater on the plaza's eastern side, is the **Old Casino of Puerto Rico**, built shortly after the American capture of Puerto Rico but harking back architecturally to the Spanish reign.

Ironically, if somewhat predictably, the path most tourists take into Old San Juan is the least characteristic of the city as a whole. **Calle Fortaleza** is, at least for three blocks, as cluttered with bar-

Left, Friday night *paseo*, Old San Juan; right, Plazuela de la Rogativa, San Juan.

gain basements, souvenir shops and second rate hotels as any place in the city.

Fortunately, Calle Fortaleza is just as crowded with architectural wonders. The first right along the street is **Callejon de la Capilla**, a romantic, lantern-lit alley-way which passes a decent *colmado* and an unpretentious outdoor cafe as it arcs uphill to Calle San Francisco. At the corner of Fortaleza and Callejon de la Capilla, the **Casa del Callejon**, an 18th-Century residence, houses two charming museums. The **Museum of Colonial Architecture**, on the first floor, has an impressive collection of blueprints, city plans and photographs, but is certainly more satisfying to those already familiar with the layout of San Juan. Upstairs, the **Museum of the Puerto Rican Family** shows a reconstructed Puerto Rican home of a century ago.

Continuing on Calle Fortaleza, turn right on Calle Tanca for a bit of relaxation in the sloping **Plaza Salvador Brau**, or left down Calle Tanca towards the piers of San Juan Port. Every weekend night, Calle Tanca is filled with throngs of San Juan's teenagers queuing up for admission to the discos and bars along the street.

Most ports which serve a large number of cruise ships end up looking rather like jungles of cranes and heavy machinery. San Juan, which takes more cruise traffic than any port in the Caribbean, is an exception. The port not only benefits from the tastefulness of its more utilitarian maritime buildings (the pink, mock-colonial **United States Customs House** is a good example), but actually boasts a beautiful cityscape as well.

Plaza de Hostos is an oasis of shade in a square full of *adoquine*. Named after the 19th-Century *independentista* scholar, it provides a haven for sunburnt tourists and locals alike; Plaza de Hostos must be the domino capital of the Caribbean. Looming over the plaza is an office of the **Banco Popular de Puerto Rico**, surely one of the great modern architectural triumphs of the Caribbean. This brawny, 10-story mass, built in the mid-1930s, is unashamedly art-deco. Heavy cameo eagles brood over the main entrance, which is lettered in sans serif gilt intaglio. Elongated windows with prominent pastel mullions run the full height of a faintly apsidal facade.

The pier area is particularly fortunate

Callejon de la Capilla, Old San Juan.

culinarily. **Calle Tetuan** has a number of first-rate restaurants and a sprinkling of clubs, though it is marred somewhat by the massive parking garage it shares with Calle Recinto Sur. Those who prefer *carnalidad* to *carne* can entertain themselves a short walk eastwards on Calle Marina.

Whether approaching uphill on Calle Cruz from Plaza de Hostos, or via Calle Fortaleza from Plaza Colon, almost all travelers pass through the workaday heart of Old San Juan, centering around the **City Hall** (*Alcaldía*) and the adjacent Plaza de Armas.

San Juan's City Hall was begun in 1602 to be an exact replica of Madrid's. What works in Europe seems rather somber for the Antilles, but it is an attractive building nonetheless, one whose charms are enhanced by the fact that small businesses operate within the same arch-covered block as the local government. The plaza is no less historic, having served, in the days before soldiers were permanently billeted in San Juan, as the training field for the Spanish soldiers defending the island (hence the name).

Nonetheless, the main streets along the **Plaza de Armas** have the unpretentious likability of a business district, rather than the imposing sense of history of much of San Juan. **Calle San Francisco** is a friendly mix of tourist shops and government buildings, while the part of Calle Fortaleza just south of the plaza is an engaging few blocks of restaurants and department stores. Worth a visit is **The Butterfly People**, an atmospheric, hanging-plants, sort of quiche restaurant, overlooking a placid courtyard. It's all very peaceful and aesthetic; walls are covered with plexiglass-mounted arrangements of thousands and thousands of native butterflies. If you're more interested in examining the lepidoptera than in eating the food, it's unlikely you'll encounter much resistance from the proprietors, who have a local reputation for viewing life a tad more cosmically than most.

Across the street, **González Padín** is the granddaddy of Puerto Rico's department stores. When built at the turn of the century, it was the tallest structure on the island. Down Calle Cruz is **The Bookstore**, with the largest selection of English titles in Old San Juan, as well as a number of North American periodicals. After examining the mosaic work on the

Vendor, Old San Juan.

facade of the apartment opposite and perhaps watching the cruise boats arrive and depart in San Juan Bay directly below, buy a copy of the *New York Times* and take it into the **Cafe de Los Amigos** next door. Natives consider the coffee here — thick, dark, and served in tiny paper cups — the best bargain in Old San Juan. Rules of conduct for Los Amigos are posted prominently behind the counter, among them *NO DISCUTA POLITICA AQUI.*

La Fortaleza

Calle Fortaleza grows more and more dignified as it approaches **La Fortaleza** itself. This chalk-white wonder of a fortress is the oldest continuously inhabited executive mansion in the New World and construction began in 1532 and was completed in 1540, and serves to this day as the residence of the Governor of Puerto Rico. La Fortaleza, known originally as Santa Carolina, is a wonder of a fortress in only the narrowest architectural sense. In fact, much of Old San Juan looks as it does today because of the strategic inadequacy of its first bastion.

This was apparent even to the Spanish architects, who decided that the nubby peninsula on which La Fortaleza was being built did not command enough of San Juan Bay to protect completely against invasion from the sea. Accordingly, construction of the massive fort at the tip of the San Juan Peninsula — El Morro — began in the 1540s. The 1588 sinking of the Spanish armada made the West Indian possessions of the Spanish Crown more vulnerable than ever, with the result that even more Puerto Rican colonists clamored for greater fortification. By 1595, Queen Elizabeth, hearing of 2 million ducats of gold stored in La Fortaleza, quickly despatched Sir Francis Drake, whose ambitions included not only the great bounty of gold, but all the Spanish lands of the New World as well. Drake arrived in San Juan in late November of that year. He stopped across the bay at Isla de Cabras, and launched a flotilla of several dozen ships. Ten would never go back to England, and 400 English sailors would rest forever beneath San Juan harbor. Drake's own cabin was torn apart by a mortar shell during the invasion.

Perhaps the Spanish grew complacent

Tapia Theater, San Juan.

after the first thwarted invasion of their colonial capital, or perhaps it was due to the death of Drake just a year later. Whatever the reason, in June of 1598, the Duke of Cumberland was able to land a force of about 1,000 men in the area of Puerta de Tierra, and march on to San Juan.

British Invasion

The 400 Spanish soldiers defending the city were suffering from a severe epidemic but put up a valiant resistance, enduring a 15-day siege inside El Morro before capitulating. The Union Jack flew over the walls of La Fortaleza. The British were hounded by the Spanish colonists almost as soon as the port came into British hands, but it was less Spanish resistance than British *lack* of resistance to the same epidemic that had beleaguered the island's defenders that led the occupying army to give in. In a matter of several weeks after the invasion, Cumberland sailed for home, having lost over 400 sailors, to leave San Juan in peace for another 27 years.

The year 1625 saw the final occupation of La Fortaleza during colonial times. A Dutch fleet under the command of Boudewijn Hendrikszoon (Bowdoin Hendrickson) swiftly moved into San Juan Bay and set up a beachhead between El Morro and La Fortaleza. Though swift response from the island's defenders had the Dutch scurrying back to their boats in short order, the Dutch burned much of the city to the ground, including several dozen houses, Bishop Bernardo de Balbuena's library (at that time the finest in the New World), and much of La Fortaleza. The reconstruction of La Fortaleza began in 1640; the building was expanded in 1800 and 1846. Guided tours of the building are trips through periods of La Fortaleza's architectural and military history.

Only someone who lives on another street would claim that **Calle del Cristo** (Christ's Street) is not the most alluring of Old San Juan's thoroughfares. It is an intoxicating avenue of sights and sounds, of romance and history. Running from a point high above San Juan Bay, Calle del Cristo arches to an even higher perch above San Juan's Atlantic shore, where El Morro looks sternly out to sea. It can claim Old San Juan's most popular park, its most underrated

Playing in Las Palomas Park, Old San Juan.

museum, most famous cathedral, poshest hotel, and finest bar.

This adventure in *adoquines* beings at the **Parque de las Palomas** (Pigeon Park), a part of the city walls which thousands of pigeons have made their home. The birds nest in little chinks in the park walls, and on certain particularly cold days outnumber the tourists and *jibarito* schoolchildren, who seem to be bused in by the flockload. The pigeons are safe to feed by hand, most of them being at least as continent as their grade-school admirers. Fabulous views of the bay make the park a popular spot for lovers and an even more popular spot for aspiring ones.

Building with Love

Love almost certainly played a part in the construction of the quaint **Capilla del Cristo** (Chapel of Christ). Story has it that during an 18th-Century horse race, one of two competing riders failed to make a left turn onto Calle Tetuan and plummeted over the massive cliffs, seemingly to his death. When he survived, astounded locals constructed a chapel to commemorate Christ's inter-cession. More cynical Puerto Ricans claim that the race was a sort of gentlemanly duel over a comely young woman between two chivalrous *enamorados.* One fell to his death in what reads like a colonial *Rebel Without a Cause;* the chapel was built both to commemorate the tragedy and to block off Calle Cristo to prevent such a mishap from occuring again.

The peninsula stretching below the Cristo Chapel is known as **La Puntilla.** Best known as the site of defunct **La Princesa Prison**, it now houses a few official buildings and a somewhat swank modern condominium complex.

A short walk up Calle del Cristo on the right is one of Puerto Rico's most enchanting and least-known museums. The **Casa del Libro** is a breezy, parqueted sanctuary chock full of some of the finest European illuminated manuscripts this side of Bobbio, as well as some fine work by local artists and illustrators and an excellent selection of postcards.

It seems only fitting in this land of paradoxes that one of San Juan's great surprises should abut one of its great disappointments. **The Museo de Arte** **Bastion de Las Palmas, San Juan.**

de Puerto Rico, housed in a pretty 18th-Century house next door, attracts only due to its courtyard. Exhibits downstairs are often one-man shows by obscure local artists, while the upstairs section, which is reputed to house fine European work, seems never to be open.

Any aesthetic overdose one suffers on the south part of Calle del Cristo can be cured with a bracing piña colada in one of the bars on the north side. A plaque around the corner on Calle Fortaleza claims that a bar which once occupied the site of what is now a jewelry store was the birthplace, in the early 1960s, of the piña colada. This is nonsense; and besides, no matter where the birthplace of the piña colada, it seems right at home anywhere in the city.

A Cathedral and a Convent

Ascending Cristo Street, even the most skeptical of travelers will begin to see what he came to San Juan for. On the right, usually bathed in sunlight at afternoon, is the Cathedral Metropolitana, or **San Juan Cathedral**, a fabulous beige-and-white structure that must count among the most important houses of worship in the west. It was here that Sebastián Ramírez, the first bishop to be consecrated in the New World, was ordained.

The beauty of the church's exterior is immediately perceptible. Its three tiers of white pilaster and arch mount to a simple cross at the church's pinnacle. The three brick-red and white cupolas atop the church are among San Juan's most photogenic objects, and must themselves lure many visitors to the island each year.

But the interior of the church is not as easy to appreciate for anyone who thinks of cathedrals primarily in their French, German, or English incarnations. For one, the floor is of a black parquet, which seems to belie the solemnity of the building. The brown and ochre *trompe l'oeil* ceiling is pretty, but too close to the worshipper's eye to seriously *trompe* anybody. In truth, the Cathedral needs several visits to appreciate, but will in time reward the most discerning.

Among the highlights of the Cathedral are **Ponce's gravestone**, with an understated virgin warrior glancing down at the body and the red script of the epitaph, and the glittering blue statue of **La**

San Juan Cathedral.

Virgen de Providencia, Puerto Rico's Patroness, located nearby. Pius' remains are to be found in a glass case containing a macabre plaster figure of the saint, to the rear of the altar. There's another such effigy, of a prostrate Jesus, in the **Chapel of Souls in Purgatory** in the Cathedral's right nave.

Directly across Calle Cristo from the Cathedral is **El Convento**, now a luxury hotel established in 1651 as a convent for Carmelite nuns, San Juan's first. When the nuns moved to Santurce in the early part of this century, the convent fell into disrepair. It was restored only after World War Two, in a multi million-dollar project that took several years. Though very few of the fixtures are originals, all the interior decor fits in harmoniously with the conception of a nunnery-turned hotel.

Bars do not often make travel guides, but **El Batey**, across Calle Cristo from the Convento, is wrapped up in the recent cultural and intellectual life of its city in a way that few bars are. Very few travelers of any renown or intellect pass through the city without at least one visit to this old-world wonder, whose regular clientele is a fairly even mix of American and European expatriates and young locals. *Batey* is a Taíno Indian word, meaning "dirt space for ceremonial games," and that is exactly what the bar is, an old San Juan home pushing its third century and left in utter disrepair for decades. Regulars claim the jukebox to be the best in the Antilles.

Steps and Statues

Across Cristo from San Juan Cathedral, between the fork of two of San Juan's oldest and most pleasant *adoquine* streets, lies the lush **Plazuela de las Monjas** (Nun's Square), a perfect spot for an urban picnic. The Square looks out on not only the Cathedral and El Convento, but also the **Casa Cabildo**, San Juan's original City Hall, which now houses an interior design company.

A walk down **Caleta San Juan** will take you to the **City Gates**, the only one of three original portals remaining. Sailors weary of their voyages used to moor their ships in San Juan Bay, ferry themselves ashore, enter through the gates, and walk to prayer services via Caleta San Juan, which describes a straight line between the gates and the Flea market, Plaza San José.

Flea market, Plaza San José.

main altar of the Cathedral. The gates are now open to one-way automobile traffic, as a continuation of Calle Sol, **Paseo la Princesa**, the route that leads below the City Walls back to de Hostos Square is certainly one of the world's most romantic city-meets-sea drives.

San Juan Bay is considered too polluted to swim in by the local authorities. But the more adventurous do often swim to the right of the big pier outside the San Juan gates.

Continuing up Recinto del Oesto past more examples of fine colonial architecture, one reaches a modern sculpture of religious women in procession. This is **La Rogativa** and commemorates the repelling of an English seige of San Juan in the spring of 1797. The legend runs that General Sir Ralph Abercromby led a fleet of British ships to take San Juan in a rapid, all-out assault by land and sea. When this plan failed, Abercromby ordered a naval blockade, which lasted two weeks, while the residents of San Juan began to suffer from dysentery, losing hope of the arrival of Spanish reinforcements from the inland settlements. The governor called for a *rogativa*, or divine entreaty, to the Saints Ursula and Catherine. All the women of San Juan marched through the town carrying torches, to the accompaniment of loud ringing of tocsins. Abercromby, fearing that reinforcements had arrived from the countryside, quit San Juan with all his ships, never to return.

The walk back to the Cathedral on **Caleta de las Monjas** is full of surprises, chief among them, the step streets leading up to the left towards Calles Sol and San Sebastián. At the top of the first, **Escalinata de las Monjas**, is the old **Palace of the Bishop of San Juan.** The second, **Calle de Hospital,** detours left around the Palace to San Juan's Hospital Rodríguez. The two streets are somewhat in disrepair, but are the only two of their type that remain in a city that was once full of them.

With all the historical legacy San Juan offers, it's sometimes easy to forget to view the city as its natives view it: as a place to have fun. Calle San Sebastián is perhaps the preeminent place in the old city to do just that. Running perpendicular to the top of Calle Cristo, it's a place of museums and old homes whose many bars and spacious plaza make it a mecca for *sanjuanero* youth of all descriptions.

Food vendor outside Museo Pablo Casals, Plaza San José.

Plaza San José serves as the centerpiece for the street, paved with rosy Spanish conglomerate about a statue of Ponce de Leon made from English cannons melted down after the first invasion. The plaza draws hundreds of partying teenagers on warm weekend evenings ("evenings" being at about 1 a.m. in Puerto Rico) and hundreds of tourists throughout the year.

San Juan's **Dominican Convent** dominates the plaza. Built in 1523, this mammoth, white, elegantly domed structure has seen as much history as any on the island. The complex proved particularly popular among foreign armies: the Earl of Cumberland used the convent to study in during the English occupation of 1598, and Bowdoin Hendrickson quartered some of his men there during the Dutch occupation. Until two decades ago, it was the headquarters of the U.S. Antilles Command.

The Convent now houses the **Institute of Puerto Rican Culture**, the body which has been more than any other responsible for the renaissance in Puerto Rican scholarship and art over the last several years. Under their auspices, the parts of the convent not used for office space have been converted to cultural ends. A beautiful indoor patio is the scene of many concerts and plays, and now serves as the focus for the magnificent San Juan Museum of History and Art. The old convent library has been restored to its original 16th-Century decor, and the nearby **Center of Popular Arts** offers exposure to local artists.

Museum Spin-Offs

A whole complex of museums has sprung up around the Dominican convent. The **Museo Pablo Casals**, which abuts the convent, is a petite, gray, two-story townhouse storing memorabilia of the legendary cellist who moved to Puerto Rico in 1957 and lived here until his death in 1973. It includes manuscripts, instruments, texts of his speeches to the United Nations, and a collection of cassettes of his music which can be heard on request.

The **Museum of Santos** includes numerous examples of that most Puerto Rican of art forms, *santo,* or "saint" carving. These small, brightly colored wood shapes were used by the early Spanish missionaries to coax the native Taíno Indians of Puerto Rico to convert to Christianity. Other interesting visits in the Dominican Convent area include the **Indian Museum**, the **Museum of Pharmacy** and the **Library of the Society of Puerto Rican Authors.**

Next to the Convent itself is the stunning and unusual **Church of San José.** Built shortly after the convent in the 1530s, San José is the second oldest church in the Western Hemisphere; only San Juan Cathedral, a half-block down the street, is older. The Gothic architecture of the structure is a true rarity; only the Spanish arrived in the New World early enough to build Gothic churches, and only a handful exist today. The interior of San José certainly has far more charm than that of the nearby cathedral. A wooden crucifix of the mid-16th Century, donated by Ponce de Leon, is one of the highlights here, as is the 15th-Century altar brought from Cadíz. The church was the original resting place of Ponce in Puerto Rico, after his body was removed from Cuba, and the great Puerto Rican painter, José Campeche, is buried here.

The Spanish colonists considered San Juan chiefly as a military stronghold, and held military architecture as their

Left, San José Church; and right, view of La Perla and El Morro from San Crístobal.

first priority. It is not surprising, then, that contemporary *sanjuaneros* are proudest of the breathtaking forts, unique in the western world, that their antecedents left them.

El Morro

El Castillo San Felipe del Morro, or El Morro, the larger of the two forts, commands San Juan Bay with six levels of gun emplacements and walls that tower 140 feet (43 meters) over the Atlantic. Its gun's embrasures were capable of aiming at any ships anywhere within El Morro's field of vision, and the walls themselves, connected with the system that circles San Juan, are 20 feet thick.

The fort's first battery was completed in the 1540s, but it was not until 1589, when Juan Bautista Antonelli arrived with a team of other Spanish military engineers to begin raising a true bulwark along the edge of the peninsula, that the fort was completed. When Drake attacked in 1595, he was roundly repulsed, but Cumberland's land attack from the Condado succeeded in piercing El Morro's still vulnerable rear approach. The English held the fort for three months until dysentery took the lives of nearly half their men. It would be the last time El Morro would fall, even holding out against the Dutch siege of 1625 and the American gunnery fire which rained upon it during the Spanish-American War of 1898.

Today, visitors appreciate El Morro more for its breathtaking views and architecture than for the protection it affords them. The approach to the fort is over a vast, 27-acre parkland, former drill square for the soldiers and current haven for kite-flyers and strolling lovers. A road through the green leads over a moat and into the massive structure, crossing El Morro's main courtyard, with its beautiful yellow walls and white archways. Here are a souvenir shop and a museum, both of which are useful in orienting the traveler to the fort's layout and history.

The massive archway facing over San Juan Bay on the west side of the courtyard is the entrance to what looks like the longest skateboard run in the world, a huge, stone, step-flanked ramp leading to the lower ramparts, the area of the fort known as the **Santa Barbara Bastion.** This is the most popular of the fort's

Cemetery, Old San Juan.

various sections, affording views of the surf crashing below, and of the fort from the ocean side, as its invaders saw it. Definitely not recommended for the acrophobic.

Back upon the upper level of El Morro, a left turn through the courtyard patio leads to another ramp, this one twisting rightwards towards the **Port of San Juan Lighthouse.** This highest point of El Morro was destroyed by an American mortar shell during the Spanish-American War, but later restored, and currently functions to mark the channel entrance to San Juan Harbor.

One note about the lovely rounded sentry boxes that line the walls of San Juan's forts. Known as *garitas,* these are peculiar to the island, and, indeed, serve as the official symbol of the island which they guard. However, they are very secluded, and as San Juan is a city short on public restrooms, they are occasionally quite odoriferous.

San Juan Cemetery, considered by many the most picturesque in the world, sits on a broad, grassy hummock of land tucked between El Morro's walls and the pounding surf. Its highlight is a tiny circular chapel, set among the bleach-white gravestones and dates from the late 19th Century.

Abutting El Morro's grounds, the **Casa Blanca** is the oldest house in Puerto Rico, having been built for Ponce de Leon in 1521. Used in the years preceding the construction of La Fortaleza as a shelter against the attacks of savage Carib tribes, it was owned by the Ponce family until the late 18th Century and now houses the offices of Puerto Rico's Institute for Advanced Studies. The nearby **Casa Rosa** is a lovely pink building overlooking the bay and serving as the office for the Puerto Rican College of Architects.

La Perla

A glance down the beachfront at El Morro will show one the most bizarre and colorful coastal cityscapes imaginable. One- and two-story shacks, seemingly piled one on top of another, crowd the coastline all the way from El Morro to San Cristóbal, running along the battlements which formerly connected the two castles. This is **La Perla**, the so-called ''world's prettiest slum,'' which Oscar Lewis immortalized in his

Below, Old San Juan street. Following page, cannonballs at Fort San Cristóbal.

study of slum-life, *La Vida*.

La Perla presents Puerto Rican governors with a number of problems, among them whether there is more to be gained by forcibly evicting the residents from the land on which they are squatting (it is public beach) or to let them be. From a scenic point of view, the second is undoubtedly the better option; there are four entrances to the neighborhood from the embankment of Calle Norzagaray above, and one can look down any of them at the spectacle of brightly clad children running between the pine green tarpaper roofs of La Perla's main street, all against the backdrop of an aquamarine Atlantic.

Nonetheless, even the toughest of San Juan residents will warn tourists against descending to this charming looking neighborhood, speaking of drugs, violence and a general lawlessness.

Though overshadowed by its more famous neighbor to the west, **El Castillo de San Cristóbal** makes as fascinating a trip as El Morro. What El Morro achieved with brute force, San Cristóbal achieved with subtlety. It sits 150 feet above the waves, reflects the best of 17th-Century military architectural thought, and has an intricate network of tunnels that was used both for transporting artillery and for ambushing invaders. The fort was first completed in 1678 as a means of staving off land attacks on San Juan, like the one the Earl of Cumberland had made to capture El Morro in 1595. But the fort as it is known today is the product of the acumen of two Irishmen "Wild Geese" fleeing the Orange monarchy, in the employ of the Spanish army. Alejandro O'Reilly and Tomas O'Daly designed a system of battlements and sub-forts that ensured that no one could take San Cristóbal without taking all of its ramparts first. No one ever did. The first shot of the Spanish-American War was fired from San Cristóbal's walls. Today the U.S. Army maintains administrative offices here.

Frequent guided tours explain how San Cristóbal's unique system of defense worked, as well as pointing out some of the fort's big attractions, like the **"Devil's Sentry Box,"** a *garita* at the end of a long tunnel that runs to the waterline. Views from the battlements are outstandingly spectacular, particularly in the direction *sanjuaneros* describe as "towards Puerto Rico": Condado, Hato Rey, El Yunque.

PUERTA DE TIERRA: BLUE-GREEN GATEWAY

It's easy to try to relegate **Puerta de Tierra** to the status of a sort of verdant buffer zone between San Juan's body and its soul, separating as it does the brawn of Santurce from the historical grandeur and romance of Old San Juan. But Puerto Rico's greatest allure must often be sought out, and so it is with Puerta de Tierra. The word means 'gateway of land,' but Puerta de Tierra is a gateway in more than this narrow sense.

A Beachfront Capitol

Commanding a fabulous view of beach and blue water, straddled by Puerta de Tierra's two main thoroughfares, **El Capitolio**, Puerto Rico's Capitol Building, serves as centerpiece to the peninsula. Designed by Puerto Rican architect Rafael Carmoega and begun in 1925, the building is a grand, white classical structure resembling the Capitol building in Washington, D.C. It's on a smaller scale of course, but there are few government employees who wouldn't move into more cramped quarters for an ocean view like this one.

The large rotunda, the last part of the building to be completed, has been stocked with symbolic baubles and seals, which the Capitol authorities seem very anxious to explain to visitors. Highlights include a lovely stained-glass mosaic of Puerto Rico's coat of arms, above which the Constitution of Puerto Rico, signed in 1952, rests in an attractive urn.

Nearby are a number of other buildings which, though less imposing, are no less beautiful. The **Casa de España**, just down the hill towards Old San Juan from the Capitolio, rates very high in the esteem of San Juan residents. This blue-tiled, four-towered edifice lies tucked into hilly greenery between the two main avenues. Once a popular gathering spot for local gentlemen, it now serves as the site for cultural events. Down Avenida Ponce de Leon is another lovely edifice, the **Archives and General Library of Puerto Rico**. Pedestals and pilasters support a graceful pediment, and throw a skeleton of white against a lovely sun-washed yellow. The style could reasonably be called "Tropical Classical." Now run by the Institute of Puerto Rican

Culture, the General Library lives up to the standards the institute has set for its other buildings, with solemn tessellation of red stone, delicate chandeliers and fine furniture. There's also a peaceful, if small, chapel on the first floor. If this seems out of place in a national library, it is because the building, built in 1877 as the last major Spanish architectural effort on the island, was originally designed as a hospital. Hotels you'll find anywhere. The **Caribe Hilton** sits on several acres of beautifully landscaped grass and sand, overlooking a little beach-lined cove that stretches to Condado. The pool is inviting, never overcrowded, and overlooked by a lavishly-accoutred bar. The *piña coladas* here are good enough to make one wish it were raining, so one could stay inside all day and drink.

As if it weren't enough that the Caribe be blessed with so many superficial assets, it possesses a historical one as well, in **Fort San Gerónimo**, a small but crucial element of the old Spanish fortification of San Juan, which stymied a British invasion of the city in 1797. The military museum inside is entertaining and worthwhile.

Preceding page, San Juan and Condado at sunset. Left, Capitol, Puerta de Tierra; and right, Muñoz Rivera Park.

CONDADO:
SAN JUAN'S FAST LANE

"Condado" in Spanish means 'county,' and many Puerto Ricans still refer to the glittering strip of land between lagoon and Atlantic Ocean as "*the* Condado." If the appellation is meant to convey anything rustic or sleepy about this part of town, it grossly misses the mark. A trip across the Puente San Gerónimo from Puerta de Tierra takes one out of history and into hysteria, into a world where gambling, dining, drinking and dancing are the life of the night, a world where conspicuous wealth and a hectic North American lifestyle are *de rigeur*. Some county!

American ties are strong and readily apparent here, and there's no place on the island you're more likely to have your "*Con permiso, senor*," answered with a "Whaddaya want, Mac?" Despite the fact, however, that Condado is a thoroughly preconceived place — one of those communities that springs up the week after a sharpie somewhere has a good idea — it has very little of the "just-thrown-up" look which one might expect to see. This is perhaps because Condado was the first of the Puerto Rican beachfront areas to absorb those American vacationers who fled their Havana resort homes during the period which led up to the Cuban revolution in the late 1950s. Many Cubans moved to Condado as well, with the consequence that there is a sense of continuity here which, while not exclusively Puerto Rican, is certainly reassuring to those whose taste does not run to the "all-new."

Ashford Avenue, Condado's main thoroughfare, looks as though it is desperately trying to run for election as the sixth borough of New York, or perhaps as an annex of Miami Beach. In a large measure, it succeeds. Its miles of beachfront are lined with chic boutiques, banks, restaurants and — most conspicuously — hotels.

Hotels are, of course, of varying quality in Condado, but the town's lodgings seldom dip very far below the "luxury" rating. Many have casinos, and most of the casinos require ties. The casinos aren't exclusive; non-hotel patrons are welcome at the tables, as long as they bring their wallets. Restaurants, both hotel-affiliated and otherwise, tend to be of good quality. There's a price to pay for quality in Condado — the pricing is extravagant. Some of the restaurants in town are almost legendary.

Restaurants with a Class

L'Escargot offers the diner some of the finest French cooking found anywhere in the Caribbean; the **Scotch and Sirloin**, with its hefty portions, quiet outdoor tables and breathtaking view ("The only thing we overlook," runs one advertisement, "is the lagoon."); the **Chart House**, in what seems a miracle, gathers an immensely diverse collection of seafood from locations ranging from Alaska to Venezuela under the roof of a lovely three-story townhouse.

To go to the beach in Condado implies more than taking the sun and riding the waves. (The surf, by the way, is positively uninspiring compared to that in Rincón and Jobos.) Here, people-watching is the chief popular pastime, and there is certainly a fine variety to watch. The beach itself is decent, if not especially wondrous by Puerto Rico standards. Like the surf, there is better to **Sunning on Condado Beach.**

106

be had. The sand, lovely and white, is strewn hither and thither with gum wrappers and empty suntan lotion bottles, but the litter shouldn't put any bathers off; the water is warm and unpolluted. The Condado strip of sand, by the way, is the first beach east of San Juan which the Department of Natural Resources considers "swimmable." One unfortunate consideration for swimming and body-watching buffs who are just visiting Condado without hotel reservations is that the wall of hotels lining the beach has made access somewhat difficult in spots. Remember that none of the beach-front is privately owned — all the beaches in Puerto Rico are public — but the big hotels aren't going to go out of their way to show anyone the easy route to the beach.

Ocean Park

Heading east on Ashford Avenue, past the Burger King and the Citibank on the right and the Howard Johnson's on the left, one approaches **Ocean Park**, Condado's wild and woolly western fringe. Here, the houses become smaller and more spread out, and the beaches grow less crowded. The ambience becomes no less American, though the observant beach bum will begin to notice something unusual. There aren't any bikinis to be seen. No, it's not because the suntanner has stumbled onto a nude beach. As one wanders westward on the beach, one will notice the number of women steadily dwindling. One might easily assume that the residents of the area were all either American, homosexual or American homosexual, and indeed one would not be too far wrong. Most of the latter tend to congregate in a number of small guesthouses on the water.

This is one of the more scenic of San Juan's beachfront panoramas, with views stretching from the palm-lined point at Boca de Cangrejos to the bright-white high-rise wall of Ashford Avenue's hotels. After a swim and perhaps a look at one of the longest and most varied stretches of Puerto Rico's north coast, retire to **Kasalta's**, an oasis of fine native cuisine in a desert of kitsch. Here you'll find all the San Juan newspapers, a range of Puerto Rican delicacies unmatched on the island, and a fresh cup of native coffee that will absolutely electrify you.

Shooting pool in Condado.

SANTURCE: BUSINESS AS UNUSUAL

Santurce is a knot of highways and main roads which connect the more touristed and, admittedly, more picturesque areas of the metropolis. It can't claim a seacoast; in fact, one could almost define the area as the set of neighborhoods one encounters moving south from more fashionable Condado and Ocean Park. It hasn't the history of Old San Juan, having been founded only about a century ago as a fashionable suburb. But Santurce does have manifold charms of its own, making it well worth a visit for those few who make the effort.

Love, Not Money

Santurce is considered by most the heart of San Juan, and not just in the sense that it's the source of the city's main traffic arteries. At a time when most world cities have razed their most charming business districts, Santurce survives as a true marketplace. The quaintest manifestation of this ethic is in the **Santurce Market** on Calle Canals, where vendors bargain and sell in much the same way as in the more renowned market in Río Piedras. The might and influence of Santurce's manufacturing and service industries are not to be underestimated, but neither is the innate charm of the place. Around the exigencies of business has grown up a decorum and custom which set the Santurce native apart from other Puerto Ricans. Here, distances are measured not in miles, meters, or even versts, but in bus stops, and a Santurce friend is far more likely to tell you he works at *"Parata 22"* than at Avenida Jose de Diego.

While many *San Juaneros* come to work in Santurce, a surprising proportion come to eat. The area has long been host to many of the island's most elegant restaurants, but its most appealing establishments are often little *fondas* as low on price as they are on pretentiousness. The arts thrive in Santurce as well, and the construction in 1981 of the **Centro de Bellas Artes**, at the corner of Avenidas Ponce de Leon and Jose de Diego, has brought the neighborhood a new share in San Juan's cultural wealth. Old movie buffs have long known that in this most cinematically impoverished of islands, Santurce is practically the only locale in which to take in a good flick.

Santurce is far more, however, than a thriving business community with a few cultural attractions. Its properties are often verdant, its streets tree-lined, especially where modern business developments meet fairly affluent residential districts, as in Santurce's western sector, near Avenida de Diego. Just south of here is one of San Juan's prettiest buildings, the **Colegio del Sagrado Corazón**, running along the north side of Avenida Ponce de Leon. With its 33 acres (13 ha) of rolling parkland and some pleasant turn-of-the-century architecture, this is an ideal location for an urban picnic.

Back on the western edge of Santurce, closest to Old San Juan, is **Miramar**, one of the most charming and paradoxical of the suburbs in the metropolitan area. Here are lovely tree-lined avenues of pretty modern residences, many with well-groomed lawns and delicate ironwork. Nearby is one of the sleazier red-light districts on the island which, whatever solace it offers its lonelier patrons, can't be such a popular institution among Miramar-homeowners.

Left, one of Santurce's many highways; and right, Condado lagoon from Santurce.

BEACH IN REACH: ISLA VERDE

Almost everyone arrives in Puerto Rico at Luís Muñoz Marín International Airport in **Isla Verde**, and almost all remark at first sight how unlike an ordinary airport town the place is. For one, it doubles as a farmer's market; the airport exit is generally thronged with local merchants and farmers selling everything from flowers to bread to beans to *pollo asao* (roast chicken). For another, once one is out of the immediate area of the airport, Isla Verde takes on a look of affluence that few areas as close to such booming noise, annoying traffic snarls and transient lifestyle possess — big, chalkwhite blocks of high-income apartment houses choke one of the most beautiful beachfronts on the island, giving Isla Verde one of the most Miami-Beachesque aspects this side of . . . well, Miami Beach.

Isla Verde is very rich, but hardly anyone in Puerto Rico would disagree that it has never quite got over being an airport town. It's a bit dull. The usual airport businesses — car rental agencies, vinyl cocktail lounges and the like — have overrun the place, and most of the residents of the area are either retired or doing their best to pretend they are. Part of the problem is, of course, location; suburbs separate Isla Verde from the historical charms of the older parts of San Juan, while water — and perhaps lack of enthusiasm — separate it from the charming rusticity of Piñones.

Riding the Waves

This is not, however, to count Isla Verde as being utterly without its charms. **Playas Punta las Marias** and **Isla Verde** stretch for over a mile of white sand from the end of the beach at Ocean Park to the lovely coral reefs at Boca de Cangrejos. The surf here is formidable, especially in winter, and the area known as **Pine Grove** is among the most popular hangouts for young people throughout the year. And when the surf is up, and young bodies are working up a thirst riding the waves, those mammoth white hotels — almost all of which have bars inside — lose any sort of sinister aspect they may have held previously.

Isla Verde.

HATO REY AND RÍO PIEDRAS

It's odd that in so many of the great cities of the world, financial brawn and bohemian asceticism have shared the same neighborhoods. Opposites attract: New York's arty districts of Tribeca and Soho rub shoulders with Wall Street: London's City is surrounded by universities and galleries. San Juan follows this rule to an unusual degree. Here, **Hato Rey**, the undisputed business and high-finance capital of the Caribbean, abuts — and often intermingles with— **Río Piedras**, the (disputed) intellectual capital of the Caribbean.

The Golden Mile

Most of the money in the Antillean Islands is filtered through a group of institutions clustered on a section of the Expreso Luıs Muńoz Riviera (Route 1) in Hato Rey known as the **Golden Mile**. Though Operation Bootstrap certainly contributed to Puerto Rico's importance as a financial center, the recent emerg-

ence of Hato Rey as a mecca for financial corporations owes a great deal to a long-standing Puerto Rican commitment to banking.

Not everyone comes to San Juan to make a buck, but everyone who visits should head down to Hato Rey nonetheless, if only to see the intriguing modern architecture banking always seems to drag in its wake. Particularly interesting is the **Banco de Santander Building** — which, with its reflecting plate-glass arching from an austere concrete shaft, looks something like a giant refrigerator. The **Banco de Ponce Building**, in which all the businesses in San Juan seem to be located, makes good use of a modernistic eclecticism, with a sleek, black-glass facade, and meets the ground ingeniously with a bowed carport-cum-mall area.

Enrique Adsuar González, a respected commentator on local custom, has mentioned that the specter of Hato Rey businessmen walking the streets in Wall-Street-cut woolen winter suits in 90-degree weather is one of the great ironies of contemporary Puerto Rican life. True, but not all the ironies of Hato Rey are as painful to those who partake of them.

Roberto Clemente Stadium, Hato Rey.

For one, Hato Rey has become something of a culinary capital, if in a modest and basic way. One can't expect gourmet food in restaurants which cater solely to men who will lose their jobs if they go for an extra course, but solid Puerto Rican fare is to be had here for prices one wouldn't mind paying in the Cordillera. Without mentioning any names, save the **Caribe**, with its exemplary *Mofongo*, one can say that Hato Rey subscribes to the rule laid down by Eleonora Abreu for restaurants throughout Puerto Rico: the more modest-looking the place, the better the food.

A mile west of the business district on Route 23 (Avenida Franklin Delano Roosevelt) are two of Puerto Rico's more adventurous recent structures. The first, on the north side of the highway, is **Plaza de las Americas**, a real *norteamericano* shopping mall replete with fountains and flowered walks, where San Juan natives flock in droves to buy everything from *guayaberas* to guava juice. Across the highway to the south is the **Estadio Hiram Bithorn**, another of those odd, hyper-modern Puerto Rican stadiums, which is site for a variety of sporting and cultural events.

Perhaps Hato Rey maintains its humanity due only to the humanizing influence of the university town of Río Piedras to the south. Within the shortest of walks, concrete and plate glass give way to cobbled paths and flower gardens. With its 25,000 students and distinguished faculty from all parts of Latin America, the **University of Puerto Rico** is certainly unique in the American university community. Among those who've taught here have been Juan Ramón Jiménez, Pablo Casals and Arturo Morales Carrión. The Jiménez Room, located on campus, contains a large collection of the poet's personal effects. The university's octagonal clock-tower, which soars out of the palms at one side of the campus has become something of a symbol for Río Piedras, and serves as a compass point useful in orienting one to the massive and often labyrinthine university grounds.

Particular high points on the grounds include the **José Lazaró Library**, the largest in Puerto Rico, and the **Museum of the University of Puerto Rico**, a splendidly laid-out series of exhibits which is perhaps the best place in which to familiarize oneself with the island's archaeological and cultural history.

The highlight of any visit to Río Piedras, however, must be the **Botanical Gardens** at the Agricultural Experimental Station a mile south of the university and reachable by following the signs after turning off at the intersection of Muñoz Riviera and Regimiento de Infanteria. Hundreds of varieties of tropical and semi-tropical plants, including many from Australia and Africa, make up one of the most extensive parks of its type in the world. The gardens will comprise 200 acres (80 ha) when completed. Suffice it to say that it's hard to imagine a botanical garden landscaped as imaginatively or as subtly as this one, with its two man-made ponds and vine-crowded gravel walkways, where lilies, ferns and ubiquitous *yautía* compete for one's attention. Near the ponds is a lush, disorderly orchid garden, whose varied vegetation is flecked with pastels of heart-stopping variety.

Río Piedras is not, however, all ivory towers and ivied lanes. Its **Paseo de Diego** is the largest pedestrian market in San Juan, with all the haggling, gesticulation and frenzy of an Arab *souk*. This is the place to go if you'd like a cultural education.

Left, Carillon, University of Puerto Rico; and right, Río Piedras, Hato Rey.

CATAÑO: RUM AND RELAXATION

New Yorkers, wishing to impress visitors, often take them to the Staten Island Ferry and brag that, at 25c a ride, it's probably the world's best transportation bargain. Puerto Ricans know otherwise. For the dime you invest on the Cataño Ferry, you'll be repaid with a few refreshing moments on windswept San Juan Bay, as well as a chance to tour the world's largest rum factory and sample some of Puerto Rico's finest seafood.

Cataño is by no means a picturesque town. It is haphazardly laid out, almost shadeless, and utterly without charm in its shopping areas. It does, however, have a beachfront area with grassy spots for picnicking and unrivaled views of Old San Juan.

Still, it's best to move out of San Juan's shadow and on to some of Cataño's own attractions. The **Bacardi Rum Plant**, five minutes west on Route 165, distills millions of gallons of its various rums yearly, and offers free tours each hour in bizarre little two-coach trolley buses. The vats are fascinating, the museum boring, and the free rum daiquiris cold and delicious.

Bathed in the warm aroma of molasses, which wafts down its streets courtesy of Bacardi, **Palo Seco**, though not in Cataño proper, lures most of Cataño's visitors with its justly renowned seafood. An almost unbroken string of restaurants, many of them named after the local pirate Roberto Cofresí, stretches through Palo Seco, parallel to the ocean.

At the end of a pine-flecked spit of land is **Isla de Cabras**, now a recreational area and hangout for local fisherman. The island originally housed the long-range artillery of **Fort Cañuelo**, built in 1608 to guard the parts of the entrance to San Juan Bay which El Morro could not reach. In later centuries it served as a leper colony. Ruins of both buildings are still visible. Cabras also boasts a beautiful — but, tragically, unswimmable — beach. Hedonists should head further west on Route 165; across coral-studded Ensenada de Boca Vieja, **Punta Salinas** is flanked by two of the prettiest beaches in the San Juan area.

View of San Juan from Isla Verde.

114

BAYAMON: HIGH-RISE HISTORY

If the good people of **Bayamon** are referred to by other Puerto Ricans as *vaqueròs* or "cowboys," it is due less to a tendency to run about roping goats than to a sort of unruly maverick quality that has for years put the city in a friendly opposition to others on the island.

Bayamon is in fact an island of paradox in an island of paradox. Founded in 1509 by a group of settlers led by Ponce de Leon and officially purchased and incorporated in the following year, Bayamon is one of Puerto Rico's oldest municipalities, which labors nonetheless under the stereotype of being an historical, hyperamericanized commercial center, a sort of glorified shopping mall. It is a place where the antiquated *fincas* and plantations of an older Puerto Rico are set in sharp juxtaposition to some of the most innovative civic architecture and ambitiously conceived public park space in the Americas. It is a city with such easy access to the capital that it could be lumped quite understandably into the category of "suburb," yet Bayamon has been admirably fastidious about retaining its regional attitudes, customs, cuisine. It is the last of the above which will most likely provide the traveler's first impression of the city; along almost every road leading into the city, especially on weekends, are *bayamonés* food vendors selling roast chicken, Bayamon white bread, and the most legendary of all local treats — the *chicharrón*, a tart mix of pork and spice baked into a great, tough, bready mass. Adult male visitors may be warned that *chicharrón* has a connotation which would make it inadvisable to ask local women if they would like a taste.

Politicos and Parklands

A first-time visitor arriving on Route 2 will have no trouble figuring out when he's reached Bayamon: he'll see the multi-winged eight-story **Alcaldía de Bayamon**, which spans five lanes of highway and access road. Built in 1978 of concrete, glass, and lemon-yellow steel I-beams, it is the only building so suspended in the Caribbean. In the same complex is the new and highly successful **Braulio Castillo Theater.**

Across the highway from the Alcaldía is its conceptual twin, the **Estadio Juan Ramón Loubriel**, a highly attractive modern baseball stadium whose massive light towers crane over the playing surface, giving it the appearance of some sort of unidentified flying colander. On the same side of the highway, Bayamon's Parque Central is no less dedicated to recreation, with a variety of historical and cultural displays including an airplane, an old locomotive, and a couple of bandstands. Nearby, the placid **Paseo Barbosa** is an unpedestrian pedestrian mall, with numerous shops ranged tastefully about the restored 19th-Century house of Barbosa.

That's hardly the only way to amuse oneself culturally in this city of seven universities. Bayamon native Francisco Oller was Puerto Rico's greatest artist; there's a liberal selection of his work at the **Museo Francisco Oller** in the Old Alcaldía at Calle Degetau, 2. Now under construction is Bayamon's **Parque de Ciencias**, a complex of scientific exhibits which, when completed, will certainly rank among the great museums of the Caribbean.

An early locomotive.

THE NORTHEAST AND THE ISLANDS

If someone arriving in Puerto Rico with the inexcusable intention of spending only a few days there were to hire a guide and ask to be shown as much as possible of the island, he would be driven directly east from San Juan. It is not that the northeastern corner of the island contains all the island's attractions; that would be impossible. It is only that the variety of landscapes and societies — none of them farther than forty-five minutes from San Juan — is mind-boggling. The ease with which one can move from one landscape to another which bears no resemblance to it will make even the crassest traveler feel he is cheating.

The palm groves and beachside settlements of Boca de Cangrejos are visible from San Juan, but a world apart. Mysterious Loíza takes you across an ocean and an eon to a world of African society and ritual. Towering El Yunque dominates the only rain forest in the National Park system, and Luquillo, almost in its shadow, guards what is perhaps Puerto Rico's finest beach.

From Farjardo, a preeminent sailor's haven, ferries depart for Vieques and Culebra, two idyllic Lesser Antillean isles that belong to Puerto Rico only politically. Here the attractions are great beaches, spectacular diving, and an intangible sense of adventure. Returning to the main island from Vieques and Culebra without a handful of colorful anecdotes and a host of new friends is not easy; in fact, returning to the main island is not easy at all.

Preceding pages: setting moon over El Yunque; El Yunque national forest; loading plantains in Naguabo. Left, horsing around in Boca de Cangrejos.

PIÑONES: PALMS,
COOL AND COLLECTED

Puerto Rico is full of surprises at every bend of the road, but nowhere are the island's contrasts more shocking than on Route 187 just east of San Juan. Here, the superhighway that links the metropolis with the Caribbean's most modern international airport passes over a bridge and turns into a rutted, barely navigable path through Edenic palm groves, herds of bony Puerto Rican cows and sheep and a cluster of ramshackle lean-tos running the length of the beach.

This is **Boca de Cangrejos** ('Crab-mouth'), as exotic a spot as one will find within 20 minutes of any major city in the world. It is at first appearance perhaps Puerto Rico at its most typically Latin American (read 'Third World'), but the ricketiness is deceptive. The flocks belong to the residents of nearby settlements around the *municipio* of Loíza. The shacks are not residences by any stretch of the imagination, rather beachfront food emporia unrivaled by any on the island, save perhaps those at Luquillo. Boca de Cangrejos is where *San Juaneros* retreat for a *coco frío* — ice cold coconut milk served in its own shell.

Grove Diggers

Long beaches under luxuriant pine groves are what draw visitors to Boca de Cangrejos. Surfers are the most devoted of such partisans, and can be seen riding the waves at the part of the beach they refer to as **Los Aviones** ('The Airplanes') for the frequent flights from Isla Verde that roar over all day.

It's commonly advised in Puerto Rico to stay away from **Piñones** when the beach is deserted, but this is seldom the case. Those who, for whatever reason, crave company, tend to stick to the extreme eastern and western ends of the beach, where, not coincidentally, the finest views of the Santurce skyline are to be had.

Piñones grows more eerie, rustic and beautiful as one moves east. At its farthest point from San Juan is **Vacia Talega Beach**, a bleak and breathtaking finger of rock capped by palms and carved into strange formations by eons of surf.

Beach at Boca de Cangrejos.

Loíza: Back To Puerto Rico's Beginnings

Few towns in Puerto Rico balance natural beauty and cultural achievement as gracefully or as charmingly as Loíza Aldea. Just six miles (10 km) east of metropolitan San Juan, **Loíza** has maintained its separateness from the capital thanks to a cluster of natural barriers. Puerto Rico's largest mangrove swamp, the massive and mysterious woodland of **Torrecilla Baja**, sits smack between the two communities, and is traversable only via the rutted coastal Route 187, which passes through Piñones. The **Río Grande de Loíza**, Puerto Rico's widest, roughest, and only navigable river, is the final bastion against metropolitanization. It can be crossed only by a hand-towed car ferry, and then only when the river is not up. Though a bridge now under construction will soon bring Route 187 and hordes of *San Juaneros* across the Río Grande, it's unlikely the unique culture and folkways of Loíza will change greatly in the immediate future.

Loíza is arguably among the purest centers of true African culture in the western world. It was settled in the 16th Century by black slaves sent by the Spanish crown to mine a rich gold deposit in the area. When the gold ran out, they became cane-cutters, and when slavery was abolished in 1873, many blacks from around the island flocked to this agricultural economy.

Loíza's blacks learned Spanish and became Catholics, but in the subsequent fusion of African culture with Spanish and Indian, the African certainly won out as the preponderant influence. At no time of the year is such influence more visible than during the Fiesta de Santiago Apostól, when the people of Loíza gather to praise Saint James, patron of the town. The week-long celebration commences each July 25, when citizens dress in ceremonial costumes strikingly and significantly similar to those of the Yoruba tribes of West Africa, from whom many of Puerto Rico's blacks are descended. Participants include masqueraders, ghouls and *viejos* (old men), and the making of costumes for the ceremonial rites is ordered by a social hierarchy quite alien to Latin America.

The most distinctive festival attire, however, belongs to the *veigantes*, most of them young men, who dress in garish and infernally gaudy costumes and parade through the streets throughout the festival. Their religious purpose is generally taken to be that of frightening the lapsed back into the Christian faith, though they can be just as much a source of celebration and mirth. Though styles vary, most true *veigante* masks are made from coconuts or other gourds, painted a primary color, speckled with shades of other colors and carved into grimaces like those of the most sinister jack-o-lanterns. At times aluminium foil are used to make the mask's teeth look more eerie.

Unfortunately, many recent developments in the Loíza festival have been somewhat less in harmony with tradition. As media intrudes more into Loízan life, so does popular culture, and it is now not uncommon to see Darth Vader masks at the festival.

Nonetheless, Loíza has material as well as spiritual resources to meet these challenges. The 1645 **Iglesia San Patricio** is the oldest continually functioning church on the island, and several other precious buildings in the village attest to a rich architectural heritage.

Spanish colonial church.

LUQUILLO: CAPITAL BATHING

There's plenty to see in Puerto Rico's northeast, but few informed visitors get to see any of the area's attractions without first making at least a day's detour to what many consider the island's finest beach. Shimmering **Luquillo** is just 35 minutes west of San Juan on Route 3, which, in traveler's terms, is about the same time it would take one to get to lovely but arduous El Yunque or Fajardo's mob scene, and about half the time it would take to get to grisly Humacao. The only liability of a trip to Luquillo is its over-crowdedness — on pleasant weekends you'll see all your friends from San Juan there.

Mountains to the Sea

Even those not terribly enthusiastic about beaching will find it hard to ignore Luquillo's appeal. This beautiful, bleachy-white town is tucked cozily between dark Atlantic waters and Puerto Rico's most imposing mountain chain, the Sierra de Luquillo, from which the town draws its name. There are few more dramatic sights on the island than that of the whitecaps of the shoreline glistening in summer sunlight while the peaks of the El Yunque rain forest just inland are suffused in purple thunder clouds. Occasionally, some of the rain intended for the forest does fall on Luquillo, and quite often the beach is under heavy cloud cover.

Luquillo is listed officially as being 2¼ miles (3½ km) long but it's linked to two other swimmable beaches— **Playas San Miquel** and **Convento**— which are every bit as lovely and almost deserted, and stretch nearly to Cabezas de San Juan, at the far northeastern extremity of the island. This is ideal beach-walking territory.

Luquillo is also the premier beachside food emporium on Puerto Rico; a seemingly endless string of shacks sells delectably rich local seafood specialties and a variety of hard and non-alcoholic drinks, including the immensely popular *coco frío*, ice-cold coconut milk served in its own shell.

There's nothing better to indulge in on a sunny day.

Below, Puerto Rico's finest beach, Luquillo; and right, El Toro Park, El Yunque.

126

THE LUSH ALLURE
OF EL YUNQUE

The only tropical forest in the U.S. National Park system and the only part of Puerto Rico administered by the U.S. Department of Agriculture, the Caribbean National Forest, known to practically all as **El Yunque**, is home to all the mystery and wonder that comes in the color green. These 28,000 acres (11,330 ha) of bucking mountain at the highest part of the Sierra de Luquillo offer one of the most extreme of the island's climates, and the most extreme of its ecosystems as well.

Showers and Towers

To begin with, there is the rain. The massive, low-lying, purplish-black clouds one sees moving across the Atlantic onto Puerto Rico's northeast coast dump most of their cargo when they hit the northern flank of the Sierra de Luquillo, with the result that this is far and away the rainiest section of Puerto Rico.

El Yunque gets upwards of 240 inches (600 cm) of rain annually — put in more alarming terms, this is 100,000,000,000 gallons per year. The fact that Pico del Toro, which commands the forest from a height of 3,523 feet (1,070 meters), is Puerto Rico's highest peak gives an even odder turn to the flora and fauna of the rain forest. Hundreds of different animal species make El Yunque their home, among them 26 autochthonous to the forest. Puerto Rico's most familiar animals are here, like the mellifluous treefrog known as the *coquí*. But more exotic ones are here as well, like the colorful but endangered Puerto Rican parrot, and the Puerto Rican boa, Puerto Rico's largest snake, which can grow up to seven feet long.

Characteristic of Puerto Rico's landscape is the preponderance of subclimates, which promote vastly different types of vegetation and fauna within very small areas. As this phenomenon is most intense in mountainous regions, El Yunque offers a startling diversity of forest types.

Forest Types

Most widespread of these is the Tabonuco forest, which ranges around the warmer, drier parts of the park at altitudes of under 2,000 feet (600 meters). Higher up are Colorado forests (which certainly look nothing like those of that state). These are mossy, somewhat more tropical looking than the Tabonuco forests. Although taking up less than a fifth of El Yunque's territory, the reserve's pine forest is the rain forest that gives the area its reputation. Perhaps this is because its beauty is so unexpected and almost unnatural. Sierra palms, which account for most of the subclimate's vegetation, can grow in very slippery and unstable soil. Thus, when they're not punctuating a fern field or running up a steep hill, they can be found in the most dramatic locations: half-submerged in riverbeds, shading tortuous mountain roads, jutting from cliffsides. Perhaps the renown of the pine forests is due as much to the fact that Route 191, which most tourists take through El Yunque and which is most responsible for its renown, never gets above the 2,500-foot (760-meter) altitude at which the palm forest stops. Areas above that altitude are more bizarre and no less fascinating. This area of dwarf pine and moss covers less than

1000 acres (400 ha), and receives the full brunt of the Puerto Rican weather. Such growth is due less to intense rain, however, than to poor soil quality.

Driving Rain

However alluring the upper reaches of El Yunque, most will see it only by automobile. The most popular and varied route leads south from the town of **Palmer**, known in Spanish as *Mameyes*, along Route 191. Palmer is a tiny, haunting town, one which seems all the more so for its striking contrast to the 45-minute drive from San Juan, which carries one through glittering, modern industrial and commercial landscapes. Nonetheless, Palmer is admirably uncommercialized and untouristed for a park entrance.

Route 191 used to lead straight through the park to Naguabo, but a landslide which damaged roads on the southern edge of the park about a decade ago has never been cleared away; a gate now blocks access to the damaged part of the road at Km 13.5. But despite the damage, and despite the fact that Puerto Rico's numerous hiking enthusiasts will tell you you have to get up *into* the woods to appreciate them, Route 191 provides a sterling introduction to the park.

Attractive Falls

Rising gradually, the road hits one of El Yunque's premier attractions at a bend in the road scant kilometers into the park. **La Coca Falls**, at Km 8.2, is a blurry cascade of ice-gray river rushing down a wall of beautiful moss-covered stones. Though the park service claims most of the water in El Yunque to be perfectly potable, and although you'll almost certainly see Puerto Ricans and foreigners alike drinking from the stream, do exercise caution here as anywhere in the mountains, as Puerto Rico has a number of river snails which produce "schisto" (*schistosoma*), a bacteria causing the highly dangerous liver disease, bilharzia. Make sure to check all sources of health information before swimming in or drinking from Puerto Rico's streams.

El Yunque's second great waterfall, **La Mina**, is just off the road a mile (two km) ahead. Unfortunately, it's invisible **Many trails crisscross El Yunque.**

from 191 and can be reached most easily from the **Palo Colorado Recreation Site** at Km 12. On your way there, you'll pass the **Sierra Palm Interpretive Services Center**, an invaluable source of information on hiking trails and outdoor camping. Adjacent to the next recreation site is the **El Yunque Restaurant**, a beautiful hacienda-like structure tucked at the bottom of a shady ravine within earshot of the roaring Río La Mina; certainly worth a visit, if only for their luscious sweet cocktails made of different kinds of Puerto Rican rum. During thundershowers, the rattle of rain on the tin roof of the restaurant is deafening.

Hoofing it through the Highlands

The landslides on Route 191 have left El Yunque a far less accessible place by car than it used to be. As such, the advocates of the ''slog-the-bog'' method of seeing El Yunque have something of a point when they speak of having to leave the main roads truly to see the park. One can only summarize the hiking attractions of the place, but a few hiking excursions are to be recommended.

The **Tradewinds National Recreation Trail**, known as El Toro to Puerto Ricans, is the island's longest nature trail, at about eight miles (13 km). Commencing a few hundred meters beyond the gate on Route 191, it tends to be rather a trail out of the park, bypassing all of El Yunque's ''big'' attractions, but does have the advantage of taking one through all the major ecosystems and vegetation types of the forest. The **Big Tree Trail**, leaving from the first parking lot along Route 191, gives one a good bird's-eye view of La Mina falls before meeting the road again at a well-situated camping site. Perhaps most spectacular of all is the **El Yunque Trail**, which leaves the Sierra Palm Interpretative Services Center for three of the most spectacular vistas in the park. To get to **Los Picachos Lookout Tower**, carry straight on; a left 2½-mile (four-km) down the trail takes one, after a southern detour of less than 100 meters along nearly untraveled Route FR10, to the **Mount Britton Lookout Tower**, perhaps the park's crowning glory; a turn left just before reaching Los Picachos brings one to the lookout tower at **Pico El Yunque** and to the fabulous vistas to be found at remote **El Yunque Rock**.

Mist settles into the rain forest.

FAJARDO AND THE OFFSHORE CAYS

Fajardo is different things to different people. To some it is merely an overcluttered dockfront town, ranking third behind Brindisi, Italy and Hyannis, Massachusetts in the "Grim Ferry Ports of the World" ranks. To others it is an eminently glamorous resort, a charming community, gateway to a handful of fabulous islands and home of the finest sailing in the Caribbean. The first major town along Puerto Rico's northeast coast, Fajardo remains a mecca for yachting enthusiasts. Originally a small fishing and agricultural village, Fajardo became in the late 1700s a popular supply port for many pirate and contrabandist vessels. The town itself, a hodgepodge of clothing, furniture, and video stores, is somewhat unprepossessing compared to the area's natural attractions — the calm, clear waters and cays and coral reefs of Vieques Sound.

Playa de Fajardo, a waterfront community at the east end of town,

docks the ferries headed to Culebra, Vieques and a small island marina nearby. Next to the ferry terminal is the pink stucco **U.S. Post Office/Customs House** and one of Fajardo's few hotels.

Just north of Fajardo, two condominium high-rises, architectural anomalies here, loom over the small fishing village of **Playa Sardinera**. Hundreds of fancy motorboats and yachts of all descriptions crowd the two waterfront marinas nearby. Local fishermen line the beach in the middle of the village with boats and tents; they supply the half dozen expensive little seafood restaurants in the area.

A road over the hill passes a comfortable guesthouse and the **Maharishi Caribbean "University,"** formerly the Hotel El Conquistador, which was taken over by the Transcendental Meditation Program in the mid-1970s.

The road continues on to **Playa Soroco,** a long, narrow stretch of crisp white-sand beach whose clean, shallow waters make it a favorite among locals. At the leftmost point of Soroco, a dirt road leads to **Playa El Convento,** an isolated beach stretching for miles. At the other end of Soroco, the **Cabo San**

Boating in Las Croabas.

Juan Lighthouse crowns a hill on the Cabezas de San Juan peninsula. Built in 1880, this pristine white neoclassical structure with black trim is one of only two operational lighthouses on the island. The view from the Cabezas de San Juan is head-spinning. As you look back towards the heart of Puerto Rico, El Yunque's formidable mountain rain forest towers over the island. In the other direction, polychromatic, Caribbean-blue waters yield a chain of cays ranged like enticing stepping stones to the isles of Culebra and far-away Saint Thomas.

The dozens of cays and islands off Fajardo provide Puerto Rico's best boating. A protective reef stretching from Cabezas de San Juan to Culebra and beyond keeps the waters calm, while swift Atlantic tradewinds make for great sailing. To see the islands, charter a yacht from one of Fajardo's marinas and spend the day sailing, sunbathing and snorkeling.

Icacos, the largest and most popular cay, offers a narrow stretch of bone-white beach, making it a nice spot for picnicking or even camping. Two rows of wood posts from an abandoned dock march into the water, and, just beyond, a coral underworld descends to the sandy bottom 20 feet below. The beach is certainly warm and comfortable, but all the action is around the reefs: elkhorn, staghorn, brain, star, and other corals host legions of underwater plant and animal life.

Other popular cays, somewhat less readily accessible, include **Culebrita,** and **Cayos Lobos** (wolves), **Diablo** (devil), **Palominos** (doves) and **Palominitos** (take a wild guess). These and many smaller cays are ripe for water exploration among numerous coral walls, caverns and tunnels.

Just south of Fajardo, one of the largest naval bases in the world, **Roosevelt Roads,** occupies about a quarter of Puerto Rico's eastern coastline. Headquarters of the U.S. Caribbean Naval Forces, the base fuels all American and Allied ships in the area. Roosevelt Roads also oversees large-scale sea maneuvers (the training range covers more than 200,000 square miles) as well as anti-submarine warfare testing and operations. The U.S. prepared and launched its invasion of Grenada from here. It is strictly off-limits to civilians.

Pigeons in Fajardo.

VIEQUES AND THE GOOD LIFE

Six miles (10 km) off the Puerto Rican mainland lies remote **Vieques**, with twice the acreage of Manhattan and twice the charm of some islands many times its size. Like Culebra, Vieques belongs geologically to the Virgin Islands, but this is not all that sets it off from mainland Puerto Rico. Despite the encroachment of the U.S. Navy and the island's growing popularity among expatriates, traditional ways live on. Islanders still refer to crossing the sound as "going to Puerto Rico," and the *Usted* form of second person address, extinct on the mainland, is still heard in conversation here.

Much of Vieques looks like California cattle-country: dry, rolling hills, scattered lazy herds and flocks of white egrets. But the island also enjoys scores of beaches, a small rain forest, exotic wild-flowers and a healthy population of tree frogs, mongooses and horses. A hundred or so beautiful *pasofino* (fine-gaited) horses descended from 16th Century Spanish steeds, roam wild over the island. (If you can catch, feed and train one, it's probably yours.)

The Taíno Indians who first settled the island called it *Bieques*, or "small island"; Columbus named it *Graciosa* (gracious). English pirates named Vieques Crab Island for the still-common land crabs they would count on for a tasty dinner. And the Spanish (who built the lighthouse and an unfinished fort) called Vieques and Culebra the Useless Islands, because neither had gold. (And who said Western civilization wasn't in decline?)

Vieques is accessible by air from San Juan or by sea from Fajardo. The latter is the preferable route, offering an exhilarating journey through brisk, choppy waters, a distant view of stormy El Yunque, and — with luck — a full double rainbow stretching for miles across blue waters. Near the ferry landing, **Isabel II,** Vieques's only town, offers the staples of any modest Puerto Rican municipality. Many of the island's 8,000 residents live here or nearby. Natives work in factories, or on ranches, in stores, and fishing, but unemployment remains a severe problem. Although the town is

King of the Castle on Flamenco Beach, Culebra.

good for procuring necessities (bank, rent-a-car, pizza), do not plan on spending much time in Isabel II.

Esperanza

Only a 10-minute drive across the island, **Esperanza**, a small fishing village, consists of little more than a strip of guesthouses and restaurants overlooking the water. Do not be fooled: this is *the* place to eat well, sleep well, sunbathe and explore.

The real gem of Esperanza is a tropical plantation house right out of a Somerset Maugham story, the **Casa del Frances** — "the world's most laid-back hotel." A near-jungle of orchids, coconuts, bananas, mangoes, aloe, bamboo and all sorts of other tropical flora surrounds the house and rises dozens of feet in the atrium. (Do not be surprised to find an enormous toad in the foyer during a rainstorm). From 17-foot ceilings, gentle fans turn. Drinks arrive on a checkered verandah overlooking a pool, stables and grazing horses and colts.

A lovesick French army general-turned-sugar plantation owner bought the house in 1910 for his pretty young bride. Word has it the spoiled girl was impressed with neither the island, the house, nor the husband, and promptly fled back to Paris. Today, irreverent Bostonian Irving Greenblatt personally oversees the general's fantasy.

Esperanza manages a lively nightlife at Banana's Tradewinds and (Saturday nights) Cerromar. At the distant NAF (Naval Ammunitions Facility), try catching a USO show and hobnobbing with chatty American officers and enlisted men. During the *Patronales* (patron saint's) festival in the last two weeks of July, things really hop.

Just outside Esperanza, **Sun Bay** glistens with a popular crescent-shaped beach. Beyond it and more secluded lie **Media Luna** and **Navio** beaches. Final scenes from the 1963 movie *Lord of the Flies* were shot at Navio, a favorite spot for locals. The other good beaches to visit are not far away but are within U.S. Navy land.

In 1941 the Navy acquired over 70 percent of Vieques to use for land and sea exercises. As part of the Atlantic Fleet Weapons Training Facility, about once a year the Navy stages maneuvers. As marines perform mock amphibious

Ponies abound on Vieques.

invasions, the blasts of artillery batteries and fighter planes' target practice can be heard across the island.

As an impediment to development, the Navy has been partly responsible for the island's charm. Though inhabitants have protested the military presence, the Navy does build roads, let cattle owners use Navy land and leave reserves open for public access to beaches.

Red, Blue and Green Beaches

With characteristic imagination, the Navy named three of the island's beaches Red, Blue and Green. Merely getting to these places is a small adventure; rocky approach roads wind through thick seagrape overbrush. **Red** and **Blue Beaches** are ideal for swimming, snorkeling and scuba. Seventy-five yards off Blue Beach floats a cay to swim to and explore for helmet shells and coral. The way to **Green Beach** is long, bumpy and tortuous. If you make the trek, stop by to see **Mosquito Pier,** a mile-long dock built earlier in the century when sugar production supported Vieques's economy.

Vieques has a good number of minor expeditions on which to embark should you muster the energy. Get a local fisherman or Pete at the Dive Shop to take you out at night in a boat to **Phosphorescent Bay**, considered the best in the world. Billions of luminescent microscopic creatures emit a green fluorescence when the water stirs. Best on a moonless night, swimming here becomes a scintillating experience (ever see *Liquid Sky?*) as the green-gold organisms sparkle everywhere.

Or climb to the cave atop **Mount Pirata**, where the ancient *cacique* Bieque allegedly hid his tribe's treasure once he realized the conquistadors' intentions. Islanders say the cave's ceaseless roar attests that the great chief's ghost still rages. And while on the subject of superstitions, on Vieques's north coast near **Roca Cucaracha** (Cockroach Rock) is **Puerto Diablo** (Port Devil), the third point of the Bermuda Triangle.

If you happen to be in Isabel II on a Sunday afternoon examining the last Spanish fort built in the Western Hemisphere, drive to the *gallera* just outside town to see the late matinee of cockfighting. This sport is not recommended for the faint-hearted.

CULEBRA'S CORAL GLORIES

From Isla Grande Airport, the short flight to isolated **Culebra** overlooks dramatic coastline, dozens of varied cays and a patchwork of blue, turquoise and green Caribbean Sea. Columbus reportedly discover this island on his second voyage in 1493. The first known inhabitants, Taíno Indians, sought refuge on Culebra after the Spanish started colonizing Puerto Rico.

Before long, pirates and privateers began to use Culebra (Pirates' Cay) as a protected hiding place and supply base before sailing off to raid ships in the Virgin Islands. Infamous corsairs, including the swashbuckling Welshman Sir Henry Morgan, may have buried treasure on and around Culebra; according to legend, a road near Punta del Soledado, a bend on Los Vacos Beach, a clump of large trees near Resaca Beach, and a rocky mound at the end of Flamenco Beach might be good spots to start looking for the 17th and 18th Century fortunes.

By 1880, settlers from Puerto Rico and Vieques were braving severe droughts and swarms of mosquitoes to build a colony which grew tamarind, mango, cashew and coconut trees. Then, a few years after the Spanish-American War of 1898, the U.S. Navy opened facilities on Culebra, making Ensenada Honda its principal Caribbean anchorage. About this time, the island's town moved from what is now Campamento to Dewey (named after the victorious commander of the U.S. Asiatic fleet, Admiral George Dewey). In 1909, one of President Theodore Roosevelt's last executive orders established Culebra as a National Wildlife Refuge, one of the oldest in the U.S.

By the end of World War Two, the U.S. Navy had begun to use Culebra for gunnery and bombing practice. Sea vessels and fighter planes from the United States and its allies pummeled target areas. Culebra received no payment for use of its lands. Islanders recall days and nights of constant bomb bursts. At one point, the Navy proposed relocating all Culebrans on Vieques.

The Culebrans bitterly opposed and protested their island's use for military targeting, and by the early 1970s, this plight of only 800 persons had been considered in the U.S. by generals, senators, governors, cabinet secretaries and presidents. In 1971, the Navy and Culebrans exchanged tear gas and Molotov cocktails, for which some islanders were imprisoned. Finally, after decades of trial and tribulation, Henry Kissinger transmitted President Nixon's decision that all weapons training on Culebra be terminated. President Ford's National Security Council reaffirmed the decision, and Culebra was left alone in 1975.

Probably the most important feature of Culebra is its arid climate; with only 35 inches of rain a year, there's always some sunshine here. Its 24 islands comprise 7,700 acres (3,100 hectares) of irregular topography and intricate coastline. Due to the dryness, most of the terrain is good only for pasture, forest or wildlife. Much of the land is administered by the U.S. Fish and Wildlife Service, which aims to maintain the diverse fauna and flora of the islands. Culebra's cays provide nesting colonies for a dozen marine bird species including brown boobies, laughing gulls, sooty terns, and Bahama ducks. The brown pelican, an endangered species, can

Left, cannon guards the coast off Isabel Segunda; and right, Flamenco Beach, Culebra.

often be spotted in mangrove areas. Rare turtles nest on many of Culebra's beaches from May through July. Turtle-watchers on Resaca Beach frequently stay up from 6 p.m. to 6 a.m. in order to see the large, lumbering amphibians deliver and protect their eggs.

Because the island has no freshwater streams, sedimentation is low, and Culebra enjoys one of the healthiest coral ecosystems in the Caribbean. Remarkable reefs make for an abundance of fish species and especially clear water.

More than 2,000 people now live on Culebra, many of them in pastel-colored houses amid scrubby hills. Roads and front yards abound with jeeps, chickens and chickadees. Time passes slowly; the atmosphere is one of tranquility, grace and bonhomie.

Dewey!

The town of **Dewey**, a 10-minute walk from the airport, covers only several blocks. (Be sure to remember Culebran law — no walking around town without a shirt!) At one end of town, the Fajardo ferry docks. Near the docks you will find a dive shop, some guesthouses and the highly recommended **Marta's Deli**. Down the road are two markets, the bank, the post office and one of Culebra's three restaurants, **El Pescador**, which has inexpensive burgers, pricy seafood and a bar where a slew of Culebrans hang around.

Just beyond town is one of the few drawbridges in the Caribbean. Nearby is **Ensenada Honda** (''Deep Bay''), surrounded by mangrove forests and one of the most secure hurricane harbors in the area, not to mention a nice spot for wind-surfing. Smack in the middle of the bay is **Pirate's Cay**, where Culebrans enjoy holiday parties of beer and *arepas* (a local favorite made of sweet, fried bread).

While on Culebra, try and make a point to see **Flamenco Beach**. A *publico* can take you there, or you can make the long walk from Dewey. This is the sort of beach you have always heard about — soft, white sand; clear, blue water and no one to kick sand in your face. The eponymous flamingos lived here until the U.S. Navy began to bombard the beach in 1945. A few hundred yards down the beach rest two archaic U.S. Marine Corps tanks, looking like the

casualties of an island war never fought. The Navy used these and eight other tanks in the nearby hills as targets. Hikers occasionally find unexploded shells in the vicinity.

Only half-a-mile uphill and east of Flamenco Beach stands **Mount Resaca**, the highest summit on Culebra, with a formidable 360-degree view of cays and some of the Virgin Islands. Resaca hosts a dry subtropical ''rock forest'' where exotic Caribbean flora thrives amid thousands of large boulders. Last officially sighted in 1932, the ''Culebra,'' a local lizard monster, is believed to survive in the forests.

The best way to see Culebra is by packing a picnic and hiring a boat for the day (try finding native Culebran Rogelio Escobar to take you — ask at El Pescador). Travel out to see otherwise inaccessible beaches, lagoons, forests and rocky bluffs on **Cayo Luis Peña** and **Culebrita.** Here you will find the most exuberant wildlife on the island. On Culebrita, you can also see an operating stone lighthouse built in 1874 by the Spanish colonial government. And buffs, be sure to do some snorkeling or scuba diving from the boat.

Below, caretaking in Isabel Segunda; and right, Puerto Rican flora.

THE NORTHWEST

Visitors to Puerto Rico may be confounded by the dazzling array of holiday choices that confront them: The neon of San Juan or the phosphorescence of Parguera? The waters at Coamo or Culebra? Cabo Rojo or Cabo San Juan Lighthouse? Other questions are more easily answered, however, and "Where would I choose to live?" generally elicits "The Northwest" as response. Here are some of the island's loveliest and most historical cities — Arecibo, Lares, San Sebastián, Isabela — with all the bustle of San Juan and none of its mind-bending frenzy, all the calm of the Cordillera and none of its backwardness.

To the connossieur of natural beauty, the northwest is also the most rewarding area of the island, owing to magnificent ranges of karstic mogotes, or limestone hillocks, whose likes are found only in a handful of places in the world. Limestone is carved with a master's hand as well in the lovely caves and sinkholes that pepper the whole karstic region. This is beauty on a human scale, true adventurer's territory. And if you're a mush-for-brains *gringo* surfie to whom "beauty on a human scale" means next to nothing, rest assured that the island's best surf is never more than a right turn away on Route 2 anywhere from Arecibo to Mayagüez.

Preceding pages: Caribbean sunset; Sun Bay Beach, Vieques. Left, one of Puerto Rico's delectable pineapples.

DORADO: FIRST RESORT

Driving west from San Juan on Route 2, the landscape opens up a bit, the first hills begin to rise, and the first-time visitor may begin to feel he's left the metropolis and is about to penetrate Puerto Rico's fabled countryside. That is, until he hits sprawling, congested Bayamon; then he begins to wonder if the big cities will ever stop. They stop in **Dorado**, 10 miles (16 km) west of San Juan, the first town which can claim to be out from under its shadow.

Dorado's a pleasant, quiet, unassuming little town. You'll miss it if you stay on the highway, and may have to look twice for it even if you should take the detour on Route 165, which leaves Route 2 and runs north across emerald marshlands before looping back to Dorado. The town introduces itself well, as they say in the wine trade. The hospitable hamlet of **Toa Baja** signals the turnoff. If Dorado is unassuming, Toa Baja is positively diffident, though it is full of charms which belie the quiet. Dividing Toa Baja from Dorado itself is the sluggish **Río de la Plata**, whose grassy banks and meandering course would remind one of some of the more timeless parts of rural England were it not for the clayey riverbed which has turned the stream's waters a rugged brick red.

Dorado follows 165 loosely on both sides. No cross streets slow traffic enough to draw attention to the small main plaza by the roadside, and the town's businesses are admirably free of gaudy billboards and other bric-a-brac. "Urban" Dorado is just clean, slow-paced, and friendly, and a disproportionate number of its business establishments — bakeries, bars, juice stands — have camaraderie as their *raison d'être*.

What do you do with an unspoiled...

Beach? Spoil it, of course. And about two decades ago, Dorado looked like the prime place on a burgeoning tourist island to develop a resort and make a killing. The Rockefeller family decided to develop a few dozen acres of beachfront Dorado landscape and turn it into a luxury sunspot in the manner of Huma-

cao's Palmas del Mar. There's little to be said about the beautifully landscaped and luxuriously accoutred grounds of **Cerromar Beach**; if you're an ordinary tourist you'll never get near it, and if you're one of those potbellied New Yorkers who head down to Puerto Rico every chance they get, all the information you need will be handed out at the front desk. Suffice it to mention that the place is as relaxing and idyllic as any resort in the Caribbean.

Dorado boasts an ancient castle, the **Casa del Rey**, whose structure has been restored and converted to government offices. Its residents included Don Lopez Canino, and it will soon be converted into a museum, as Don Lopez and his wife were good to all classes. Illustrious Puerto Ricans who spent time there included José Celso Barbosa, José De Diego and others.

But Dorado is not all culture. Its beaches are inviting and easily accessible via the *guaguas* that leave from near the town plaza. A mile northwest of town, through a spinney of mangroves and a bone-white graveyard on Route 693, is the irresistibly lovely beach at **Playa Sardinera**.

Vega Baja:
Bizarre Beachfront

A fast, 35-minute drive west of San Juan on Routes 2 and 686, **Vega Baja** is one of the most popular of San Juan's metropolitan beachfronts, and benefits not only from spectacular juxtapositions of sand and sea, but from lush and unusual surrounding countryside as well. The beach itself draws most attention for its weird and haunting rock formations. It runs for 2,500 feet (760 meters) from the snug, palm-lined cove of **Boca del Cibuco** to craggy **Punta Puerto Nuevo**.

At Puerto Nuevo a line of coral islands runs parallel to the seashore and meets a rocky headland tangentially. This odd, almost unique formation has sheltered most of Vega Baja while causing its western end to resemble at times a sort of preternaturally large jacuzzi. Further along, and accessible by Route 686 where it runs by the base, is **Puerto del Tortuguero**, the largest and most palm-lined of the area's beaches. Half a mile (800 meters) inland, **Laguna Tortuguero**, while not officially a nature reserve, provides a rushy and silent haven for local bird life.

Foliage and Joviality

The town of Vega Baja has grown into a fairly modern and uniform Puerto Rican municipality; new settlements like **La Trocha** and **Pugnado Alfuera** are worth passing through only if one is on one's way to the Cordillera. The town does have a sense of humor about its reputation as something of a hokey place, however; an official town bulletin offers not only the usual information of town history and famous residents, but a tongue-in-cheek roster of *Personajes tipicos de Vega Baja*. These include the tallest man in town, the drunk, the beggar, the basketball fan and others. A town that can parody itself so remorselessly deserves a visit.

But not so much as the surrounding countryside. Vega Baja sits in the middle of the lovely and fertile coastal flatlands just west of San Juan. Visitors will be rewarded with long vistas over old canefields and marshes, and an array of deciduous foliage most impressive for an island full of tropical trees.

Playa Marchiquita.

ARECIBO: EMERALD CITY ON THE ATLANTIC

There are prettier cities on this island, but certainly none is prettier to approach than **Arecibo**. Forty-eight miles (77 km) west of San Juan, Route 2 takes a torturous turn and reveals the second capital city of Puerto Rico's north coast backed by the blue Atlantic. The coastal road, Route 681, affords one an even more dramatic perspective. This is in itself one of the most spectacular drives in Puerto Rico, running from Palmas Altas through Islote, past Desvio Valdes, through a settlement at Punta Caracoles, and by the big radio antennae of the Arecibo station WCMN, before hitting the bay at Puerto de Arecibo. Here one meets the city in truly spectacular fashion. Middle-sized apartment blocks and business premises seem to loom large and blue across an even bluer bay, and Arecibo takes on something of the air of a western Puerto Rican Eldorado.

The reality of Arecibo is a bit more worldly than one would assume from its externally Arcadian aspect. It's one of the oldest of Puerto Rican towns, and since its foundation in the 16th Century has enjoyed one of the highest levels of prosperity on the island. Operation Bootstrap, the project designed by Muñoz Marín and the U.S. Congress to boost Puerto Rico into the industrial world, and Section 936, the American legislation which has offered tax incentives to companies investing in Puerto Rico, have accelerated Arecibo's advance in the business world. Puerto Rico produces more pharmaceutical products than any other country in the world, and Arecibo lies at the center of Puerto Rico's pharmaceutical industry. Valium, Qaaludes, barbiturates . . . commenting on the slow-paced lifestyle of their island, more than one Puerto Rican has remarked, "It's not as if we need them."

Still, Arecibo has been a leader in the art of manufacturing products that ease one along the troubled road of life since long before the pharmaceutical boom. Ron Rico, one of the great rums of the island which is the rum capital of the world, is probably the major industry in town. It's hardly the greatest (the greatest is Barrelitos Three Star, brewed

Across the lagoon to Arecibo.

just outside of San Juan), but it's eminently drinkable, and Arecibo is eminently proud of its part in the Puerto Rican rum trade. Arecibo's Chamber of Commerce even goes so far as to acquaint the tourist with the saga of Don Juan Piza Bisbal, the Catalán who left Barcelona "*con lágrimas en los ojos*" to come to Puerto Rico and introduce to Westerners *Ron Llave*, "the key to happiness." Those visitors who have toured the Ron Rico plant tend to agree with this appraisal of the salubrious properties of Puerto Rican libations.

What Salubrious Properties?

For a town so situated, Arecibo is center to a surprising variety of terrain. It forms a northeasterly-pointing semi-peninsula at the delta of two rivers: the **Rio Grande de Arecibo** and the **Canal Perdomo**. To its east recede swamps of unmeasured depth and gloom. This is why the roads from San Juan hug the shoreline to give such pleasant views of the city from afar. *O! Felix culpa!* But not too *felix*...the place is chock-a-block with mosquitoes in wet season.

Arecibo itself disappoints some tourists who use the city as a way station on their ineluctable search for all that is mundane and tacky on the island. It takes an intelligent person to realize that Arecibo is one of the finer and more livable cities, not only on the island, but anywhere in the Caribbean. Its streets are broad, its citizens relatively well-off, and its shopping district has far more variety than one might expect from a city of only 75,000 inhabitants. It has cafes and theaters — not as commonplace as one might think in Puerto Rico — and its oldest, a distinctive wooden structure, dates from 1884. **Calle Alejandro Salicrup**, at the tip of the semi-peninsular wedge, is one of the best thoroughfares on which to see such timbered architecture, which is as unique to Arecibo as the southwestern townhouse style is to San Germán. In a somewhat different vein, the **Iglesia San Felipe**, between Calles José de Diego and Gonzalez Marin, boasts an unusual cupola and an anti-nuclear, anti-torture mural.

The **Alcaldía**, tucked at the intersection of Calles José de Diego, Romero Barcelo and Jaurregui, is among the prettier offices in Puerto Rico, and its inhabitants are among the friendliest and most receptive. A trip there will garner you information galore — their pamphlet, *Historia de Arecibo Como Capital de Ron*, is a big favorite among rummies — and perhaps a cup of coffee.

Formerly the Plaza Mayor, now the **Plaza Luís Muñoz Rivera**, this must be the prettiest plaza in Puerto Rico, with the cathedral facing over an idiosyncratically-landscaped park surrounded by wrought-iron railings and particolored Spanish colonial architecture. The plaza has undergone an astounding number of changes in the past century. In the mid-1890s, it was burnt to ashes during a fire that consumed much of the city. In 1899, a hurricane and the ensuing surf, which was not far short of a tidal wave, pounded it into disrepair. Arecibo was one of the first of Puerto Rican cities to jump off the Spanish imperial bandwagon to honor its native heroes. The monument in honor of Queen Isabela II of Spain, which for so long stood in the middle of the plaza, was replaced in 1927 with an obelisk honoring Luís Muñoz Marín. It's the centerpiece of the town to this day, and is one of the things that makes downtown Arecibo most scenic.

Below, selling grapefruits; and right, rum distillery, Arecibo.

We Are All in the Gutter..

Notwithstanding its history of natural disasters, about the only bad thing one can say about the layout of the town is that the Rio Grande de Arecibo is a volatile creature, and the town does flood with alarming frequency. This, however, only enhances its prestige as an attractive shopping town; floods mean flood sales.

...But Some of Us
Are Looking at the Stars

Anyone who has ever taken sixth-grade or first form science should have some familiarity with Arecibo. On one of those big, full-page spreads that fill up space in astronomy textbooks, in black-and-white or color, in pen-and-ink or photography, the **Arecibo Observatory** is generally featured prominently.

A complicated trip twenty miles (13 km) south into the karst country will bring you to the mammoth complex. From downtown Arecibo, follow de Diego to Route 129. Bear left on Route 651 and follow it for the four miles (Seven km) before it becomes 635. Travel about the same distance until you come to a T-intersection, at which you'll turn right (onto 626) and travel a few hundred yards before making a left on 625, at the end of which is the renowned observatory.

The place's reputation precedes it. Owned by Cornell University, it houses the world's largest radio-telescope, which is tucked snugly into a basin formed by karstic *mogotes*. It is massive — 1,320 feet (400 meters) in diameter, with a surface area of 40 acres (16 ha). The lattice looming 600 feet (185 meters) above the dish itself is what makes Arecibo a "radio-telescope"; its spectroscopic apparatus allows scientists to measure radiation from, and to determine chemical compositions of, stellar bodies.

Those who find all of this disconcertingly modern can take refuge at the **Cueva del Indio**, a cave west of Arecibo where Indians met in pre-Columbian times for religious rituals. The cave-paintings here rival those of Lascaux and Altamira in beauty, though certainly not in age.

Right, grocery shopping in an Arecibo market.

FEARFUL SYMMETRY: THE KARST COUNTRY

Puerto Rico is undeniably one of those places blessed to an almost unfair extent with an enormous variety and beauty of landscape. But such places are legion, and what do you give in Puerto Rico to the tourist who has everything? The answer is not hard to arrive at: the dark green sector of the island's northwest where the land rises in regular green-and-white hillocks and appears to be boiling, the area known as the karst country.

Old Limestone

Karst is one of the oddest rock formations in the world and can occur only under the most fortuitous circumstances. Some geologists claim that there are only two places on earth where rock formations resemble those of the northwest of the island: one, just across the Mona Passage in the Dominican Republic and one in Yugoslavia.

Karst is formed when water sinks into limestone and erodes larger and larger basins, known as "sinkholes." Many erosions create many sinkholes, until one is left with peaks of land only where the land has not sunk with the erosion of limestone: these are "mogotes," or karstic hillocks, which resemble each other in size and shape to a striking extent, given the randomness of the process that created them. All this leads one to realize that the highest point on the highest mogote in the karst country is certainly below the level the limestone ground held in earlier days when the first drop of rain opened the first sinkhole.

It's hard to say where the karst country begins. Some say at Manatí, though there are two hills not 10 minutes drive west of San Juan which look suspiciously karstic. From Manatí, they carry on as far west as Isabela, and are at their most spectacular a short drive (five miles, eight km) south of the major cities of Puerto Rico's northwest.

It's just as hard to say wherein their appeal lies. Part of it must be in the odd symmetry of the things — despite

Left, karst formations near Arecibo.

the fact that it is the holes, not the hills, which have undergone the change over the eons. These karstic mogotes, crammed tightly together, appear too similar not to give the feeling that *someone put them there.* There is also the fact that they *are the wrong size,* and man will always be fascinated by nature's ability to trump him that way. Eighteenth-Century Viennese royalty entertained itself by keeping midgets as companions. More recently John McPhee expressed the beauty of dwarf-pine forests. Obviously neither had seen karst.

These hills are impressive mountains only a hundred feet high — they are probably the grandest landscape humans can feel a sense of scale within. They encompass a startling variety within their regularity; certain mogotes can look like the Arizona desert tucked in for bed in the Black Forest.

The Karstic Forests

The Department of Natural Resources is to be credited for recognizing the beauty and fragility of this unique landscape. It has created four national forests in which it is protected: **Cambalache, Guajataca, Río Abajo** and **Vega.** Not all the karst country is limited to these forests; in fact, they are woefully small, comprising only about 4,000 acres (1,600 ha) in total, with Río Abajo accounting for over half of these.

All are ripe for hiking, yet the trails in the karst country never seem as crowded as those up El Yunque and other Puerto Rican mountains. This is due perhaps to the fact that the northwest is still the most isolated part of Puerto Rico, but perhaps is also due to the dangers involved with this sort of landscape. Sinkholes are not like potholes, but they can come as unexpectedly, especially in heavy brush. Get a trail map from the visitors' center at whatever reserve you try. Otherwise, *The Other Puerto Rico,* by Kathryn Robinson, offers helpful advice, and one read of it will convince you there's no place in Puerto Rico that's not worth risking your life to see.

Cars to Karst

One of the great pleasures of the karst country is that it is located in the idyllic Puerto Rican northwest, full of prosperous towns, cheerful bars and decent roads. No one should miss experiencing this landscape out of a fear of being forced out the front door of his rented car. Driving is easy in the karst country, with none of the coronary anxiety most tourists experience in the Cordillera Central.

Arecibo is the capital of the karst country, and some fine drives can begin from there. The easiest is certainly Route 10 south to **Embalse dos Bocas**. Taking 129 southwest to Lares is a pleasant *colmado*-flanked jaunt, which never lets one stray into the Cordillera, as the Route 10 trip is prone to do. If you like karst a lot, though, head west on Route 2, turn left on Route 119, and follow it to **Lake Guajataca** for the finest views of the water and limestone that made the whole unfathomable landscape possible.

Make it a point, if at all possible, to get out to the karst country. The unique beauty is staggering, and is worth a visit by itself. Even more, though, visions of karst will add another dimension to this tropical paradise too often labeled as a place for a "beach vacation."

Below, Lake Dos Bocas, near Arecibo; and right, rolling cigars.

LARES: TRADITION ON THE FRONTIER

If this tiny island has a frontier town, surely **Lares** is it. It sits at the western edge of the Cordillera Central's main cluster of peaks, and rests at the southernmost spur of the karst country. Lares is about as far from the sea as one can get in Puerto Rico, and to its west stretches a placid corridor of plains land running just north of the hills of La Cadena and just south of Route 111 and the sleepy Río Culebrinas.

Like many of the towns in this area where plains meet uplands to produce eerily spectacular vistas, Lares is as scenic to approach as it is to leave. Arriving from the south on either Route 124 or Route 128, the traveler is greeted by a tiny, toylike and close-packed community perched on a gentle rise across a valley and shadowed by rugged twin karstic mogotes. Emerging from the east on Route 111 from the karstic clusters of the Río Abajo Forest Reserve, one is hit by surprise at Lare's anomalous urbanity.

Left, Arecibo window; and below, Arecibo man keeps watch.

The town itself exudes much of the toylike ambience one perceives from afar. It's an attenuated cluster of little businesses, bars and shops snaking along two main one-way streets that run in opposite directions. In the center of the town is an imposing 19th-Century Spanish colonial church, whose pale pastel facade and gracefully-arched roof give it something of a Middle-Eastern look, especially when seen from across the valley at sundown.

If Lares has a stern side, pride rather than inhospitability is its source. For as the scene of the *Grito de Lares*, Puerto Rico's glorious and ill-fated revolt against Spanish colonial rule, the town is felt by many to be the birthplace of modern Puerto Rican political consciousness.

The Grito de Lares

The *Grito de Lares* ('Shout of Lares') was not merely a Puerto Rican historical event; its roots lay in political grievances that were to sweep Spain's Caribbean colonies in the mid-19th Century and result, some decades later, in their ultimate loss.

When in 1867, native Puerto Rican guards demonstrated in protest at discrepancies between their own salaries and those of Spanish guards, many liberals were expelled from the island, including Ramón Emeterio Betances, a distinguished physician and certainly the most prominent voice in Puerto Rican politics at the time. Betances went to New York, Santo Domingo and Saint Thomas, where he rallied support for abolition and self-determination and met Manual Rojas, a Venezuelan farmer who lived in Lares. With Rojas, he planned an agrarian revolt in the area.

On Sept. 23, 1868, despite the fact that their organization had been infiltrated and their plans discovered, hundreds of Betances' followers seized Lares and began to march on nearby San Sebastián. There they were met by Spanish forces, and easily routed. Though Betances was merely exiled to France and the revolution came to nought, the *Grito de Lares* led Puerto Ricans to think differently of their land and their aspirations for it, and the spirit of that September day lives on not only in the streets of Lares, but in the hearts and on the tongues of Puerto Ricans throughout the island.

SAN SEBASTIÁN: PRIZING PROVINCIALITY

Of all the prosperous and provincial towns of Puerto Rico's northwest, **San Sebastián** stands out as the most representative of the region and in the most noticeable contrast to the gloomy villages of the Cordillera Central to the south and east. Perhaps this is because it is the first of the towns which is truly out of the highlands and secure in its footing as part of the low-lying northwest. Perhaps too it has something to do with the cornucopia of food products the region around San Sebastián produces, for this is the heart of many of Puerto Rico's oldest food industries.

San Sebastián is surrounded by green and moist rolling grassland, and stood as one of Puerto Rico's sugar boom towns in cane's heyday. Now, the area is given over to scattered dairy farming and various other agricultural pursuits which used to be associated with other parts of the island. Tobacco grows in many a valley, and coffee plants, once the preserve of Yauco and other towns in the island's arid southwest, can be seen growing on many a hillside.

With close to 40,000 residents, most of them living in the shady main streets that cluster about a lovely plaza, San Sebastián has more of an urban ambience than most of the northwest. It lacks the historical reputation of Lares just to the east, and as a commercial center is utterly overwhelmed by Mayagüez just 10 miles (16 km) away. But San Sebastián is within easy driving distance of all of these places and has a number of charming features that they all lack.

Primary among these is its existence as the most provincial of moderate-sized Puerto Rican cities. It is at once a city with a thriving local culture and one whose residents are not deprived of modern amenities: big salsa groups like El Gran Combo de Puerto Rico play here, as do first-run films.

This is not to say San Sebastián is devoid of scenic charms. There's hardly a better spot from which to explore Puerto Rico's wondrous karst country. To the north, lovely **Lake Guajataca** boasts natural nature walks and a *parador*. And any drive into the countryside will lead to scenery and surprises.

Plaza, San Sebastían.

158

UNDER THE ISLAND: THE CAMUY CAVES

Camuy is an unspectacular town just far enough west of Arecibo, just far enough north of Route 2, to appear almost untouched by the life of modern Puerto Rico. What appeal Camuy has is more primordial—a bewildering maze of one-way streets that will never accommodate automobiles; a lifestyle tranquil to the point of torpor; a few vestiges of an older era, like shops that sell salves and incense for the appeasement of various saints; and, most primordial of all, one of the largest cave systems in the western world.

Speleology and Scatology

Most easily reachable by driving due south on Route 486, the cave system is actually a series of karstic sinkholes connected by the Camuy River, which burrows underground through soft limestone for much of its course from the Cordillera to the Atlantic. The largest of these entrances has been developed for

North Coast, near Camuy.

tourism, with attractions of the "fun for the whole family" variety. A bandstand draws local groups of the stature of El Gran Combo, numerous picnic tables offer respite for those famished by the drive from San Juan, and a small bar proves a good spot for a Corona and a gaze up at the karstic hills. In cages along the walk to the caves proper are massive and majestic tropical birds to the ornithologist's delight.

The cave entrance looks like a cathedral facade, with a broad row of toothy stalactites descending from the bushy hillside. Inside the cave's overhang, the light becomes bluish, and a weird silence descends, broken frequently by the chirp of bats on the ceiling and minute distant echoes. Could it be the sound of water dripping through yet undiscovered passages? It could be, but it's not. It's bat-shit, and you won't have to travel more than a dozen steps to realize that much of it is going to fall on you in the course of your perambulations. Natives claim the droppings are potentially very toxic. But don't let this keep you away from the caves. Wash up afterwards, and bring covering if you must, but visit. There's nothing else quite like it.

WAY OUT IN QUEBRADILLAS

The most amazing story Puerto Ricans tell about **Quebradillas** concerns basketball. During a close regular season game between the Quebradillas team and archrival Isabela, the score became close, and tensions and tempers began to run high. When Isabela took the lead on a surprise basket and its supporters began to cheer and taunt, Quebradillas's Mayor Hernández rose from the stands with a revolver and fired into the opposing stands, injuring several spectators.

Anything Can Happen

This is not to point to the people of Quebradillas as being especially violent — if anything, their friendly and welcoming attitude will convince you the opposite is the case — but rather to show that in this isolated northwestern municipality, anything can happen, and quite often does. Quebradillas adds to the appealing oddities one expects from the towns west of Arecibo — spiritualist herb shops, narrow streets and florid houses sloping suicidally towards the waterline — and some geological oddities that make it a town well worth going out of one's way for.

A short drive or walk northwest of town, **Playa Guajataca**, described by locals as a "nice, dangerous beach" is to be taken with caution. Deep waters, white sands and raging surf make it highly attractive for surfers and bathers, but highly dangerous for those incapable of swimming the English Channel or disinclined to bring life preservers. Even experts should exercise caution.

The **Río Guajataca** is another spot as beautiful as it is forbidding, and pocked with a cave system, which, though not completely charted, appears to be as extensive and awesome as that of the Camuy. Nearby **Lake Guajataca**, seven miles (12 km) south on Route 113, is man-made, as are the rest of Puerto Rico's lakes, but offers a splendid natural retreat, with two *paradores*, Vistamar and Guajataca, serving as convenient bases for hikes into the rolling **Aymamon Mountains** in the **Guajataca Forest Reserve**, just to the west.

Urbanization in Hatilio.

ISABELA:
SNOW-WHITE WONDER

Isabela is a florilegium of all the charms of Puerto Rico's northwestern corner, with a cluster of brilliant, whitewashed houses tumbling out of the hills to some of the island's most justly renowned surfing and swimming beaches. The city has that look of stability and purposefulness so characteristic of the region, due perhaps to flourishing shoe and textile industries. Lest it be thought that Isabela has bought its serenity at the price of industrial over-expansion, it should be mentioned that the *municipio* has retained a far higher proportion of its small farms than most other island communities.

If history has been somewhat kind to Isabela, nature has not. Located just south of the tectonically fickle Milwaukee Trench, Isabela has been victimized by earthquakes and tidal waves for as long as it has been settled. The most memorable of the quakes — on Oct. 11, 1918 — destroyed much of the town, including the renowned **Iglesia de San Antonio de Padua**. The reconstructed church on Calle Celso Barbosa, built in 1924, is still worth a visit; the subtle beige facade and delicate double cupolas recreate aspects of the original design.

Horse enthusiasts should head to **Arenales**, in the southern part of the *municipio*, where a number of fine *pasofino* stables have made Isabela almost as renowned as Coamo and Vieques for breeding the noble animals.

Most visitors to Isabela, however, come to ride waves, not steeds, and **Jobos Beach**, just west of town on Route 466, is the place to do that.

The beach is made even more beautiful by the high cliffs which back it. One of these, **El Pozo de Jacinto**, is the source of a charming local custom. A farmer named Jacinto used to pasture his cows near the edge of the cliffs. One day, part of the cliff collapsed and Jacinto's finest bovine tumbled to her death. Jacinto, enraged, ran to the cliff's edge and cursed Fate. Fate disapproved; Jacinto too fell off the cliff and died. Today, Isabela schoolchildren stand at the edge of the cliffs and yell: "*Jacinto! Damne la Vaca!*" (Damn the cow!) It's supposed to bring good luck.

Pounding surf at Isabela.

AGUADA AND AGUADILLA

These two lovely seaside towns have a running rivalry over which was the spot where Columbus first landed in Puerto Rico. As such, its residents might be taken aback to find that most of the handful of visitors who come each year have a hard enough time telling the two apart, let alone judging the primacy of their respective claims.

Aguada has erected a seaside **Parque de Colón** a mile northwest of town on Route 441, dead center of **Playa Espinar**, a 2,500-foot (760-meter) white sand beach so enticing that Columbus buffs will wish their man had landed there, regardless of historical fact. Aguadillans, meanwhile, certainly have logic, if not an airtight argument on their side in claiming that Columbus's men stopped for water at the spring which now forms the focus of their own **Parque El Parterre**.

Aguadilla is the more prosperous and picturesque of the two towns. It's laid out like a Mediterranean resort, bleeding along a mile of coast with very little penetration inland. **Avenida José de Jesus Esteves** (Route 440) is a prim and polychromatic seaside boulevard, a little Caribbean equivalent of the Promenade des Anglais in Nice; parallel streets are punctuated with attractive if unspectacular parks. *Mundillo* lace and wicker hats are the twin prides of Aguadilla's active artisan community; both are ubiquitous in the commercial district.

Flyers and Playas

Many though its charms may be, Aguadilla can't claim, like Aguada, to have a pleasant *balneario* at its doorstep. Aguadilla's is just a bit too rocky for sane people to have a go at. Most of the townspeople, therefore, head north on Route 107 to **Playa Boquerón Sur**, known locally as **Crash Boat Beach** for the vessels which used to take off from the beach to rescue errant fighter planes from **Ramey Air Force Base** just to the north. Ramey is quite a base, with the longest runway in the Caribbean (and apparently the longest odds against returning to base safely, given the proximity of Crash Boat).

Crossing the plaza, Aguada.

162

RINCÓN: GEE IT IS SWELL

Rincón is certainly not a place for bathing enthusiasts, excepting those whose idea of a good time is being thrown face-first onto rock flats or jagged reefs. Nor, although nightlife here is fast and loose enough for any taste, is it partying that draws so many young people to Rincón from San Juan, 100 miles (60 km) away. It is rather a dazzling and varied offshore surf which has drawn board enthusiasts for decades, and has made Rincón, since the World Surfing Championships were held here in 1968, the surfing capital of the Caribbean area.

Though *rincó* means 'corner,' the town actually sits at the flat, regular end of a peninsula shaped like a pointer's snout. This is **La Cadena Hills**, the westernmost spur of the rugged Cordillera Central, and nowhere in Puerto Rico do mountains meet coast more dramatically. The view most surfers see from offshore is of deep green hills and shimmering groves of mango backing bright, white sand and turquoise sea, and it's highly possible that this unique vista draws as many surfers to Rincón as the sport itself.

Tunnel Vision

Still, it's hard to imagine better surfing anywhere. Rincón is not just one beach, but six, bordered by picturesque and prominent coral reefs and shoals, stretching from Puerto Rico's rough Atlantic coast on the north side of the peninsula to the placid and eminently swimmable turquoise waters of the Caribbean south. The surf varies all the way along the peninsula, leaving boardmen with a choice of rides at all levels of difficulty. The effect is rather like that of a ski resort with a great number of delightful trails.

The town of Rincón is pleasant and quiet, with a number of trendy, surfer-infested restaurants ranged along Route 115. An old disused nuclear power plant standing next to the town's quaint, little lighthouse lends the area an eerie look and gives Rincón an otherworldliness perceptible even to nonsurfers.

Going for a ride in the Aguadillan surf.

CORDILLERA CENTRAL

The Cordillera Central, or "central spine" towers over the middle of the island, its peaks and valleys stretching 60 miles (96 km) east to west. It is a region of superlatives and extremes — the highest, the deepest, the roughest. And also the remotest; most visitors to the island choose to ignore its allure, staying on the beaches or in San Juan. This is perhaps due to lack of publicity. It is true that the charm of the Cordillera has little to do with the shops of old San Juan or the sun-drenched beachfronts of Dorado and Humacao. Rather, it offers cool mountain lakes and streams, isolated green spots and remote country inns. The temperature in the mountains drops one degree for every 500-foot increase in elevation. This means that when San Juan is broiling, you just might need a sweater on Cerro de Punta. So if you've seen one too many sunburned tourists on the beach, or if you've fallen victim to the lobster tan yourself, head for the hills and cool off. The contrast between Puerto Rico's urban industrial character and its countryside is both delightful and thought provoking.

The best way to see the Cordillera is by automobile. Allow at least two full days, and find a good road map of the island. Getting around in the mountains is half the fun. Two-lane blacktop is the rule for mountain roads; some two-lane roads are major ones, others minor, and still others turn into dirt tracks half-way up deserted hillsides. Be prepared for some arduous driving on hairpin and switchback curves. The roads connecting most mountain towns run from plaza to plaza, making for easy navigation. Along these roads, you are never more than a few minutes away from the next *colmado*, a roadside store selling cold drinks, groceries and perhaps a sandwich or two.

The Cordillera is the last retreat of the once-ubiquitous *jíbaro*, the hardy Puerto Rican mountain peasant, whose exploits have been the stuff of legend and literature from the chronicles of the early settlers to the stories of Emilio Belaval. *Jíbaros* are to the Puerto Rican consciousness what cowboys are to the American, or bushrangers to the Australian. The *jíbaro* is shaped by an exacting landscape, possessed of a pride, resourcefulness and wry pessimism—his is the story of Puerto Rico. Anyone who speaks a little Spanish and wishes to penetrate the Puerto Rican character will find no better instructor than one of these diminutive, scythe-swinging philosophers.

CAGUAS: KEY TO THE CORDILLERA

Two roads connect San Juan with **Caguas**, 20 miles (32 km) to the south; Route 52, the fast modern tollway that runs all the way to Ponce, and the older and slower Route 1, with no toll collectors. Caguas, whose 110,000 people make it the largest city in the island's interior, lies in the broad and fertile **Turabo Valley.** Three different mountain ranges form the valley's walls, accounting for its unusual expanse. To the north and east rises the **Sierra de Luquillo**, which runs almost to the coast. To the south, the **Sierra de Cayey** climbs rapidly, blotting out the horizon. And to the west, the Cordillera Central stretches up and across the island.

Caguas is named after the Taíno Indian *cacique* Caguax, who ruled the Indians of the Turabo Valley area at the time of the Spanish Conquest. Caguax was one of the two *caciques* who made peace during the Indian uprisings of 1511. The Indians, fearing reprisal after drowning a Spanish boy, revolted. Several *caciques* led guerilla bands on raids in the following weeks, but Ponce de Leon, with help of peaceful *cacique* soon restored order. A large allegorical painting exists depicting his conversion to Christianity.

In many ways Caguas typifies the Latin American city of moderate size. **Plaza Palmer,** one of the most charming plazas in Puerto Rico, is the center of civic and spiritual life. Almost as large as the one at Ponce, it is dominated by two ancient rubber trees with benches built into their huge trunks. Pigeons inhabit the plaza, some in an aviary and others flocking freely from one end to the other. In the middle of everything, a solemn statue of 19th Century poet José Gautier Benítez, Caguas' most famous son, stands on a pedestal. Goldfish sun themselves in a mossy pond next to the aviary, and on weekends, musicians bring salsa rhythms to a small bandstand. There is also the Daliesque **Relój Florido**, a giant clockface planted with flowers.

The large **Cathedral of Caguas** faces one side of the plaza, directly across from the *alcaldía* with its 1856 facade. The church has been rebuilt and enlarged several times as hurricanes have struck in this century and the last one destroyed the original building. On any afternoon the plaza attracts a good number of people. Couples sit quietly holding hands, old men move from bench to bench, always keeping in the shade, and kids plan may-hem while their mothers shop in nearby stores. An evangelist, accompanied by a lone guitarist, exhorts a small crowd, which keeps its distance. Every city or town in Puerto Rico has its plaza, but few are as lively or picturesque as this one.

A walk down Calle Ruíz Belviz reveals a tiny 19th Century **Baptist church.** Farther along, on a side street, the historic **Piedra de Polanco** can be found. This large rock was once used by ladies and gentlemen to mount on and dismount from horses and carriages when visiting town. Today it is part of a jewelry store.

The outskirts of Caguas offer a variety of sights. The southern tip of **Lake Loíza** may be reached by taking Route 796 northeast out of town. The road skirts the lake's sleepy banks before circling back to join Route 1 north of Caguas, with several likely spots for picnic or fishing.

Scenes near Caguas: left, Route 52; and right, aspiring Roberto Clementes.

AGUAS BUENAS TO CAYEY

The six miles (10 km) between Caguas, and **Aguas Buenas** to the west, mark a profound change in the landscape. Route 156 begins to climb as soon as it leaves the city behind. Aguas Buenas is perched on a hill that is part of the far northeastern extension of the Cordillera Central. Mountain palms and bamboo start to line the roadside. The lush green miniature valleys glimpsed through the breaks in these trees are a rugged preview of the contours of the Cordillera, and the hills and curves of Route 156 serve as a beginner's course in Cordillera driving. Is it the change in temperature? The sweet, cool air? The first sight of a little boy leading a skinny black-and-white island cow? Whatever it is, the city seems much farther than a few miles away, and the intangible yet universal mountain mind-set of isolation and wonder begins to take hold.

Aguas Buenas is dashed across the hillside as if with one hurried stroke of a paintbrush. The town extends much farther along the face of the hill than up or down. A modern church and a school struggle for space on the smallish **Plaza**. When school lets out, the plaza fills with young people of all sizes including some very beautiful girls of high-school age.

The town was once known for the nearby **Caves of Aguas Buenas.** The Department of Natural Resources once ran tours on weekends, but the caves have been closed for some time. It is however possible to enter them off **Route 794.** Only experienced spelunkers should attempt serious exploration. Route 794, at any rate, has some interesting views as it leads down out of town and then up to rougher country. For the not-too-timid, fresh milk can be bought from one of several farmers along the road. The number of houses with signs announcing *Se Vende* or *C.V.D.* for short (for sale) attests to the cityward migration in Puerto Rico that threatens almost to depopulate the Cordillera.

Dammed Cidra

Nine miles (14 km) southwest of Aguas Buenas is **Cidra.** Cidra can also be reached from Caguas on Route 172. This road offers excellent panoramic views of the entire **Turabo Valley,** including Caguas. Several roadside fruit stands sell local fruits and vegetables, some varieties of which are never seen in San Juan. They also sell flowers, fresh and colorful enough to brighten the drabbest hotel room.

With over 30,000 residents, Cidra is a larger town than it seems. There is always a line of young people waiting to play video games at **Café la Estrella**, one block off the plaza. **Lake Cidra**, five miles (eight km) long, supplies water to San Juan, Cataño and other cities. The lake, an artificial one, was dammed in the 1940s. While there is no boating, residents claim that the fishing is worth a try. The houses around the lakeshore, with their serene views, give quiet testimony to the gracious lifestyle of their lucky inhabitants. A restaurant on the shore with outdoor tables shares the view, luckily for visitors.

An interesting local legend of buried treasure dates from the turn of the century. One night during an epidemic of smallpox, a wealthy peasant fearful of losing his fortune rode his horse into the forest and buried a quantity of gold.

Left, entrance to caves, Aguas Buenas; and right, passersby in Cayey.

Upon returning home, the man fell sick and soon died without disclosing the location of his treasure. To this day the old peasant appears as a skeleton atop a black horse, unable to rest because his sons inherited nothing.

Between Cidra and Las Cruces on Route 787, **Rancho Pepon** provides a pleasant family *pasadia* (picnic ground). Rancho Pepon looks like the country ranch that it is. Its facilities include a large covered patio, a swimming pool and a restaurant open on weekends. The Caraballo family, Luis, Sonia and their son Peponcito, run the facility which can accommodate groups of up to 300.

Cayey

Following either the tollway or the lesser Route 1 south of Caguas, the next major town is **Cayey**, 12 miles (19.2 km) away. The first view of Cayey is of a modern strip-cum-shopping-center at the highway exit. A Pizza Inn and a twin cinema share the space with other stores. Cayey is a city of nearly 50,000 with a university and bustling industry. The city sits on the northern slope of the Sierra de Cayey. Southeastern Puerto Rico is a tobacco-growing region, and Consolidated Cigars has a large plant in Cayey. Here popular brands like Muriel and Dutch Masters are manufactured.

Cayey's **Plaza** features a large church built in 1813. Of unusual design, the church has an extremely long nave, a single square tower and a dome overlooking the transept. For culture lovers, the museum at the University displays works by major Puerto Rican artists.

The Ruta Panoramica avoids Cayey, passing several miles to the south, but that doesn't mean the city's vistas are second-rate. It does mean, though, that Cayey is a good place to pick up the Ruta Panoramica from San Juan, little more than a half-an-hour's drive from Condado. Route 1 becomes the Panoramica about two miles (three km) past town. Care should be taken, for the Panoramica shifts to Route 772 after another three miles (five km).

The Ruta Panoramica, as its name suggests, is rich with vistas for the eyes to feast upon. Cordillera driving is no picnic however; be sure to pick up a map for winding road navigation, and pack some Dramamine — you never know.

COAMO:
SPAS AND STEEDS

Coamo is probably most famous for its hot springs, where even before the Spaniards came the Taínos considered the waters holy and healing. In the early part of this century, **Coamo Springs** was a major Caribbean resort with an international clientele. Franklin Roosevelt took the waters here in the 1930s. After World War Two, however, the resort went bankrupt and fell into decay. Moving westward across the mountains from Aibonito, Route 14 goes directly to Coamo. Coamo is also relatively close to Route 52. One of the oldest cities in Puerto Rico, Coamo was founded in 1538. On the plaza, a **historical museum** located in a sunny courtyard displays 450 years of artifacts, documents and pictures. Several rooms of the museum are furnished with antiques in an attempt to create a typical (and prosperous) 19th-Century household. The museum must be entered through a pediatrics clinic just off the plaza.

Today a new resort stands on the ruins of the old one. The **Parador de Coamo,** part of the system of *paradores,* was built in 1975. The crumbling 1848 walls of the original hotel are cleverly used to help support some of the new structures, lending an air of the picturesque to the site. Water at 110 degrees Fahrenheit (45 degrees Celsius) is pumped from the springs into a large pool. The mineral content of the water is remarkably high; a card listing its contents is available at the desk.

A Mediterranean health spa in the mountains of Puerto Rico? That's what it seems, with healthy young men and women jogging on the road outside the parador and tanned bodies sunning by the swimming pool with iced juices in hand. The jet set no longer stops here, though. Most guests are vacationing Puerto Rican families. There are also public baths at the springs for those who come only for the waters.

Find the springs on Route 546. Signs point the way to the parador. Outside Coamo, farms and ranches raise beef cattle and fine horses with an island-wide reputation. The tradition of the gentleman farmer still lives here, after four centuries.

Left, horseplay in Los Banos. Below, shopping for peppers and plantains.

AIBONITO AND BARRANQUITAS

Aibonito is a pretty jewel of a place set in a narrow valley. The Ruta Panoramica narrowly misses the town, which can be reached from Cayey via **Route 14**, a road rivaling the Panoramica for valley viewing and for its number of curves. Aibonito, at 2,500 feet (800 meters) has the highest altitude of any town in Puerto Rico, and the lowest average temperature. In 1911, the temperature reached 40 degrees Farenheit (8 degrees Celsius). One story of how Aibonito was named has a wandering half-starved 17th Century bandit who stumbles onto the valley and then exclaims "*Ai, que bonito!*" (How pretty!) In 1887 Aibonito was the provisional capital of the island for seven months. In that year, known as *El Año Terrible*, an independence movement was bloodily suppressed by a military governor, the hated General Palacios Gonzales. The General moved his troops and government to the mountains in order to be better prepared to chase down the hated *Independentistas*, and also perhaps to enjoy the cooler clime. The plaza here has a movie theater, a diner that would not be out of place in Des Moines and a shining white 19th-Century church with two small towers. Weathered wooden porches around the plaza give an air of genteel neglect.

A Slit in the Hills

Near Aibonito is the **San Cristóbal Canyon**, the deepest gorge on the island. Formed by the Rio Usabon, this canyon, with walls up to 700 feet (230 meters) is so deep and narrow that from the air it looks like a slit in the hills. From the ground, the only way to see it is to stand on the very rim. The view, is indeed impressive. To approach the canyon, follow Route 725 to the north. In this area, businesses tend to call themselves *El Cañon* — Tienda el Cañoni, Ferrenta el Cañon, and so on. One of the most *simpático* of these establishments is the **Bar el Cañon**, at Km 4 on Route 725. Among its attributes: a juke box and canned beer at country prices. The canyon can be reached from here, but it is a rough hike. Better to go on to Km 5.5, where a narrow unmarked side road comes a little closer to the edge. From there it is a short hike down to the canyon, where, with a little effort, it is possible to find a 100-foot (30-meter) waterfall.

Barranquitas: Hills and Heroes

Four miles (seven km) north as the crow flies, but double that by car, the town of **Barranquitas** overlooks the other side of San Cristóbal Canyon. The best place to view the canyon in Barranquitas is on Route 156 east of the town. At Km 17.7 the Lion's Club has a view which gives more perspective than the close-up views at Aibonito.

Barranquitas is known as the birthplace of Luís Muñoz Rivera, the famous autonomy-minded statesman. Muñoz Rivera and his equally famous son Luíz Muñoz Marín, governor of the island from 1948 to 1964, are buried here near the plaza in a small complex that also includes a museum full of Muñoz Rivera artifacts. The complex is located on Calle Muñoz Rivera.

Sad to say, Barranquitas lacks the charm of its cross-canyon neighbor. Its narrow streets and tightly packed houses

Left, Lake Caonillas; and right, Barranquitas.

have a sinister feel despite the mountain setting. Even the people seem more sullen. Perhaps the lack of an inspirational and mellifluous name like Aibonito has something to do with it. In Spanish, *una barranca* means a cliff or gorge, but it can also mean great difficulty or an impassable obstacle.

There is another more direct route from San Juan to Aibonito and Barranquitas, a pleasant drive through hilly country. Take Route 2 from San Juan to Bayamon. From Bayamon take **Route 167** south until it intersects **Route 156**, which goes to Barranquitas. This route looks less taxing on the odometer; in reality, it involves nearly 30 miles (48 km) of demanding two-lane roads. If you plan any mountain driving beyond Aibonito or Barranquitas, it is probably better to take the Autopista to Cayey.

Route 167, though, is worth a trip in itself, especially on a Sunday afternoon. Immediately south of Bayamon, the road begins playing a game of peek-a-boo with the **Plata River** and its subsidiary streams. The streams jump back and forth across the road with increasing frequency until at last, near **El Ocho**, a panorama of the broad Río de la Plata,

named after the mighty South American River, unfolds.

Another feature of the road, starting just outside Bayamon and continuing its entire length, are the green and white colors of the PIP (Puerto Rican Independence Party) splashed on walls, houses and trees with great regularity. Whether this attests to a rural base of support for the *Independentistas* is a matter of conjecture; perhaps the graffiti are more noticeable for the lack of other signs in the country.

Route 167 passes through or near settlements with rustic names: *Pájaro Puertorriqueño, Sabana, Naranjito* (Puerto Rican Bird, Savannah, Little Orange). On Sunday afternoons in nearly every one of these little towns, musicians will be tuning up in bandstands and in *colmados*. They will start to play as the sun's rays stretch out, singing to audiences of 20, 30 or 50. If there are no musicians around, a group of men in a bar will begin to sing and keep singing until long after sunset. This happens all over the mountains. Thus the country people (and the city people who come to the country) squeeze every moment out of the weekend.

ASCENT TO TORO NEGRO

In the southwest of the Cordillera, the town of **Villalba** is surrounded by some of the most incredible scenery on the island, including Puerto Rico's highest peak. From Coamo, Route 150 reaches Villalba in 14 mountainous miles (22 km). Villalba itself is not as interesting as the nearby peaks and forest reserves. A drive on its streets, choked and dusty at midday, awakens the desire to escape back to the cool green heights. North of town, Route 149 begins to climb in earnest. And you thought you were in the mountains! A stop at the *colmado* **La Collaloma**, within sight of the intersection with Route 514, feels like a reward for leaving civilization behind. Here you can catch your breath while sipping a *bebida* and sitting on a handmade bamboo bench. From this vantage, Villalba and **Lake Toa Vaca** spread out far below, and in the distance — yes, the blue Caribbean shimmers. High above, terrace gardens line the slopes. Farther up, the peaks disappear into the mist.

Route 149 continues to climb until it intersects Route 143 inside the **Toro Negro Forest Reserve. Route 143** is an east/west road that follows the backbone of the Cordillera Central from Adjuntas to a point near Barranquitas. This 30-mile (48-km) section of road is the longest continuous stretch of the Ruta Panoramica. Views along this road stretch north and south to both coasts.

To the east of the intersection is the **Dona Juana Recreational Area**, a *pasadía* that features a large freshwater swimming pool and several trails through dense forests of large mountain palms. There is a campground here, and a ranger station. The pool was closed for repairs in May 1985, but at time of press will be reopen soon. A trail leads from the pool to a deserted lookout tower about two miles (three km) away. The first quarter of the trail is paved with uneven, mossy stones. Moss turns very slippery with the smallest amount of water, watch out on wet days. The **Dona Juana Falls**, a 200-foot (61-meter) waterfall, is nearby.

West of the intersection, the road climbs into the silent peaks. **Lago**

Lake Patillas from Sierra Cayey.

178

Guineo (Banana Lake), the highest lake on the island, hides at the end of an unmarked gravel road. A dam across the Toro Negro River keeps the lake full. It's difficult to find, walled about by steep red clay banks choked with bamboo. Only the high-pitched chatter of the *coquí* disturbs the perfect isolation of this little round lake. The clay banks demand caution; clay is another surface that gets very slippery when slightly moistened.

Cerro Altitude

Farther west (and higher up) the road passes **Cerro Maravillas**, a lofty peak that bristles with antennae and microwave towers. Across the road from the peak, a grassy picnic area overlooks the entire south coast. A gravel parking lot on the north side of the road at Km 16.5 marks the base of **Cerro de Punta**, at 4,400 feet (1,350 meters), the island's highest peak. The peak's summit can be reached on foot or by car up a treacherously steep paved road considerably less than one lane wide. On top, the solitude is shared by more antennae and a bunker-like shed. The view of the north coast includes San Juan unless of course a stray cloud gets in the way. To be on Cerro de Punta when the mists roll in is a powerful experience.

A few miles directly north of Cerro de Punta, **Jayuya** nestles in its valley. Fortunately for the unspoiled forest, and unfortunately for the driver, no road connects the two. Take Route 144 to the town from either east or west. In Jayuya, a visit to the stately **Hacienda Gripinas**, a *parador* situated on an old coffee plantation, might prove more tempting than a long drive home, especially if the day is almost finished. A wide porch on the restored 200-year-old house overlooks a cool valley. As the sun goes down so many *coquí* begin singing that the *parador* lists this performance as a distinctive feature in its brochure. A trail connects the *parador* with Cerro de Punta a short distance away.

The astonishing variety of terrain, combined with the beautiful views afforded by heights such as Cerro de Punta make a trip to the southwest Cordillera well worth the time. It's there for the asking — the mountains, waterfalls, and, in the distance, the omnipresent blue of the Caribbean.

Near Barranquitas.

THE FAR WEST: ADJUNTAS TO MARICAO

West of Toro Negro, the mountains change character once again. The stately peaks give way to rougher, lusher country. The valleys are smaller, shallower, more numerous. The tall mountain palms yield to bamboo, ferns and hardwoods like teak. Flowering bushes sometimes line the road. The town of **Adjuntas** marks this area of transition. A rugged town filled with nononsense hardware stores and lumberyards, Adjuntas also has the **Monte Rio Hotel**, a clean establishment near the plaza. The **Cafeteria Adjuntas** on Route 10 sells fresh juices and huge wedges of plain yellow cake. Adjuntas is nicknamed "the town of the sleeping giant," a reference to the outline of the mountains above.

Guilarte: Land of the Jíbaros

The **Guilarte Forest Reserve** west of Adjuntas is another good place to get back to nature. A hillside *pasadía* is set

near a eucalyptus grove. The fragrant, blade-shaped leaves litter the ground. A few hundred feet up the road, a well-marked trail leads to the top of 1,200-meter (3,900-foot) **Monte Guilarte.** Watch out for slippery clay on the trail. The view from the desolate summit is unrestricted by the usual telephone company junk: not a single antenna to be found on this mountain.

Between Adjuntas and Monte Guilarte are many small farms, farmed by small farmers — the last of the *jíbaros*. This area is one of the few places on the island with such a concentrated population of these legendary people. The Ruta Panoramica passes right through their farmland, and the colorful little men like nothing better than talking to travelers in a Spanish that is nasal, twangy and high-pitched.

Following the Ruta Panoramica west from Monte Guilarte will bring you to a town called **Los Rabanos** on the map, but known to residents as **Castaner.** A real one-street country town, Castaner has a formidable number of jeeps, pickup trucks, and land rovers, and feed stores seem to be its busiest establishments. Surprisingly, the town has a rather large community of mainland U.S. expatriates. The hills above the city are planted with evenly-spaced coffee bushes, and the air has the dry, hot feel of Puerto Rican coffee country.

North of Adjuntas toward **Utuado**, the Cordillera begins its descent to the coastal plain. But that does not mean the land gets flat. The haystack karstic hills north of Utuado march all the way to the Atlantic. Utuado boasts the usual plaza with the typical 19th-Century church.

Caguana: Land of the Indians

West of Utuado on Route 111, the **Caguana Indian Ceremonial Ballpark** should not be missed. Built by the Taínos nearly a millennium ago, the ballpark includes ten *bateyes* (ball courts) on which the early Indians played a lacrosse- or pelota-like game in a blend of sports and religious ceremony. Overlooking the courts, a small rocky peak has been guarding the park for centuries, and looks as though it will continue to do so for centuries to come. Strange sounds echo back and forth over the landscaped grounds. An owl hoots. A dry leaf rasps across one of the

Left and right, views from the Ruta Panoramica.

bateyes. The Taíno gods *Yukiyu* and *Huracán* continue to make their presence felt here.

North of Utuado on Route 10, **Lago Dos Bocas** (Two-Mouthed Lake) curves into a U-shape around steep hills. Near its shores, a roadship stop called **Los Chorros** provides a restaurant, swimming pool and *pasadía*. The restaurant takes its name from a nearby cave which can be reached on foot. At Km 68, Route 10 skirts the lake shore. From there, a launch service carries passengers back and forth across the lake. Boats leave every two hours, starting at seven in the morning, on what is a pleasant and worthwhile side-trip.

Maricao: Land of the Baby Fish

On the far western edge of the Cordillera, not far from Mayagüez, is **Maricao**, the smallest *municipio* in Puerto Rico, with just over 3,000 people. Route 120 approaches Maricao from the south through the **Maricao Forest Reserve**. By the roadside in the middle of the forest is a castle-like stone tower, four stories tall. A boy's backyard dream-come-true, the tower overlooks the entire western half of the island from 790 meters (2,600 feet). The forest reserve also has a tidy campground.

Maricao's tiny plaza features a rustic cream-and-brick colored church. Just outside town is the **Maricao Fish Hatchery**, where many species of freshwater fish are hatched and raised. The 20,000 fish raised here annually are dumped in 26 lakes around the island to replenish the sportfish population. On the road to the fish hatchery is a mountainside shrine, a haven of serenity and dignity.

The **Hacienda Juanita** in Maricao is yet another coffee plantation converted into a *parador*. The inn to this day is surrounded by groves of oranges, bananas and avocados. Guests are invited to pick their own breakfasts. For the lazy ones, bowls of fragrant fruit are always within reach, and bunches of bananas hang from 150-year-old beams. Some of these beams are hewn from precious *ausubo*, a type of ironwood native to Puerto Rico. This wood, prized for its resistance to rot and termites, was once plentiful, but today it is among the rarest of the world's hardwoods.

THE SOUTH COAST

Until the completion a decade ago of Route 52, the San Juan-Ponce toll road, San Juan natives considered the prospect of driving to Ponce only slightly less daunting than that of swimming to Miami. Indeed, Puerto Rico's south coast used to be so isolated by the Cordillera and its tortuous one-lane roads that a majority of Puerto Ricans saw their southern compatriots in terms of a number of bizarre and often unflattering stereotypes. These were the proud, stubborn farmers whose accent was slightly odd. They were a simple people with something of a gift for politics but with a culture you wouldn't envy if you lived at the bottom of the ocean. Their only inheritance was a landscape as gorgeous as it was remote.

All that has changed, and it's no longer even possible to entertain those stereotypes. The south has charms that are drawing northerners an hour down the highway to take residence. Ponce, with a glittering double plaza and the greatest art museum in the Caribbean, is as pleasant and cultured as any city of its size anywhere. Salinas' seafood restaurants rival San Juan's best, and Jobos Bay is as pleasant a spot for picnicking as it is for sailing. All along the coast is the alluring, typically southern landscape of golden plain stretching between lush mountain and blue Caribbean. And from Ponce, it's now only an hour to get to San Juan. Most Ponceños would tell you it's not worth the effort.

Preceding pages: petroleum and sugarcane, the two major industries, side by side near Yabucoa; Spanish colonial house, Guayama. Left, Punta Tuna, the island's westernmost point.

HUMACAO: SUGAR AND SPICE

Humacao is a first-rate industrial center with pretensions to bring a first-rate resort. Some of these pretensions are justified. The city, only a 45-minute drive from San Juan via Route 30, is within two miles (three km) of some of the most dazzling beachfront Vieques Sound has to offer. Add to that its convenience as a starting point for excursions in the southeast, and Humacao becomes a place to be taken seriously as a holiday retreat.

The best way to begin a beach tour of this part of the island is to head north to **Playa Humacao**, probably the best equipped public beach on the island. The beach boasts not only miles of bright sand and a handful of offshore cays, but also a veritable arcade of lockers, refreshment stands and other amenities. The beach benefits from its size, drawing heavily enough from local and tourist groups alike to assure there's always something going on, if only a pickup volleyball game: Don't be bashful

— the games are friendly.

Halfway down the eastern coast and a 10-minute drive south from Humacao is **Palmas del Mar**, Puerto Rico's largest vacation resort. The self-appointed "New American Riviera," this 2,700-acre (1,093-hectare) holiday heaven comprises just about everything but a monorail: 20 tennis courts ("One free?" "No, sir, not 'til Thursday"), a gorgeous beachfront golf course, riding stables, fine beaches, deep-sea fishing, eight restaurants, numerous bars, an ice cream shop, and so on. Palmas del Mar proves popular among families and conventioneers.

Monkey Business

A little less than a mile off the coast of Playa Humacao lies an anomalous island that few have had the opportunity to visit. This place, **Cayo Santiago**, means home for approximately 700 rhesus monkeys.

With a grant from Columbia University, the animals were brought from India to Puerto Rico in 1938 for research into primate behavior. Never before had such a social troupe of monkeys been transported into the Western world and placed in semi-natural conditions. The comfortable climate and undisturbed environment of Cayo Santiago still left many experts skeptical on the question of whether the primates could survive and breed.

For two years, tuberculosis scourged the colony. Then, during World War Two, grant money ran out and the monkeys faced the threat of starvation. Townspeople from nearby Playa de Humacao supported the colony by taking bananas, coconuts and other available foods out to the island several times each week for the duration of the war. (Nowadays the animals feed on commercial monkey chow.)

Since 1938, more than 300 scientific articles have been published about the colony. Unfortunately though, due to possible health hazards (and the fact that rhesus monkeys have large canine teeth and can at times be very aggressive), visitors are not allowed on the island.

No matter however: head over to Yabucoa and maybe you'll be able to observe some of the peculiar eating habits of the wildlife there. The rats in Yabucoa, according to local lore, aren't monkeying around.

Left, bathing at Palmas del Mar; and right, on the links at Palmas del Mar.

THE ROAD TO YABUCOA

From Humacao to **Yabucoa** (a native Indian term meaning "Place of the Yucca Trees"), rolling hills, semi-tropical forests, sugarcane fields and cow pastures highlight an exceedingly pleasant drive. Just before reaching Yabucoa, Route 3 passes the **Roig Sugar Mill**, a rusty piece of antiquity which is one of the few survivors of the southeast's agricultural economy gone belly-up. During the harvest season (January to June), you can see how masses of cane get shredded and pressed to extract juices which later become refined sugar.

Yabucoa marks the beginning of an industrial circuit that continues southwestward. Taking advantage of low-wage labor and liberal tax laws, oil refineries, pharmaceuticals, textile manufacturers and industrial chemical plants border the small towns all the way down the coast.

Leaving Yabucoa, Route 901 takes you on a scenic drive southward (part of the Ruta Panoramica) through arid coastal headlands which form part of the **Cuchilla de Pandura** mountains.

Ghost Beach

A few kilometers away from town along the **Balneario Lucia** shore, abandoned seafood restaurants indicate that, at one point, this spot was believed to have potential as a popular bathing retreat. Now it's a ghost beach; few bother with it. Rows of planted coconut palm trees grow in awkwardly misshapen directions along the beach. The trunks of these trees are wrapped with sheet metal, apparently to prevent rats from climbing them. According to a native writer:

when there are no such bands, rats with a penchant for primitive piloting climb the trunks, nibble a hole in the coconuts, lap out the milk, crawl through the hole into the nut, gnaw off the stem and sit inside the shell as it makes its break-neck descent to the ground . . .

Those crazy rats — they're either out surfin' or they got a party goin'.

Route 901 curves upward into a series of hills overlooking rugged shoreline and a Caribbean expanse, with Vieques hazed in the distance.

Built on an impressive vista point, **El Horizonte**, a touristy-looking restaurant, gives occasion to savor reasonably priced local seafood while looking out to sea.

Down to Punta Tuna

The road descends from the hills to **Punta Tuna**, where one of Puerto Rico's active lighthouses rests. Built in the 1890s by Spain, the lighthouse is now run by the U.S. Coast Guard. Adjacent to Punta Tuna, a little-known beach ranks among the nicest on the southeastern coast. Farther down the road, on the opposite side of Punta Tuna, another good beach arches more than a kilometer around tiny **Puerto Maunabo**. Pack a lunch in the morning before setting out from Yabucoa. A lunch break on one of these lovely beaches is the perfect interlude on this circular trip.

The Ruta Panoramica continues past the town of Maunabo and winds up a narrow road past cliffside houses and damp verdure over the Cuchilla de Pandura and back to Yabucoa.

Below, playing dominoes at Maunabo; and right, two in a hammock, Playa las Palmas, near Punta Guilante.

GUAYAMA, ARROYO, AGUIRRE, SALINAS

You can tell you're in the southeastern corner of Puerto Rico when the residents stop having preconceptions about their part of the island. This place is not karstic or dry or cosmopolitan. Nonetheless, it's Puerto Rican landscape at its least spoiled.

Jobos Bay

Guayama and **Aguirre** hold little in common besides the fact that both border on Jobos Bay, one of the finest protected shallow-water areas on the island. Ichthyologists and ornithologists will love the area—several species of Puerto Rican birds unseen elsewhere on the island frequent the place, and fish are well-served by the bay's healthy quantity of microorganisms. The fishing is good everywhere, but legal only outside of protected waters. This takes a boat, but boating is a popular pastime in Jobos Bay, and Ponceños frequently include the area in daytrips from Caja de Muertos. Winds tend to be better than average in the area, though it's no place for the city-slicker to unwind—the joke about the travel-writer who went looking for a rollicking good time at Jobos Beach and wound up at Jobos Bay rings all too true in some circles.

Arroyo

Arroyo, with what some consider its sister city Patillas, is one of the most down-to-earth of Puerto Rican towns. The landscape surrounding the city is fetching, if unspectacular—it's a rushy, reedy, bushy sort of place. The beaches by both towns are uncrowded and pleasant, and weather generally makes beaching even more secure a prospect than it is in San Juan. The **Embalse de Patillas**, a short drive up Route 184 from that city, makes for a fine picnic on the way into the Cordillera.

Salinas

Salinas is one of the most enjoyable and undersung cities on this island. It has more of a southwestern ethos than the cities surrounding, perhaps because it maintains a shade of cosmopolitanism of the sort practiced in Ponce and Mayagüez, or perhaps because its many excellent seafood restaurants serve up redfish, lobster and other *criollo* specials of a quality that puts the Mona Passage in one's mind.

Eastern Allure

Despite its western orientation, most of Salinas' allure lies to the east. Its downtown is an attractive one, but you'll want to get on the road to Aguirre to visit one of the most lively and patronized *galleras* on the island. Here, men knowledgeable about fighting cocks wager hundreds of dollars on the local birds. Be careful though. The sport is bloody and hardly for the fainthearted, and there will be plenty of people willing to take your wagers. (And there aren't any odds posted.) Not too far away, **Punta Salinas** offers a slew of unpretentious seafood restaurants, several of which look out on the irenic **Bahia de Rincón**, and all of which serve seafood the likes of which would cause the most finicky chef in all of San Juan, and perhaps even some of the east coast's most scrupulous fishermen to order another plate.

Activities in Guayama: strolling, left; and right, taking in the sun.

PONCE: LA PERLA DEL SUR

No one ever claimed that Puerto Ricans were not a proud people, but it still shocks even San Juaneros to hear a Ponceño refer to his birthplace as "La Perla del Sur," or "The Pearl of the South." It's to be expected that tourism companies and travel agencies will exploit such a sobriquet, but . . . natives? Remember that this is Puerto Rico's second largest city, and that there are close to 200,000 people running around doing this.

Perhaps most surprising is the fact that **Ponce** actually is a pearl of sorts. Though not so distant in the imagination of travelers as Mayagüez, it's still far enough away from the San Juan/ Cerromar/Palmas del Mar circuit most travelers hew to. But now Ponce is an easy hour's drive from San Juan on the new Route 52, and there's very little excuse for not heading south to see what all these southerners are bragging about. On an island where self-congratulation is a way of life, the people of Ponce have

the reputation of being almost haughty. And anyone outside deepest San Juan will admit that Ponceños have a right to be.

Hot Stuff

To begin with, Ponce has the best weather on the island. It's located in what ecologists call a "rain shadow": the afternoon storms which beleaguer the north coast are stopped dead by the peaks of the Cordillera Central. You can see the rain — it's in those purple clouds pulsing about the hills ten miles (six km) north — but you're not going to feel any of it. The landscape surrounding the city shows the same typical southwestern pastiche of purple and lavender skies against tumbling grasslands, parched to gold by the Caribbean sun. This is not the Atlantic — although a place as far south as Puerto Rico can take on its hostile cobalt aspect — as a look south from the hills above town will demonstrate. Especially from El Vígia Hill, a look across Ponce shows the coral and white of the town's stately houses, the turquoise waters of its Caribbean harbor and the stripes of green mangrove and

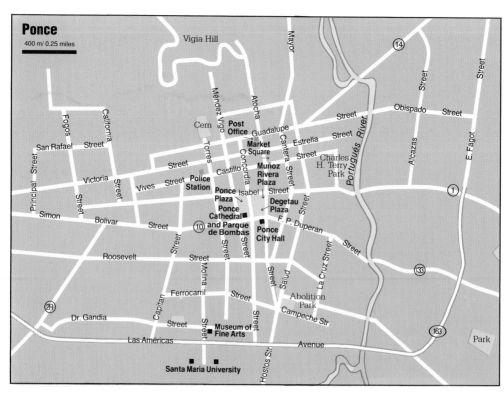

194

travertine coral formations of the archipelago surrounding the big isle of Caja de Muertos.

This is not the impression you'll get as you enter the town on Route 2, the antiquated proto-expressway. One's first sight of Ponce is of the Ponce bypass, which links the highways 52 and 2, traveling through a neighborhood of unmitigated tedium. This is where the shopping malls, the roadside fruitstands and the gas stations are.

The Inland Port

But Ponce proper — and if there's a proper city in Puerto Rico, it's Ponce — is not as far away as one might expect. This is perhaps the archetype of a strangely Puerto Rican sort of city: a bustling port with an enviable natural harbor which has nonetheless developed around a city center some distance inland. A left turn will take you, not to the center of a bustling waterfront town, but to the interesting outpost at **Playa de Ponce** and the wharf at **Muelle de Ponce**. To get into the heart of Ponce, one continues in a northwesterly direction on Route 133 as it passes over the sluggish Río Portugues and becomes **Calle F.P. Duperan**, the main commercial street of the town, sometimes known as "Calle Comercio."

A Square Deal

At the end of Calle Duperan is the cluster of architectural beauties which gives Ponce its reputation as one of the most Spanish of Puerto Rican cities. Here the magnificent **Plaza Central**, lush and beautifully landscaped, sits pounded by sunlight amidst a pinwheel of centuries-old streets. It's actually a double-plaza, with **Plaza Degetau** and **Plaza Muñoz Rivera** sitting kitty-cornered across Calle Cristina. Both are similarly landscaped, with huge fig-trees in lozenge-shaped topiary and large, shady islands of grass. Broad paths of rose-colored granite weave through the parks; they're lined with slender old lamp-posts which make the plaza both attractive and accessible in the evening.

Plaza Degetau is dominated by the **Cathedral of Our Lady of Guadelupe**, named for the patron saint of Ponce. It's a pretty, low, pinkish structure, reminiscent in its colors and rounded tur-

Bird's eye view of Ponce.

rets of San Juan Cathedral. Though not as old as San Juan's, having been begun in the late 17th Century, Ponce's cathedral makes ample use of the flood of reflected sunlight from the plaza. Its silvery towers — a characteristically Puerto Rican touch in religious architecture — are shaped like little hydrants, and glow oddly at midday. This gives it a bright, inviting look, with which the eerie stillness of its interior is a shocking contrast.

Photo Opportunity

Our Lady of Guadelupe may hold the religious high ground, but the building right behind it cuts more ice with the tourist crowd. This is the **Parque de Bombas**, Ponce's Victorian firehouse, and it's surely the oddest building on an island that has never been shy of architectural improvisation. With its red and black walls and playful collection of poles, sideboards, crenellations and cornices, it's a gaudy and riotous building with a playful, truly Ponceño spirit. It's also the most photographed building in Puerto Rico. The **Alcaldía**, diagonally across the plaza from the two buildings, has a pleasant hacienda feeling to it and contrasts in a lively way with its two more renowned neighbors.

Around Town

There are plenty of peaceful perambulations to be made in this most historic part of Ponce. **Calle Cristina** and **Calle Mayor** are particularly renowned for the wrought-iron grill and balcony work which evoke in Ponce, as in San Juan, the spirit of European cities. Even the highly commercialized Calle Duperan boasts a number of quaint shops and shady marketplaces. The finest market in town, however, is in the **Plaza del Mercado**, two blocks north of the Plaza Central on Calle Atocha between Calles Estrella and Castillo. Here, merchants haggle with customers over anything that can be worn, ogled or eaten, in an ambience as charged with excitement as any market in San Juan.

Deep In the Art of Puerto Rico

Ponce's **Museo de Arte** on Avenida de las Americas, is the best art museum — by far — in the Caribbean. Designed

Below, Parque de Bombas, Ponce; and right, Cathedral of Our Lady of Guadeloupe, Ponce.

by Edward Durell Stone, the architect in charge of building New York's Museum of Modern Art, the Ponce Museum is a beautiful museum indeed. A honeycomb of skylit hexagonal rooms, it looks somewhat like the inside of a white waffle-iron. Inside, paths run through a network of ponds and pools, into which those overly absorbed in the art displays have been known to fall. The building's interior highlight is perhaps its modernistic, scallop-shaped, wooden central staircase, which leads to a cluster of Renaissance paintings and sets the tone of the place.

The Europeans

Of course, it is the artwork itself which is truly spectacular. The Puerto Rican artists — notably Oller — are well-represented, but it is the quality of the European exhibits which astounds. Some fine works by Rubens and Van Dyck stand out among the Dutch collection, while a surprisingly strong English collection includes work by Gainsborough and a slew of pre-Raphaelites.

Much of the Latin-American work of distinction — which has a representative selection of Murillo, Rivera and others — was donated by the artists and their countries. But responsibility for the Ponce Museum's great success must go to Luis Ferré, former governor of Puerto Rico and scion of one of Ponce's most distinguished families. Ferré conceived of the museum and donated much of his own art collection to help get it underway. Suffice it to say here that there's nothing on the island more worth a visit than the Ponce Museum of Art.

The People and the City

Ponceños have always been a breed apart from other Puerto Ricans. Their insularity and haughtiness is legendary, and some Puerto Ricans claim that even the dialect here differs slightly from that spoken almost universally on the rest of the island. They're also racially different: you'll see more people of African descent in town than anywhere else on the island save Loíza Aldea, due to the fact that Ponce's prominence as a port antedates slavery times.

As such, a great deal of African and other regional custom lives on in the city. Every February, at the Festival of Our Lady of Guadelupe, Ponce natives parade around the city in weird, spiked horror-masks made of local gourds. The tradition actually derives from medieval Spain, but it's unquestionable that such a transoceanic transplant required a soil as culturally fertile as Ponce's to take root.

A Walk on the Nice Side

There's no better way to take in all the beauty and diversity of this city than to stroll north of the Plaza Central on Calle Méidez to **El Vígia**. This hilly neighborhood is so beloved of the natives, that you'll surely be directed to the place if you show the slightest interest in the city. From the winding road to the top you can see the mansions of Ponce's great families, the roofs of its 17th- and 18th-Century townhouses, and the greenish-blue Caribbean, which does more than any questions of demography, government or economics to shape the daily life of the proud Ponceño.

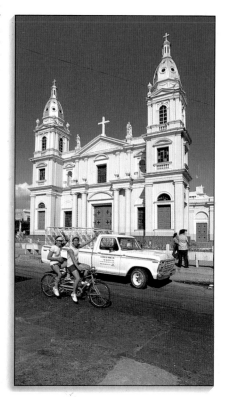

CAJA DE MUERTOS AND THE SOUTHERN ISLES

It's almost true, as mentioned above, that it never rains in Ponce. But at times the weather on Puerto Rico's sun-bombarded South Coast can get so hot and steamy that you wish it would. Fortunately, the environs of Ponce offer strategies for cooling off as diverse as they are effective. Nautical enthusiasts head their boats into the breezy waters for a trip to the fascinating rock archipelago eight miles (13 km) south.

This string of Caribbean islets centers around **Caja de Muertos** ('Dead Men's Coffin'). Largest of the islets at two miles long and a mile wide (three km by 1½ km), Caja de Muertos is as popular with birdwatchers and botanists as it is with boatmen. This being one of Puerto Rico's driest regions, the majority of Caja de Muertos' flora resembles that of Guánica Forest Reserve on the Puerto Rican mainland. Some of the more prevalent plant species include certain herbs, dwarf forests of white mangrove, and loads of bindweed. Four of the plant species on Caja de Muertos are extinct on the Puerto Rican mainland and classified as endangered. Caja de Muertos is also a haven for endangered reptiles; iguanas and wall-lizards abound, and two species of "culebra" lizards live on Caja de Muertos.

In Different Keys

Caja de Muertos is only one of the three isles that make up the **Caja de Muertos Nature Reserve**. The others, though far smaller, are no less enticing. **Cayo Morillito**, just a few hundred yards across flats, is the smallest, with only a few acres of territory, but contains more endangered birds than the other two islands combined. Among these are a variety of gulls, pelicans and seaeagles.

Cayo Berbería, closest of the cays to the mainland at three miles (five km), is blessed with a fauna no less extensive and no less idiosyncratic. Most of the fish — many of them endangered species — for which the southern isles are famous populate the waters around its shores.

Right, Playa Corega, near Ponce.

THE SOUTHWEST

The part of Puerto Rico furthest from San Juan is, not surprisingly, the part most tourists would choose to visit had they an inkling of what awaits them there. This is Puerto Rico at its best, and, in many ways, at its most typical: maritime, mountainous and metropolitan. Mayagüez sits at the center of the region, a city with a vibrancy and beauty which has led Puerto Ricans to ruminate, despite Ponce's recent boom, "What's Puerto Rico's second city, Ponce or Mayagüez?" None of the surrounding area, however, will make one sorry one left Mayagüez: there is San Germán, home to some of the few examples of Gothic architecture in the Western world and Puerto Rico's second oldest city; Boquerón, surf capital of the southwest; Parguera, with a phosphorescent bay many consider the best in the world; Guánica, where, for better or for worse, the U.S. Marines were to stage an invasion in 1898 which was to transform Puerto Rico forever; Punta Jagüey, which boasts not only spectacular beaches, but also one of the most beautiful lighthouses in the Atlantic.

All right, you're lazy and having a helluva time in San Juan. Go to the southwest. Don't worry. It's civilized there; they have *piña coladas.*

Preceding pages: country cemetery; Cabo Rojo and Salinas Beach. Left, cutting sugarcane in the southwest.

GUAYANILLA
AND GUÁNICA

Though the charms of the rippling, brown-green, semi-arid landscapes of Puerto Rico's southwest are well-known, few travelers take the effort to visit this charming tandem of cities. Nonetheless, the scenic, historic and hedonistic pleasures **Guayanilla** and **Guánica** offer are enough to repay a visit of several days.

Route 2 moves swiftly westwards out of Ponce, and within minutes is running along one of its most inspiring stretches, where it hugs the shore for about two miles (three km). Where Route 2 meets the coast it meets one of Greater Ponce's most popular beaches.

Playa El Tuque, three miles (five km) outside the city, is one of the tinier swimmable beaches on the island. It lies on the western shore of a tiny node of land, most of which is occupied by the marshy lands surrounding the **Laguna de las Salinas** five miles (eight km) outside Ponce. From certain points are good views of Ponce and its bay,

and the views to sea include turquoise waters and isolated coral islands. The beach you'll pass just to the left of the highway is formally known as **Balneario Las Cucharas** ('Spoons Bathing Area'), and the name is apt: it appears to have been gently scooped into a crescent by calm Caribbean waters.

See Ya in Guayanilla

From Las Cucharas, Route 2 runs the pretty six miles (10 km) into Guayanilla. This is a pretty town with a very southwestern flavor. It lies a little over a mile inland, though, and is somewhat quiet. The real attractions of Guayanilla are to the south. A mile away, at the mouth of the Río Guayanilla, is the desolate and hushed fishing port at **Playa de Guayanilla**. The bay itself is an amazing natural formation: three miles (five km) wide and embraced by two large peninsulas — **Punta Gotay** and **Punta Verraco** — it is surely one of the most auspiciously-formed natural harbors in the Caribbean. A number of peninsulas within the harbor give it at least five sheltered sub-inlets.

The Isle of Java

That's hardly the last you'll hear of Guayanilla Bay — the landscape that surrounds it is full of some of the lushest protected semi-arid forest in the world, and crowded with reminders of a signal episode in both Puerto Rican and American history. But not to make a circuit of the area is to miss the forest for the trees.

The charming town of **Yauco** lies three miles (five km) west of Guayanilla on Routes 2 and 127. The latter is probably the more pleasant route, except when it rains, which is about once every millennium. Anyone with the most cursory experience driving in the southwest knows that those little oily bushes huddled on the brown hillsides are coffee trees, but few know just the preeminence that the Yauco area holds as a coffee capital. By the late 19th Century, Puerto Rico had developed the most advanced coffee industry in the world. In the coffeehouses of late-colonial Europe — in Vienna, in London, in Paris, in Madrid — Puerto Rican coffee was considered the very best one could drink. "Yauco" was that coffee's name.

For whatever one can say about its other effects, the 20th-Century presence

Left, Casa Gordo Beach, Guánica; and below, in Patillas.

of Americans on the island removed Yauco from its position of preeminence, as emphasis on manufacturing and cane production sapped the industry's resources. Fortunately, vestiges of that halcyon era remain — the stately homes of Yauco's coffee barons are a testament to the wealth and pride the industry brought the region. Owing to the variety of sub-climates in the southwest, coffee was a "mobile" industry, and its scions and their residences were no less itinerant than their crops. Thus, Yauco shares with San Germán and Mayagüez an architecture that is distinctively Puerto Rican and among the best Spanish-influenced work of its day. Some of these old residences are open to the public; for information on the southwestern style and how to see it, the best source is the **Collegio de Arquitectos**, located in the Casa Rosa, near El Morro in Old San Juan.

Even more fortunate is the fact that Yauco has regained some of its old prominence as a coffee-producer. Still one of the world's great coffee concerns, Yauco makes a pungent, aromatic, snappy coffee you'd do well to order anywhere on the island.

Warships by Woodlands

On to Guánica, 5½ miles (nine km) past Yauco on Route 116, about the same size as Guayanilla, but with an understandably more oceanic ambience, Guánica might be worth visiting even without the historic significance which draws so many travelers and historians. In the mid-summer of 1898, at the height of the Spanish American War, General Nelson Miles, having had no success in a month-long attempt to break Spanish defenses around San Juan, landed in Guánica with a detachment of troops before going on to Ponce. He had come, he told residents:

"to bring you protection, not only to yourselves but to your property, to promote your prosperity, and to bestow upon you the immunities and blessings of the liberal institutions of our government."

Out of this promise came American Puerto Rico, and the degree to which it has been kept or breached has circumscribed almost all political arguments on the island for the past 90 years. Predictably, the American arrival can be referred to as either an invasion or an "inva-

sion" — the commemorative stone placed at the edge of Guánica Harbor by the Puerto Rican chapter of the Daughters of The American Revolution certainly takes the latter line.

The Birds

Though they weren't arriving for the bird-watching, the American forces who landed at Guánica chose as their target the ornithological capital of Puerto Rico. Covering 1570 acres (630 ha) of subtropical dry forest, the **Guánica Forest Reserve** is home to half of Puerto Rico's bird species. Most treasured among these is the highly endangered Puerto Rican whippoorwill, but if you're frustrated in your trip to see one, there are plenty of festively-colored and mellifluous creatures to satisfy your curiosity. This low-lying area also houses 48 of the island's endangered plant species, 16 of which are autochthonous to the forest. Well-kept hiking trails and a pleasant if unspectacular beach make the forest reserve an eminently deserving spot for a leisurely respite in a hectic schedule of sightseeing. One shouldn't miss these, at all costs.

Below, oyster stand, Boquerón; and right, Lake Yauco.

LATIN-AMERICAN GOTHIC: SAN GERMÁN

Seeds of colonization in the New World have not always brought culture, but they have generally brought over-population, and the capitals of the Americas, with their millions of citizens, were generally in place, if only as minor outposts, a couple centuries ago. **San Germán**, with its population of 30,000, is a different sort of history-crammed locale — it's one of those major towns of the 16th Century which has been blessed by never having been too thoroughly dragged into the squalid rat race of the modern world. Inch-for-inch, it is the most historic town in all Puerto Rico, perhaps in all the Caribbean.

A Capitol History

San Germán is a diamond in an emerald setting, a pearly-white town tucked in an uncharacteristically lush and verdant section of the island's south coast about halfway between Ponce and Mayagüez on pretty Route 119. Neither of these two latter metropolises is Puerto Rico's second city: San Germán is. Founded in 1573 by the second wave of Spanish colonists, it was San Juan's only rival for prominence on the island until the 19th Century. Forces invading or retreating from San Juan, notably the English, French and Dutch, not uncommonly stopped in San Germán to arm themselves or lick their wounds. In the 19th Century, it became one of Puerto Rico's great coffee towns, with magnates of the bean building some of the truly unique homes on the island. Today, San Germán owes its prominence and cultural vibrancy to the Inter-American University, with its 8,000 students and well-tended grounds, and the diligence with which it has preserved some of the earliest European architectural works to survive in the Western hemisphere.

Gates to the West

The **Porta Coeli Church** is San Germán's — and arguably Puerto Rico's — greatest architectural inheritance. Founded in 1606, it is the oldest church under the U.S. flag (not that one flies too conspicuously over its facade). It is also one of only a handful of Gothic churches in the western world. The others are in San Juan, Colombia and Mexico — it is one of the great glories of Spanish colonization that it came about early enough to assure that this neo-medieval style, which peppered all the countries of Europe with some of the greatest monuments to man's artistry ever known, could flourish in the New World as well.

Porta Coeli means 'heaven's gate,' and, indeed, its portals are of great importance in its artistry. It's a squat little whitewashed building standing at the top of a broad, spreading stairway of scrabbly brick and mortar. Its doors are of beautiful *ausubo*, a once-common Puerto Rican hardwood, and are larger than the walls of many New York City apartments. These are framed by an irenically austere pediment, above which is a battened skylight of the same wood. Inside, the pews and altar are all original, with embellishment. The altarpiece was painted by the first great Puerto Rican artist, José Campeche, in the late 18th Century, a fact that would indicate the church was fairly well-established as an historical landmark even by then. Porta Coeli overlooks one

of the most beautifully-landscaped plazas in Puerto Rico, with its terraced benches and beautifully-groomed trees.

Name that Church

San Germán, like Ponce is a two-plaza town, and its second, the **Plaza Mario Quiñones**, is no less impressive, with the same lovely walks, period lamplights and marvelous topiary. But it also has a church to rival Porta Coeli in appeal, if not in age. The **Church of San Germán de Auxerre** commemorates the French saint who is the town's patron. Its steeple does not face the superscribe plaza directly, but plays a sort of 90° trick on the town by having its facade on a nearby side-street. While less important than much of San Germán in historical terms, it dominates the town, and is particularly impressive when viewed from the surrounding hills on a sunny day.

Ancient Homes

San Germán's oldest attractions have always captured the attention of visitors, but few have stopped to examine

the general layout and ambience of this ancient town with the rigor and delight that tourists have always brought to San Juan and Ponce. This of course owes in some degree to the fact that San Germán remained so small until very recently that it cannot boast a great number of typically-Puerto Rican, wrought iron and stone residences, which tend to be most attractive in long rows in large neighborhoods.

But San Germán has a treasure trove of more recent architectural masterpieces, as Jorge Rigau and others at San Juan's Collegio de Arquitectos have recently brought to public attention. Marvelous haciendas of the late 19th Century coffee barons are abundant, and demonstrate a style which, while it can be seen throughout the southwest — in Yauco, for example — is as much San Germán-own as Porta Coeli.

These houses must be entered to be appreciated, as much of their charm lies in the way the interior spaces are divided. Beautiful *mediopunto* carvings — delicate lacy half-screens of snaking wood — create conceptual divisions between rooms without putting up a physical barrier. Some of these are astounding harbingers of art nouveau. The same can be thought of the simple and sinuous stencilings which grace the walls of many of these houses.

They're generally recognizable by the broad-porched opulence and gracefully-set wood of their facades, but it's not advisable to try to have a peek inside without consulting the owners. Those interested in learning more about these spectacular examples of Caribbean architecture should perhaps write the tourism company in San Juan.

Inter-American University

San Germán's **Inter-American University** is a hive of 8,000 students tucked into one of the oldest cities in the Americas. The University infuses the place with a cultural spirit that saves San Germán from being one of those cities which is cultured only so long as the tourists stay around. Its multinational student body and faculty is one of the most important sources of scholarly information in this infinitely fascinating town, and those interested in understanding more deeply the past and present of the place would do well to take advantage of its many cultural offerings.

Left, Parador Oasis; and right, Porto Coeli Church, San Germán.

White Nights at Parguera

Puerto Rico is blessed with several phosphorescent bays, but none as renowned as **Parguera**. Around this southwestern curiosity has developed a town just as curious and a farrago of fascinating things to do once one is finished soaking up the nature.

Those who arrive in Parguera town without realizing that the famous bay is somewhat east will be surprised by the hubbub and urbanity of the place. Parguera is not a quiet little nature-seekers' haven by any means; it's a jampacked, neon-lit beehive of hucksters and fast-food joints, which on summer nights is alive with partying youngsters and thrill-seeking tourists. This is not to say the place is spoiled; it serves the very useful function of diverting the inevitable crowds from the area's more delicate attractions.

Boats ply the waters between the village and the bay itself with reassuring frequency. For a few dollars, you'll most likely get an hour in the flying Caribbean spindrift and one of the rare opportunities Puerto Rico affords to make use of a warm sweater. Leaving the docks, cruises run through the yachts and fishing boats of Parguera's poorly-sheltered harbor and past a tiny chain of islets whose focus is **Isla Magueyes**. Most of the islets are used for scientific and veterinary experiments; Isla Magueyes, for example, hosts a large colony of lizards.

As cruise boats enter the bay itself, their wakes turn an eerie pale-green. Captains invite the passengers to scoop their hands over the gunwales and into the water to produce odd, remarkable patterns. A bucket is generally brought on board for the curious to play with, and in the cupped palms of the agitated water breaks into shapes resembling nothing so much as splattering mercury.

The phosphorescence is produced by billions of microorganisms which belong to the family of dinoflagellates known as *pyrodinium bahamense*. Try to see this unique phenomenon on a cloudy night with a light breeze, when no other light sources muddle the brilliance of the waters, and wavelets make ever-changing patterns on the surface of the bay.

In the drink at Parguera.

CABO ROJO'S
SECRET SPLENDORS

Surrounded by coral-studded Caribbean waters, bathed in dry tropical heat year-round and sculpted into an odd network of cliffs, lagoons, promontories and swamps by fickle surfs and tides, the *municipio of* **Cabo Rojo** shows Puerto Rico's seaside landscape at its eeriest and most alluring. Stretching south along 18 miles (30 km) of coast from Mayagüez, this area is among the remotest on the island; whether approaching from Ponce or from Mayagüez, one notices the landscape growing drier and more hummocky, the population more sparse and the scenery more beautiful.

From the Town Down

For those to whom the name "Cabo Rojo" has been made synonymous with isolated retreats and breathtaking vistas, **Cabo Rojo Town** can come as something of a disappointment. It is unquestionably a quaint and pretty town,

El Combate, Cabo Rojo.

however, and full of history. Its 10,000 residents are well up on local lore, including tales of the infamous Spanish buccaneer Roberto Cofresi, who made this part of the island his home during 17th Century raids on European merchant ships.

Four and a half miles (7½ km) northwest of the town lies **Laguna Joyuda**, a mangrove swamp which has been made a sanctuary for birds autochthonous to the region. Mangroves are among the most hospitable of environments for semi-tropical bird life, and Cabo Rojo boasts them in higher concentration than any other area in the western half of Puerto Rico. This 300-acre (120-ha) expanse is home to various herons, martins and pelicans, including the lovely maroon pelican. The lagoon itself is full of fish, and is phosphorescent on moonless nights, due to a preponderance of the dinoflagellate *pyrodinium bahamense*.

A Battery of Beaches

Everyone in Puerto Rico has his favorite beach, but **Playa Buye**, just southwest of Cabo Rojo on Route 307, gets more votes than many. With its wispy

rows of pine hooking around a promontory to the bay known as **Puerto Real**, and with pleasant views of the tiny village of Elizabeth across the water, Buye makes up in charm what it lacks in size. The landscape changes with shocking suddenness just south of Buye, as the cliffs of **Punta Guanaquilla** give way to the swamps and mangroves of the tiny **Laguna Guanaquilla**. The cliffs and lagoon are best reached either by making the ¾-mile (one-km) walk south or by taking the dirt road that leads out of the tiny settlement of **Boca Prieta** at the southern end of Buye.

Competing Beaches

Seven miles (12 km) south of Cabo Rojo on Routes 4 and 101, **Boquerón** is a fishing port of staggering beauty. Like Laguna Joyuda, it is blessed with a mangrove forest which shelters some of Puerto Rico's loveliest birds — the Laguna Rincón and surrounding forests have been designated a bird sanctuary as one of the three parts of the **Boquerón Nature Reserve**. But it is hardly birdwatching that brings most visitors to the town. For Boquerón sits at the mouth of a three-mile-long (five-km) bay whose placid, coral-flecked waters and broad sands backed by palm groves make **Playa Boquerón** almost without question the finest beach on the island. On an island where regional rivalries are as intense as on Puerto Rico, the fact that even some Luquillo residents will admit as much is significant. Every weekend, fisherman bring their fresh catches to Boquerón to sell to the bathers. The cabins which circumscribe Boquerón's beach are popular among weekenders; to rent one, contact the Department of Recreation and Sports in San Juan at least four months in advance. Tucked in Puerto Rico's southwestern corner at the end of Route 301, a circuitous six miles south of Boquerón, **El Combate** is yet another beach of renown. Here is a charming little row of fishing shacks and a jetty that draws large crowds.

But, to the Point

Route 301 travels even farther south past **Pole Oleja**, a not-terribly-inspiring salt settlement which is worth only a short look. Two miles (three km) south, however, at the southwesternmost extremity of Puerto Rico, is the crowning glory of Cabo Rojo and one of the most scenic spots in the entire Caribbean. This is **Punta Jagüey**, a kidney-shaped rock outcrop connected to land by a narrow isthmus and straddling two lovely bays, the **Bahia Salinas** and the **Bahia Succia**.

Herons and Eelgrass

Here too is a nature reserve of grand proportions; both the peninsula and the surrounding waters are protected as part of the same Boquerón system that embraces Laguna Rincón. But there is more to Punta Jagüey than herons and eelgrass. **Cabo Rojo Lighthouse** is a breathtaking specimen of Spanish colonial architecture, with its low-lying, pale-sided main building and squat, hexagonal light tower. It perches atop dun-colored cliffs at the very extremity of the peninsula and commands views of almost 300 degrees of Caribbean. With wide-open prospects to both east and west, the lighthouse is at its most awe-inspiring when its walls are given a faint blush by either sunrise or sunset. It's more likely you'll see the latter; many trips to Cabo Rojo are conceived as daytrips and somehow carry on.

Below, Boquerón Beach; and right, selling oysters.

MAYAGÜEZ: PLAYGROUND OF THE WEST

The third largest of Puerto Rico's three major cities is the only one which can claim the sort of cosmopolitan-cum-hedonistic lifestyle that makes a certain type of traveler fall in love with a city. San Juan and Ponce have other, perhaps deeper, charms, but both are a bit too hardworking and serious to compete with the relaxing atmosphere of their little sister out west. There's something about **Mayagüez's** modernism — this is not to say lack of history — which lends an irresponsible, vaguely Californian ethos to life there. Add to this beautiful ocean breezes and the best swimming and surfing on the island, and one is left with a holiday spot for those who wish to relax, rather than restlessly sightsee.

This would tend to draw droves of adipose *norteamericanos*, and, to be fair, Mayagüez does share with Vieques the distinction of being the greatest hangout for professional expatriates in Puerto Rico. But the beach-bums here tend to be of a more contemplative bent. For all its charms, Mayagüez remains difficult to get to. Those who reach it tend to be of superior mettle, and guzzle the local India beer with the vengeance only those who have worked hard for their holidays can understand.

Fishy Business

Not all is beer and skittles in this western metropolis; in fact, the isolation of those who engage in high living from those who are stuck making a living is in large degree responsible for the particular pace of life in Mayagüez. Pared down to its most basic, Mayagüez is a fish-packing town with a university. The town lives on tuna, at least indirectly; over 60 percent of the tuna eaten in the United States is tinned at Mayagüez, and a substantial number of residents make their living off the stuff. Since 936 funding has lured so many foreign (primarily American) businesses to Puerto Rico, the city has also taken a larger share of Puerto Rico's monolithic pharmaceutical industry from Arecibo. Mayagüez's College, located on Route 108, is an outpost of the **University of Puerto Rico**. It's primarily an agricultu-

ral college, so the ferment over issues political and literary which is so much a part of UPR Río Piedras doesn't really penetrate much here. But the College is right next to one of the finest places for learning what Puerto Rico has to offer, the **Tropical Agricultural Research Station**. Run by the U.S. Department of Agriculture, these gardens, built on the site of a former plantation, boast one of the largest collections of tropical and semi-tropical plants in the world. Nearby is the new and somewhat hypermodern **Parque de los Proceres** (Patriots' Park), okay for a picnic.

Ladies of Barcelona

All this is only about a half-mile north of Mayagüez's main plaza, the **Plaza Colón**, which is oddly beautiful for a city of this size. A statue dead-center commemorates Christopher Columbus. Round about are 16 different bronze statues of courtly ladies brought from Barcelona. The ground in the plaza is as smooth and shiny as an ice-skating rink, and the buildings around it are dignified and imposing, particularly the neo-Corinthian **Alcaldía**, with its lovely

Left, Tuna Plant, Mayagüez; and right, cleaning tuna in Mayagüez.

crimson and white facade.

There is plenty more happening around Mayagüez. The **Mayagüez Zoo**, about 15 miles outside of town, is one of those zoos that is something like a nature park, as animals roam about not in cages but in an environment as close to their native one as is possible in a climate where it almost never drops below 70° F (21° C) or rises above 80° F (27° C). It's an enjoyable family place, as small town zoos always are, with such wild animals as ringtailed lemurs, Bengal tigers and Puerto Rican children.

As it was

Mayagüez is not without history. The native Taíno Indians found the place every bit as alluring as today's beach-bums and pharmaceutical companies, and when Columbus landed here on his second voyage to the Caribbean, he found a great number of welcoming natives. The name Mayagüez means 'place of many streams' and the confluence of so many tributaries gives an open-to-the-sea feeling to the city. One of these, the Río Yagüez, gives the city its name. Could the Spanish and Taíno constituents of this odd body of water be translated into similar English, we'd be left with the infinitely descriptive monicker of the "Water River."

Devastation

As a Spanish settlement, however, the city dates only from the end of the 18th Century, when fishermen found the Mona Passage too alluring to pass up. Tragically, Mayagüez's history under Spanish dominion has been all but lost to us. The earthquake which in 1918 rocked the entire western part of the island fairly devastated Mayagüez, with the result that the town was almost depopulated. This need to build afresh an entire city has given Mayagüez a very playful, 20th Century architecture, something like that of San Francisco, California. Its similarity to the warmer parts of the United States in that regard is given a further dimension by the fact that Mayagüez was given strong consideration by the Disney Corporation as a possible site for Disney World.

Just five miles (8 km) south of Mayagüez is the tiny *municipio* of **Hormigueros**, which is a suburb only in the

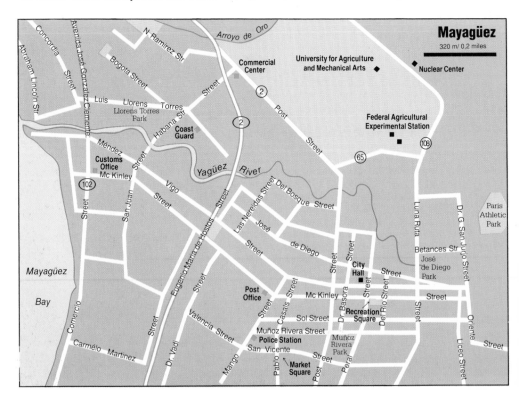

sense that it is below its parent city on the map. This is a city with the pace of the Northwest and the layout of a Cordillera town, with narrow, winding streets and one of the finest cathedrals on the island. The **Cathedral of Our Lady of Monserrat** is at once awesome and unassuming. Bone-white towers of varying dimensions rise to domes of crimson topped with austere white crucifixes of wood. Elevated slightly above the town, it appears to soar into the sky with an effect that is, oddly enough, best appreciated on a cloudy day. Yet its proximity to the streets which surround it, its everyday color scheme and something in the unassumingly ordinary way with which Hormiguerans go about life with such a treasure in their midst keeps the Cathedral a friendly-looking place. Hormigueros itself is worth a day-excursion from Mayagüez, if only for a glimpse of the cathedral, a cool tin of India in a side-street bar and a bit of shopping on the city's main avenues.

Isle of Mona

Throughout the Caribbean, it's hard not to feel that, however beautiful the landscape may be it must *really* have been heart-stopping before the European settlers arrived. There are still a few places that the hand of civilization has not reached, though, and one of them, the tiny **Isle of Mona**, belongs to Puerto Rico. Stuck 45 miles (75 km) out to sea, halfway to the Dominican Republic in the Mona Passage, this rugged island of 25 square miles (70 sq km) is a haven for some of the oddest wildlife in the Antilles, and remains as bizarre and uninhabited as it is hard to reach.

Protected Beauty

Mona is now protected by the Department of Natural Resources, which supervises the use of Cabo Rojo and other spots of great scenic beauty on the west coast; nobody lives there now. But Mona has a long history of inhabitation. Columbus found Taíno Indians there when he landed on the island, and Spanish settlers visited for many years in hopes of finding livable spots to settle. For centuries it was the stronghold for some of the most notorious of European and Puerto Rican pirates, and it is rumored that treasure lies buried on the island to

Mayagüez.

this day. For a brief period a century ago, certain prospectors carried out a brilliant scheme to mine not gold, not silver, not copper from the caves of this remote island, but . . . well, bat-droppings. For fertilizer. Since then, only a few naturalists and hermits have visited the place.

As They Left It

The landscape these solitary types have found is reported to be astounding. Except for a solitary lighthouse on a remote promontory, Mona is much as the Taínos left it. Cliffs 200 feet (65 metres) high ring the tiny island. The cliffs are laced with a cave network which some say rivals that of the Camuy. Much of the island's ground is covered by small cacti which resemble a miniature version of Arizona's organ pipe cactus, and tiny barrel cacti are common as well. Some of the vegetation on the island is known nowhere else in the world. The fauna is even more astounding. Here are found the biggest lizards in Puerto Rico, ugly iguanas growing to three feet (one meter) long. Besides a variety of gulls, there lives on Mona a red-footed bird beloved by visitors and known as the "booby."

The Perils of Travel

There are those who would claim that anyone who wished to visit Mona could be called a booby as well. Those hardy souls who are not dissuaded would be best advised to charter a boat or private plane in Mayagüez. It is claimed that planes can be chartered from San Juan's Isla Grande Airport as well. Official information on hiking trails and on the island's topography is hard to come by, but try writing to the **Departmento de Recursos Naturales** in San Juan.

Right, Plaza Colon and City Hall, Mayagüez.

LET'S HABLAR BORICUA: THE LANGUAGE OF PUERTO RICO

Even before Columbus' fleet "discovered" the island of Puerto Rico in 1493, the smallest of the Great Antilles was in a state of cultural unrest. Invading Carib tribes from South America were threatening the native Arawaks as they had many other cultures throughout the Caribbean. When the local Arawaks met the invading Caribs, what language was created? The Arawak name for the island, *Borínquen*, is still used ('*La Borinqueña*' is the Puerto Rican national anthem), and the Caribs live on in the word Caribbean. Many Puerto Rican municipalities go by their pre-Colombian names: Caguas, Arecibo, Mayagüez, Yauco, Guaynabo . . . to name just a few. The Arawaks feared the god *Huracán*, while we fear hurricanes. And the *hamacas* in which the early Indians slept are just as popular today under the name of hammocks.

If the Arawaks welcomed the Spaniards as a strategy to ward off the Caribs, they certainly miscalculated. Instead, a wave of Spaniards and Spanish swept across the island. Eventually there came battle and disease, which obliterated the native Arawak population. In some cases there was sex, which produced the first Puerto Ricans, and the first men who could claim to speak a truly Puerto Rican Spanish. The Spanish of the earliest Puerto Ricans, like that of their 1980s descendants, can be said to reflect either a pronunciational sloppiness or an Arawak love of diphthongs. For example, Spanish words which end in *ado* are pronounced as if the *d* were silent. Humacao is an Arawak name, but *pescao* will get you fish anywhere on the island. A good stew is an *asopao*, but if your *fiao* isn't good, you won't be served one in any restaurant.

Puerto Rico's first Africans were brought as slaves, mostly from West-central Africa. These slaves brought with them another language, *santería;* numerous musical instruments, including the drums; and countless customs and attitudes which have found their way into the lives of all Puerto Ricans. The *baquine*, a festival of mourning for the death of an infant, is a ritual of African origin, and is usually the cause of a great deal of rum, dancing and *lechón asao* (roast suckling pig). By the mid-19th Century, the Africans made up 20 percent of the population, and such customs penetrated Puerto Rican society proportionally. Integration of the races has worked smoothly in Puerto Rico, and it is said that *él que no tiene dinga tiene mandinga*, a phrase which attributes some amount of African ancestry to virtually all Puerto Ricans. The Mandinga were one of the more populous of the West African tribes whose populations were brought to Puerto Rico to harvest sugarcane, coffee and tobacco.

Sugar, coffee and tobacco farmers, black, white and mulatto, gradually became the archetypal Puerto Rican *jíbaros*, or hillbillies. The most famous record of the customs and speech patterns of the *jíbaro* was written by Manuel A. Alonso, a doctor whose writings fit into the Latin American literary movement known as *costumbrismo*. In 1849, his book *El Gíbaro* was published in Barcelona, and in it there are invaluable accounts of a *jíbaro* wedding, dances, cock—fights, Christmas celebrations and the arrival of the magic lantern in the hills. Equally important is the portrait of mid-19th Century *jíbaro* speech patterns. In Alonso's verses we can hear the *jíbaro* dialect in its purest form. He mentions foods such as *lichón asao*, *toytiyas* (tortillas) and *mavi* (a tropical fruit used in making a number of drinks).

For all the eccentricities of the Puerto Rican tongue, it is important to remember that the language of the island is Spanish, albeit a Spanish heavily influenced by other nationalities, and that Puerto Rican Spanish shares many eccentricities with the Spanish of its Caribbean neighbors. One such trope is *seseo*, by which *s* sounds are muted, and sometimes disappear altogether, at the end of syllables. Thus, matches are *loh fohforoh* rather than *los fosforos* and *graciah* means thanks. *Yeismo* is another variation confusing to non-Puerto-Rican speakers; this involves pronouncing the Spanish *ll* and *y* sounds as English *j*s, so as to render a word like *Luquillo*, the island's most popular beach, "Look here, Joe." Let's not forget the truncation of words with terminal *e* sounds, like *noch*'. In Puerto Rico, go into a coffee shop for a cup of *café co' lech*.

The granting of United States citizenship to Puerto Ricans in 1917 signaled the advent of English as the first Germanic language to become part of the Puerto Rican dialect. The startling result of this last infusion is Spanglish, a colloquial Spanish which may be as familiar to a North American as it is to a Spaniard. Spanglish consists not only of a shared vocabulary but also of the terse sentence construction characteristic of English. The first penetration of English into Puerto Rican Spanish seems to have been concomitant with the introduction of English labels on a majority of consumer products. Indeed, men still sit at bars nursing *un scotch* while their children look on, chewing *chicletes*. The introduction of American commerce was no less confounding in other ways. When the first American cash registers were introduced in San Juan's grocery and department stores, a whole generation stood paralyzed at checkout counters when the "No Sale" tab, marking the end of the transaction, flipped up. *No Sale* means "Do not leave" in Spanish.

Spanglish truly entered its heyday only with the mass migration of Puerto Ricans to the United States in the 1940s. This exodus created a generation of so-called *Neorriqueños*, or "Newyoricans" who returned to their native island with the baffling customs and speech patterns of the streets of New York. Or they would send letters home with news of the *bárrio*. If they had no money, they would send the letter *ciodí*. Letters to the Cordillera would have to be transported by *el trucke*. Perhaps there would be bad news, that a son had been *bosteado* by the *policías* for dealing in *los drogues*. More often it was just idle chatter, discussions of the decisions of the world *líders*, or of how a brother had won a pool game by sinking the eight ball in the corner *poquete*.

Puerto Ricans love pool, but if Puerto Rico and the Spanglish language have an official sport, it has to be *el béisbol*. Everyone knows that Roberto Clemente (from Carolina) and Orlando Cepeda (from Santurce) were Puerto Rico's greatest hitters of *jonrones*, *dobles*, and *carreras impulsadas* (RBIs). Most Puerto Ricans would say their ball-players were *wilson*, meaning "very good." Anything that is truly spectacular on the island can be referred to as *wilson-wilson-willie-mays*.

The growth of Spanglish has changed little in the way Puerto Ricans feel towards their native tongue. Dollars are sometimes called *dolares*, but more often *pesos*. Quarters are *pesetas*, nickels *vellones*, and pennies *centavos*.

The beaches of Puerto Rico have been the stage for dialogs in many languages, but none are as spicy as those you'll hear on the beach at Pine Grove between two *playeros* when the mid-winter swells are up:

PAPO: *Oye, 'mano, que pasa?* (Hey brother, what's happening?)

RAYMOND: *Cómo estamos, broki?* (How we doin', brother?)

PAPO: *Na' mas se me estallo la tabla.* (I just cracked my surfboard.)

RAYMOND: *Qué chavienda!* (What a drag!)

PAPO: *No me digas. Oye, mi pana, tienes Marlboro?* (You don't say. Hey, my friend, have a cigarette?)

PAPO lights a cigarette under a towel, and continues: *Estuve gufeando en un tubo y fua! se me fue la tabla contra esas rocas por ahi.* (I was goofing around in a tube, when, boom! my board flies into those rocks over there.)

RAYMOND: *Ea rayo!* (Geeze!)

PAPO observing another surfer's antics: *Qué chivo! Por poco se comió el cable.* (What luck! He almost wiped out.)

RAYMOND: *Ese tipo yo lo conozco. Es bien buena gente.* (I know him, he's a good guy.)

PAPO: *Vale. Ay, pero mira a esa jeba. Vamos a rapiar.* (Cool. Oh, will you look at this babe. Let's rap.)

RAYMOND: *Oye, guapa, ven aca un momento.* (Hey, cutey, come here a minute.)

MARTA: *No seas cafre o te rompo el coco.* (Don't be a rude boy or I'll break your head).

PAPO: *Me quede pasmao.* (I'm awed).

MARTA: *Pues, mira, mijo. No soy chica plástica ni na'.* (Look boy, I'm no plastic chick or nothin'.)

PAPO: *De dónde tu eres?* (Where you from?)

MARTA: *De Guaynabo y a tí que te importa?* (Guaynabo, and what do you care?)

PAPO: *A ver si quieres pon pa' San Juan que se me rayo la tabla.* (To see if you'd like a lift to San Juan, 'cause my surfboard has cracked.)

MARTA: *Bueno, vale.* (Well, okay.)

PAPO: *Cógelo suave, Raymond.* (Take it easy, Raymond.)

Like any people with a rich lore, Puerto Ricans love to talk, and, with at least four linguistic families from which to cull their idiom, enjoy a speech at once cryptic and colorful.

Preceding pages: ecological blight in El Yunque; a shell-hunter's paradise; talking it over, El Combate.

Christopher Columbus brought sugarcane to the Antilles from the Canary Islands on his second voyage to the New World in 1493. In 1515, settlers planted cane on the island of Puerto Rico. Three years later, they imported African slaves to grow the cane. Demand for sugar, a relative novelty on European markets, seemed insatiable, and settlers were willing to exert tremendous effort to establish sugar plantations in the Caribbean. But sugar was not the only substance produced from cane that promised profit.

The Spanish settlers soon discovered that the liquid by-product in the manufacture of sugar crystals—molasses—fermented naturally. They invented a method of processing this molasses into rum and the popular liquid was on its way to becoming a symbol of the Caribbean good life.

Sugar is produced by "expressing" the juice from boiled cane by pressing, rolling, or pounding it. The juice is boiled down to a concentrated syrup, placed in vats and spun at high speed, causing crystals to form. The early mills were called *ingenios* and powered by human and animal labor. Today, machines spin the syrup at a rate of 2200 revolutions per minute.

Removing the crystals leaves a heavy, sweet molasses. This, the early settlers observed, fermented easily when exposed to the open air — free-floating yeast spores thrive in sugary environments and produce alcohol during their culture cycle. Not satisfied with the flavor and proof of this molasses wine, (which many Puerto Ricons have enjoyed in times past as a beverage called *aquardiente* or *madilla*) the Spaniards distilled it, filtering out impurities and increasing the concentration of alcohol. Here, was a beverage a man could enjoy. This was rum!

Rum took hold quickly as an important Puerto Rican export. In the first half of the 16th Century its popularity grew with the increasing demand for sugar. Then a slump in the sugar industry as a result of Spain's mercantile policies led to a parallel decline in the production of rum. Decade after decade, rum claimed a smaller share of the Puerto Rican export trade. In the late 18th Century, the Spanish government taxed Puerto Rican rum so heavily that it could no longer compete with foreign producers. During the reforms made by the Spanish Republic in 1812, the introduction of a new type of sugarcane and incentives for the development of colonial agriculture and industry fostered a resurgence in the sugar and rum markets. They limped along for a hundred years, rising and falling with the tides of politics in the turbulent 19th Century. In the early part of this century, the island profited from the decision of Cuba's great rum scions, the Bacardí family, to move their center of production to San Juan. Today, located in a computer-age facility across San Juan Bay in Bayamon, Bacardí remains the largest producer of rum in the world. Finally, in the 1930s a program for the development of the Puerto Rican rum

industry was established under New Deal legislation. Since gaining status as an associated free state in the 1950s, the government of Puerto Rico has included rum in all of its programs for economic development, including Operation Bootstrap. Today rum is one of Puerto Rico's most profitable exports.

Over the centuries, Puerto Rican rum distillers have refined their methods to produce the appealing liquid available today. Rather than depend on air-borne yeast spores, they add select cultures to guarantee consistent quality. Water and old mash from cane boiling are also added. For two to three days the mixture ferments in thousand-gallon tanks. When it is removed, it is 7 percent alcohol. Distillation in a still can bring it up as high as

160 proof. The higher the proof, the lower the congeners, the lighter the body, and the more neutral the color.

Puerto Rican rum is distinguished from the rums of other Caribbean countries by its light body and smooth flavor. A fine rum to consume neat, it possesses a subtlety which makes it a good mixer. There are three categories of Puerto Rican rum. White, or silver rum is year old rum that has been leached and filtered. This pure liquid is quite dry, and only a very slight trace of molasses flavor is evident. Amber, or gold rum is aged

Daiquiri
Boil one part water with two parts sugar for five minutes to make a sugar syrup.
Mix: ½ jigger of sugar syrup
   1½ jiggers lime juice
   6 jiggers gold rum
Stir with ¾ cup crushed ice and strain over ice.
Frozen Daiquiri
Whip:
   2—3 cups crushed ice
   3 tablespoons powdered sugar
   1½ jiggers lime juice

for three years. Producers add caramel to give it a rich, sunny color and mellow taste. Gold rum is usually sold at eighty proof. Liqueur rums are the cognac of rum. Aged the longest, they are dry, but possess an elegant mellowness and a deep flavor. They are sold as Red Label or Heavy Dark rum.

Puerto Rican rums are the best choice for cocktails but use the darker rums of Jamaica and Guyana for punches — the flavor of the Puerto Rican rums is too subtle.

Here are recipes of the most popular rum drinks:

Preceding pages, luscious rum concoctions. Left, rum casks, Arecibo; and right, Bacardi tasting garden.

   6 jiggers rum
in a blender until snowy.
Hot Buttered Rum
Into a mug, pour
   1 teaspoon powdered sugar
   ¼ cup boiling water
   ¼ cup rum
and stir. Flavor with a generous dash of nutmeg and a pat of butter.
Hot Rum Toddy
Into a mug, put
   1 teaspoon powdered sugar
   1 jigger rum
   1 stick cinnamon
   3 whole cloves
   ½ lemon slice
Fill the mug with ¾ cup hot water.

FLAVOR OF THE TROPICS: PUERTO RICAN CUISINE

Carib and Spanish destruction of Puerto Rico's native Taíno tribes, for all its ruthlessness, was far from complete. It has been said that Puerto Rican society today reflects its African and Indian origins more than its Spanish ones, and there is much truth in that. Non-Spanish ways live on in customs, rituals, language and all aspects of life, and one can see in many facial features the unfamiliar expression of the Taíno, a race otherwise lost to us forever. But nowhere is the Taíno influence more visible, or more welcome, than in Puerto Rican cuisine, one of the great culinary amalgams of our hemisphere.

Imagine a Taíno tribesman — call him Otoao and set his caste at *naboría*, one of the higher agricultural castes in the Taíno hierarchy — rising one sunny morning after having won the previous day a glorious victory over the invading Caribs. This victory was cause for an *areyto*, the ritual Taíno celebration which either preceded or followed any happening of even the remotest importance. Births, deaths, victories, defeats . . . it's *areyto* time. *Areytos*, like other socio-religious Taíno festivals, required intricate preparations for whatever food and drink was to be served, and, as a *naboría*, Otoao was in charge of hunting and fishing for the tribe.

Not that Otoao's wife Tai had it terribly easy. As a *naboría* woman (women's caste was determined by that of their husbands), Tai was responsible for the cultivation and harvesting of the fields (*conucos*) as well as the preparation of the meals. These were elaborate, and the Taínos managed to get an astounding range of food on the primitive banquet table. The menu that evening included roast *jutías* (early guinea pigs) seasoned with sweet red chili peppers, fried fish in corn oil, fresh shellfish and a variety of freshly harvested vegetables. Among the vegetables were *yautías* (starchy tubers similar to potatoes and yams), corn yams, cassava and the same small red chili peppers used to season the *jutías*. Bread was *casabe*, a mixture of puréed cassava and water cooked between two hot rocks. For dessert, the Taínos had fresh fruit picked from the exten-

sive variety available throughout the island. The culmination of the celebration was the drinking of an alcoholic beverage made from fermented corn juice. This activity was accompanied by the ceremonial inhalation of hallucinogenic fumes thought to make the warriors fitter for battle. The Taínos made hallucinogens of many sorts, the most common of which used the hanging, bell-shaped flowers of the *campana* tree to make a potent and mind-bending tea.

Most of the dietary staples mentioned above survive in the Puerto Rican cuisine of

today, albeit some in altered form. Puerto Rican cooking is now an amalgam of the Taíno, the Spanish and the African traditions. Much of this interpenetration took place early in the island's history, with Spanish colonists incorporating a variety of their own ingredients and techniques into the native cuisine, most of which were found to blend surprisingly well. A tremendous addition to this culinary melange was made by the Africans brought as slaves shortly thereafter. The African tradition is responsible for what is perhaps the greatest achievement in Caribbean cooking — the combination of strikingly contrasting flavors which in other culinary traditions would be considered unblendable. One of these savory concoctions is *piñon*, a

Preceding page, roasting pig. Left, picking green peppers; and right, *frituras*, a local favorite.

Local Cuisine **239**

highly-popular combination which uses ripe plantains layered between well-seasoned ground beef and almost invariably served with rice.

Food from Around the World

As different ingredients and cooking techniques were introduced to the island by its early settlers, a local cooking tradition began to take shape. Most important of the early imports were the Spanish cattle, sheep, pigs, goats and other grillable creatures the islanders had never tasted and took to with zeal. Along with the animals were brought an almost infinite number of vegetables, fruits and spices from the farthest reaches of Spain's colonial empire. A subtler, but no

Rican coffee, for example, especially that from the region around Yauco, was long considered by Europeans the best coffee one could get in the world. And the plantain, arguably the most popular staple in Puerto Rican cuisine, is something of a national symbol, almost as the leek is to the Welsh; a man who is admirable for his straightforwardness and country-style lack of pretension is said to have on him the "*mancha del plátano*," or "stain of the plantain."

Myths and Misconceptions

Puerto Rican cuisine is as eclectic as it is varied. Local food has earned a reputation it most decidedly does not deserve for being hot, fiery and spicy. In actuality, although it

less important, influence on the Puerto Rican food supply was the introduction of European farming methods and agricultural equipment.

Surprisingly, many of the agricultural staples which look authochthonous to the island were actually brought to Puerto Rico from other parts of the world. Among the great variety of crops imported were coffee, sugarcane, coconuts, bananas, plantains, oranges and other citrus fruits, ginger and other spices, onions, potatoes, tomatoes, garlic and much more. These products, in combination with those already present, were to mold what was to become the Puerto Rican culinary tradition. It is ironic that among these imports can be counted several for which Puerto Rico was to become renowned. Puerto

is prepared with a multiplicity of richly varied spices and condiments, Puerto Ricans tend to season their food more subtly than one might imagine. The base of a majority of native dishes is the *sofrito*, an aromatic and well-seasoned sauce made from puréed tomatoes, onions, garlic, green peppers, sweet red chili peppers, coriander, anatto seeds and a fairly arbitrary handful of other spices. This *sofrito* adds a zesty taste to stews, rices, stewed beans and a variety of other dishes, but only the blandest of palates would consider it piquant.

Native Caribbean flavors are evident in the majority of Puerto Rican recipes. One common denominator in Caribbean cooking is the ingredients used in the preparation of the various dishes; Puerto Rico fits neatly into the stereotypes of Caribbean food supply. The most popular dinner dishes are stewed meats, rice and beans, an enormous selection of fritters, and desserts made from local fruits and vegetables.

Social Traditions of Old

Puerto Ricans have very successfully kept alive not only the culinary, but also many of the social traditions of their Taíno forebears. Christmastime out on the island is not complete without rice, "pigeon peas," *lechón asao* (roast suckling pig), *pasteles* (tamales made from plantains and *yautías* filled with a flavorful meat stuffing), and, as dessert, a *majarete* made with rice flour, coconut milk,

coast from Salinas to Cabo Rojo. The same is true of the great variety of fritters available in the food shacks of Luquillo, a most rewarding 30 minute visit from San Juan for anyone interested in meeting with local cuisine on its own terms. Bayamon and environs boast a truly unusual snack in *chicharrón*, a sort of massive pork-scratching sold on the highways in and out of the city. It's definitely an acquired taste, but once you've acquired it, you'll understand why there are so many slightly hefty individuals wandering the streets of Bayamón.

HoJo's a los Criollos

The island offers a great variety of restaurants for tourists and local consumers.

grated coconut pulp, sugar and spices. For the Lenten season, seafood dishes include the traditional *serenata*, codfish in vinaigrette sauce served with tomatoes, onions, avocados and boiled vegetables.

Though Puerto Rico is far too small to have a large number of truly regional cuisines, a number of dishes are limited to particular areas of the island. For example, seafood dishes tend to be accompanied by *sorrullos* (corn fritters similar to hush puppies) in most of the restaurants on the south

Left, a family outing; and right, everything under the sun.

Typical restaurants serving local food are only rarely luxurious or expensive. In fact, among Puerto Ricans, a rule of thumb applies that the shabbier the establishment, the better the food. The best native creations are found at modest little local *fondas*, where the prices are as reasonable as the food is distinguished. In a *fonda*, you can pick up a generous plate of rice and beans, *biftec criollo* (steak), *tostones* (fried plantains), salad, a can of Corona beer and dessert for about eight dollars. If you can afford to splurge for the extra thirty cents you can pick up one of the better cups of coffee you've had in your life. At the low end of the economic scale are delicious sandwiches made with a mixture of red meats, cheeses, tomatoes and other ingredients. Among the most popular are *cubanos* and *media noches*. At the pricey end of the scale is *asopao*, probably Puerto Rico's most widely loved native dish. This thick stew can be made with chicken, pork, or fish, and is invariably worth every penny one pays for it.

International Cuisine

Besides the local restaurants, you'll find a large assortment of places in which to savor food from different continents and countries. There are Chinese, French, Spanish, Cuban, Italian, German and Mexican restaurants in the San Juan area. And if gourmet international food is not your style, rest assured that sleazy little joints serving hamburgers, hot dogs, crispy fried chicken and other exquisite

junk-food are ubiquitous throughout the island.

Making In on Your Own

Armchair connossieurs who will never go to Puerto Rico and live far enough from New York City to be completely unable to procure a pre-cooked Puerto Rican delicacy can rest assured that the stuff is fairly easy to cook—once one gets the correct ingredients—and provides a rewarding change-of-pace from the wimpy little *nouvelle cuisine* they've probably been "enjoying" otherwise. Here's a recipe for *Mofongo*, a hearty, typically Puerto Rican plantain dish that makes a first-rate luncheon or dinner.

Mofongo abreu

Ingredients:
  3 green plantains
  ¼ cup olive oil
  1½ tsp. salt
  ½ cup grated pork rind
  2-3 cloves garlic
Cut plantains into sections like *tostones* (about 6 pieces each). Fry in corn oil until slightly browned. Drain off oil. Mix with the other ingredients, using — if you want to be really Puerto Rican about the whole thing — a mortar and pestle. Shape into balls and serve in chicken stock. Chicken soup's okay, but chicken stock is the real thing. Otherwise, shape the stuff into hamburg-shaped patties and serve with *carnecita*.

Those familiar with Jewish cooking will recognize the first way of cooking *Mofongo* as somewhat similar to putting matzoh balls in chicken stock. If therefore you worry that *Mofongo* will be nothing new, try it with *carnecita*, which was left sufficiently vague in the preceding recipe for us to make the formula available here:

Carnecita

Ingredients:
  2 lbs. pork (the leaner the better)
  1 cup *adobo*
Cut pork into cubes about an inch square. Marinate in *adobo* 24 hours. Fry in olive oil. Serve with *Mofongo*.

Yes, but as you're obviously no closer to enjoying your *Mofongo*, since you probably haven't the vaguest idea of what *adobo* is, we'll give you a bit of help.

Adobo

Ingredients:
  2 cloves garlic, ground
  1½ tsps. olive oil or to taste (many Puerto Rican chefs suggest 1 tsp./lb., though 1½ should be plenty for this recipe)
  ½ cup vinegar
  3 tbsp. olive oil
Stir all this up well. Slather it on the *Mofongo* and forget about it for a day or so. Fry it all up, eat it, and you'll realize that *Mofongo*, although it sounds like inner city slang for "very bad person" is a tasty concoction indeed. It just might make you want to head down to the island and sample the full range of a truly unusual cuisine.

Left, *frituras*, the pizza of Puerto Rico; and right, Santurce Market, San Juan.

ART AND ARDOR IN PUERTO RICO

If you don't know what you're in for, be warmly warned that Puerto Rico's art scene offers delights to the mind and senses as meaningful and alluring as those of its landscape. This may mean entering a room of carved religious figures (*santos*) in the middle of a bustling city and finding yourself enveloped in their holy silence; or wandering into a museum or gallery in Old San Juan, only to find yourself as taken by a beautifully-landscaped 17th-Century courtyard as by what you see on the walls; or talking to a local artist or scholar and finding that in almost no time his passion for the island and its craftsmen is yours.

As art is still merely a way of leading one's life in Puerto Rico, almost all visitors who feel at home on the island will feel at home in its art world. To be sure, there are frustrations to be encountered. In San Juan the problem centers around a glut of a good thing; finding the best is often a confusing task, with charlatans working next to some of the great artists of the day. Difficulties out on the island are more clearly logistical, with many of Puerto Rico's most fascinating local museums hiding in forgettable outbuildings on the edges of towns. Nonetheless, even the most cursory foray into the island's artistic past and present will show you many avenues to the very best.

Museum Isle

The Institute of Puerto Rican Culture, located in the dazzling Dominican Convent in Old San Juan, owns a vast amount of the island's cultural inheritance, and can guide you to almost anything you fancy. Old San Juan itself is particularly fortunate as an artistic center; besides its nine museums, it boasts a dozen solid contemporary art galleries, a few cooperatives and craft shops of all description. Some of its exhibition spaces are ingenious, perhaps the chief among them being the Arsenal, an army barracks now given over to shows by local artists.

If buying art interests you as much as just looking at it, Old San Juan is certainly the spot to begin your shopping spree. You'll find Pre-Columbian pieces at Galeria Los Arcos; Primitives at Galeria Eugenia; and prints as well as paintings at Botello, Coabey, Marrozini and Las Palomas. More avant-garde artists display at the charming

Galeria 59 on Calle del Cristo. All these spaces are within minutes of each other. In Condado, Casa Candina is a charming gallery in a beautiful and quiet hacienda. It's not only the island's center for ceramic arts, but the site of many important art shows and exhibitions as well. Other galleries await at the Plaza de las Americas.

The Museum of the University of Puerto Rico in Río Piedras exhibits only a fifth of its collection, but that small proportion is of absolutely superior quality, from Pre-

Columbian art right up to the strongest painters of the present day. But the last word on Puerto Rican art must go to the Ponce Museum, envisioned by former governor Luis Ferré and executed by architect Edward Durrell Stone. You'll find a more detailed discussion in our Ponce chapter. It will be enough to say here that in a series of dramatically sunlit hexagonal rooms is art reflecting the full range of the drama of human life. From the simplest of faces in Jan van Eyck's "Salvator Mundi" to an over-populated "Fall of the Rebel Angels" to Rossetti's wonderfully confrontational "Daughters of King Lear," you'll find it impossible not to be moved. Go out of your way to get there.

Art for Heart's Sake

Many of Puerto Rico's greatest achievements have been in the folk arts, and these retain a broad appeal, whether in the form of *mundillos* (tatted fabrics), *cuatros* (four-stringed guitars) or the festive masks of both Ponce and Loíza. The Ponceño masks are particularly captivating, shaped in forms of animal and devil heads, with hollowed horns, jagged cartoon-style teeth, protruding tongues and furry skin flecked with particolored stippling. Such masks originated in medieval Spain, where, during the Lenten season, town rowdies would make the rounds dressed as devils, in an effort to terrify women and other sinners to the point of returning to the church for salvation. A

simplicity, the chosen saint's inner meaning being revealed immediately rather than in the enumeration of detail.

The proof of the healing powers of *santos* is said to be attested to by the presence of *milagros* ('miracles'), small silver appendages in shapes of parts of the body. These were donated by people who had prayed to particular saints for intercession in healing parts of the body that were injured or ill. You can find such *santos* in the Capilla del Cristo in Old San Juan. Though *santos* by the great masters are difficult to come by, there's hardly a home on the island where you won't find at least one *santo* of some sort, greatly revered and passed on from generation to generation.

If funding can be found, there will soon be

habit long since fallen into desuetude in the Old World, it's alive and well in Ponce every February at the Festival of Our Lady of Guadeloupe, Ponce's patron saint.

By contrast, there is an uncanny spiritual quiet to be found in the Puerto Rican *santos*, arguably the island's greatest contribution to the plastic arts. These wooden religious idols vary greatly in size and shape. Their images have been carved in the name of every saint known to Western Christianity. The Baroque detail of the earliest pieces reflects both their period origins and the tastes of a Spanish clientele. But as Puerto Rico began to develop a stronger sense of colonial identity, as well as an artisan tradition, *santeros* began to carve figures of a striking

established a large museum dealing exclusively with Puerto Rican folk art. In the meantime, there are exhaustive books by Theodoro Vidal on *santos, milagros* and Ponceño masks. And, amidst a preponderance of contemporary art, *santos* are available in the Botello and Palomas Galleries in Old San Juan.

The Indian Ceremonial Ballpark at Utuado gives haunting echoes of pre-Columbian life and culture. Here, early Taíno Indians played a more civilized version of the balancing game favored by Mexico's Mayans, in which one had to keep a small ball suspended in the air for long periods of time, hitting it only with shoulders, head and ankles. We say "more civilized" on the strength of the fact that the early Taínos were not sacrificed to the gods if they dropped the ball, as their Mexican counterparts were. The dolmen-like stones surrounding the *bateyes*, or playing spaces, show an admirable feeling for the ideal spatial relationship art and nature can hold.

One finds similar evidence of the vast and various Taíno legacy at the University Museum in Río Piedras, which holds the cultural patrimony of the island. Digs from the last 10 years have been especially abundant in discoveries, some of them dazzling in quality. Amidst the expected artifacts — amulets, potsherds, tools — are some baffling cultural curiosities, like stone collars, great solid yokes at once regal and unbearable. In one intriguing case concerning Puer-

pastel clouds, but the inner peace which Campeche succeeds in displaying in his main holy figures dispels all doubt as to his stature as a truly inspired artist. There are two such masterpieces in the Ponce Museum, but it is in a formal portrait which hangs in the Institute of Puerto Rican Culture that one sees Campeche at the height of his powers. The eponymous "Governor Ustauriz" stands in a magnificent room, sunlight entering from behind. In his left hand are the first plans to pave the streets of San Juan; outside in the distance are men laboring busily to make his dream a reality. It is truly a triumphant picture.

A more accessible painter, and something of a local hero on Puerto Rico, is Francisco Oller (1833-1917). His work is housed in all

to Rico's early Arawaks, men bend and sway together in entranced harmony. In another are two partially exposed skeletons, a few broken possessions at their sides.

For all the diversity of her many cultural traditions, it was not until the 18th Century that Puerto Rico produced her first major artist in the Western tradition: José Campeche (1752-1809). In spite of never having left the island and having been exposed to European painting only through prints, he still managed to create paintings of mastery. His religious works show a weakness for sentimentality, with their glut of *putti* and

Left, Ponce Art Museum. Above: left, Hammock maker's studio; and right, veigante mask artisan.

three main sources: the Institute and the museums at Ponce and Río Piedras. To this day, the extent of his influence on Puerto Rican painting is immeasurable. Unlike Campeche, Oller lived and traveled abroad throughout his life. He studied under Courbet, was an intimate of both Pissarro and Cezanne, painted European royalty, and yet remained loyal to—and fiercely proud of—his island homeland. He was a Realist with Impressionist ideas, able to paint gorgeously everything he faced. He was adept at all genres: portraits, still lifes and landscapes like "Hacienda Aurora," reproduced here, which resonates with colors of Puerto Rico just as much in evidence today. A piece of work which defies reproduction and is worth

a plane ticket to Ponce is Oller's "El Velorio" (The Wake). An enormous painting, it covers an entire wall in the Museum at Río Piedras and illuminates the common man's universe in a fashion not unlike that of Breughel. Here people laugh, cry, drink, sing and dance about, while on a lace-covered table an almost forgotten, stone-white dead child lies strewn with flowers.

Oller's legacy to Puerto Rican painters has been one not only of technique but of theme as well. Since his time, island painters have taken an overwhelming pride in Puerto Rico's diverse populace and landscape. Miguel Pou and Ramon Frade were among the earliest to follow Oller's lead, doing some spectacular genre work in the early part of this century. At the Institute, Frade's painting "The Jíbaro" is a splendid homage to Puerto Rico's country farmers. Shyly surveying us with a bunch of plantains in his arms, this tiny old fellow appears a giant, with the land miniatured at his feet and his head haloed by a cloud.

The 1940s saw a rise in printmaking which has left that medium one of the most vibrant in Puerto Rico to this day. Funded by the government, printmaking projects lured a slew of fine artists, many of whom are still active today. One thinks in particular of Rafael Tufiño, Antonio Martorell, José Rosa and Lorenzo Homar. The poster by Ramon Power reprinted here shows some of the clarity and power which the best of Puerto Rican artists continue to draw from the medium.

Over the last 30 years, almost all Puerto Rican artists have studied abroad, and the consequence has been a broadening and increasingly avant-garde range of artistic attitudes. Some artists have remained abroad, like Rafael Ferrer, whose work is as popular in New York as it is in San Juan. Others have returned to work and teach, producing an art with a distinctively Puerto Rican flavor. Myrna Baez is such a painter, her canvases interweaving past and present, inner and outer space. Her "Homage to Vermeer," reproduced here, shows a lone figure in an interior surrealistically touched by landscape. Reflectively, she seems to have loosed a phantom of tropical hubris as she opens the drawer of a nearby table.

The work of Puerto Rico's newer artists is radiant with color and imagination. Among the up-and-coming painters are Juan Ramón Velázquez, Ivette Cabrera and Consuelo Gotay; among the photographers, John Betancourt and Frieda Medín. Arnaldo Roche, one of whose self-portraits is reproduced here, has a strong and innovative style.

SALSA: RHYTHM OF THE TROPICS

Just prior to his death, the world-renowned Argentinian composer, Alberto Ginastera, visited Puerto Rico in order to attend the world premiere of one of his works commissioned by the Pablo Casals Festival. During an interview at the Caribe Hilton, Mr. Ginastera's thoughts turned to the song of the *coquí*, the tiny frog-like creature that is found only in Puerto Rico and is famous for its persistent and ubiquitous nocturnal calls. "It is the only natural song that I know of," said Mr. Ginastera, "which is formed of a perfect seventh." The *coquí* sings a two-note song — "co . . . kee!" — and these two notes are a perfect seventh apart. It should come, therefore, as no surprise that the island's natural sounds have their unique man-made counterpart. The music of Puerto Rico is *Salsa*.

From Settlement to Salsa

Puerto Ricans have always excelled in music, and the somewhat haphazard course of the island's development and history have given it a multitude of traditions from which to build a distinctively Puerto Rican sound. The earliest settlers were as enthusiastic about their music as any Spaniards, but deprived of their native string instruments, found themselves in the position of having to create their own. As a result, there are at least a half-dozen string instruments native to the island, and about which more will be said below. Regardless of the ingenuity of the early Puerto Ricans in inventing and manufacturing new instruments, such instruments remained scarce. In the absence of tonal instruments, the settlers made do with percussive ones, which were ready at hand in the various gourds, woods, shoots and beans native to their land. The arrival of West African slaves, who brought with them a well-developed and long history of percussion, accelerated this percussive trend.

Even now, Puerto Ricans are great adepts at making music with whatever happens to be within grabbing distance. No one *owns* a musical performance in Puerto Rico, as one does in countries where musical performances are more formalized: play a Puerto Rican a piano tune he likes in a barroom or cafe, and you won't believe your ears when you hear the rhythmic sounds he gets out of a spoon, a wood block, a bead necklace or even his knuckles on the table.

No Lack of Formality

To be fair, there is a somewhat formalized genre of this very type of music. It's called *plenas*, and generally involves a handful of young men creating different rhythms on an amazing variety of hand-held percussion instruments. Some resemble hand-held tympanies, some Irish *bodhrans*, some tambourines, and many of them are homemade. The custom of *plenas* originated among the early blacks of Ponce, but today you can hear its distinctive sounds at any patron saint's festi-

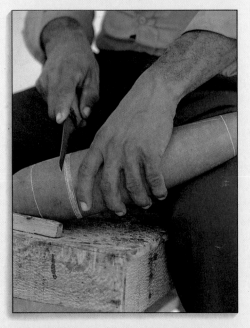

val and in many bars in Old San Juan on summer nights.

This is not to neglect the achievements of this small island in the more traditional forms. Puerto Rico's achievements have been proportionately very large indeed. It is a haven for the opera, and has its own company; Justino Díaz, the island's finest male vocalist, has impressed critics from New York to Milan. The Puerto Rico Symphony Orchestra, despite being relatively young, is probably the best in the Caribbean, and has premiered works by some of Latin America's finest composers, many of them at the famed Casals Festival.

It is Pablo Casals who, more than any other Puerto Rican, is responsible for the upsurge of interest and proficiency in classical performance in Puerto Rico in recent years. Born in Catalonia in 1876 of a Puerto Rican mother, Casals was recognized almost before World War One as one of the greatest cellists of his era. After leaving Spain in 1936 as a protest against the Spanish Civil War, he settled in the French Pyrenees, where the first Casals Festival was held in 1950. He visited his mother's homeland in 1956, and spent the final years of his life in Puerto Rico. At the invitation of Governor Luís Muñoz Marín, he founded a Puerto Rican Casals Festival in

1957, which must rank as the greatest cultural event in the Antilles, and a formidable one by world standards. In later years, Casals went on to form the Puerto Rican Symphony Orchestra and the Puerto Rican Conservatory of Music. On his death at the age of 97 in 1973, he considered himself a Puerto Rican; his countrymen considered him one of the greatest Puerto Ricans ever to have lived.

This, then, is the musical background of contemporary Puerto Rico: half-ingenuous;

A quiros maker artisan at work; and right, music making is still a favorite pastime today.

half-provincial, half-worldly. And utterly otherworldly.

Rhythm of the Tropics

Salsa is what happens when Afro-Caribbean music meets Big-band jazz. Its roots may be found in the early explorations of Tito Puente in New York City clubs following World War Two. After serving three years in the United States Navy, Puente studied percussion at the Julliard School on New York's West Side. Puente was soon playing and composing for top bandleaders like Machito and Pupi Campo, and he quickly proceeded to establish his own orchestra. Puente's Latin Jazz Ensemble continues to delight audiences throughout the world.

In a recent interview in *Latin US* magazine, Puente was asked to define Salsa:

> "*As you know*, salsa *in Spanish means 'sauce,' and we use it mostly as a condiment for our foods . . . salsa in general in all our fast Latin music put together: the* merengue, *the* rumba, *the* mambo, *the* cha-cha, *the* guaguanco, *boogaloo, all of it is salsa . . . in Latin music, we have many different types of rhythms, such as ballads* (boleros), *rancheros, tangos, and, of course, salsa.*"

The salsa band is usually composed of a lead vocalist and chorus, a piano, a bass, a horn section and a heavy assortment of percussion instruments (bongos, conga, maracas, güiros, timbales, claves, and the ever-present cowbell). The overall effect is mesmerizing, the rhythm contagious.

Traditional Music for the World

Salsa has placed Puerto Rico on the international map of popular music. Says Puente: "It's totally unexpected to see Belgians, Swedes, Finns and Danes swing to the Latin Beat . . . The bands there are playing more salsa than we are." Puerto Rican music has evolved into the salsa beat; music has played a crucial role in Puerto Rican society and culture for as long as there have been Puerto Ricans. During Spanish rule, the *danza* was the chief form of entertainment for the *criollo* aristocracy; it reached its high point in the late 19th Century when Morel Campos and other masters gave it a popularity that re-dounded back to Spain. This highly stylized tradition of music and its accompanying dance movements are preserved by several local ensembles in Puerto Rico. The *danza* is characterized by a string orchestra, wood-winds, and a formal ambience. *La Borin-queña,* the Puerto Rican national anthem, is a danza.

A more popular and widely practised Puer-to Rican musical tradition is the *aquinaldo*, a song performed around the Christmas and Three Kings holiday, usually in the form of an *asalto*. The *asalto* is a charming tradition which dates back to the 19th Century, and perhaps earlier. It goes along with the un-restrained partying of the holiday season. It is customary at an *asalto* to feast on *lechón*

décima consists of a number of three-, four- and six-stringed instruments (called appro-priately the *tres*, *cuatro* and *seis*); a minimal rhythm is kept up by *claves* or the *güiro*. The trademark of the *décima* is verbal improvisa-tion. Often, two singers will alternate stan-zas, trying to outboast each other with rhym-ing tales of luscious fruit, pretty women or physical prowess. The verbal jousting is fueled by the cheers and jeers of the audi-ence. The similarity between the *décima* and the verbal duelling of rap DJs is striking.

In contemporary Puerto Rico, salsa is king, but who is the King of Salsa? Close to the top of anyone's list are Willie Colón, Hector Lavoe, El Gran Combo de Puerto Rico and the Fania All-Stars. Younger salseros might clamor for Willie Rosario or Grupo Fascina-

asao (roast suckling pig), *yucca* (a local potato-like root), *arroz con pollo* (chicken with rice), *gandules* (local peas) and *palos de ron* (well, okay, so they have some rum). Following the feast, a group of celebrants stumbles from house to house, waking the residents and singing *aquinaldos*. The mem-bers of each household are expected to join the *asalto* as it moves throughout the neigh-borhood. Recordings of these genial songs are available as performed by a *trulla*, any professional group of *aquinaldo* singers.

The *décima* is arguably the most appealing form of traditional Puerto Rican music. It is the vehicle through which the *jíbaro* express-es his joys and frustrations; it is the poetry of the Puerto Rican soul. Instrumentation for the

ción to be on that list. Residents of Ponce would certainly favor the Sonora Ponceña for the throne. The pre-pubescent vote favors Menudo; young *puertorriqueños* have prob-ably stained more fanmag photos of Menudo with tears than men have stained tissues during the Isabel Chacón show. But that's a book in itself. Whatever the individuals taste, salsa continues as one of the hottest forms of popular music in the world.

Willie Colón and his band have produced some of the most inspired salsa to date. The album "Siembra," a collaboration with the Panamanian Ruben Blades, is easily one of the hottest discs around. The songs on "Siembra" demonstrate the rhythmic com-plexity which is at the core of salsa, as well as the thematic motifs which tie all of salsa together. The song "Pedro Navaja" tells the story of a street tough and his inevitable demise. Blades croons the final verse, describing the scene after a gunfight:

Y créanme gente, que aunque hubo ruido, nadie salió. No hubo curiosos, ni hubo preguntas, y nadie lloró. Solo un borracho con los dos muertos se tropezo, y cogió el revolver, el puñal y los pesos y se marchó; y tropezando, se fue cantando desafinao el coro que aquí les traigo dando el mensaje de mi canción. La vida te da sorpresas, sorpresas te da la vida, Ay, Díos!

He who lives by violence dies by violence; Colón and Blades are not the first salsa

Siembra con fe, con humildád y a la larga, tu verás.

Colón's talent sparkles in other collaborative efforts. His 1977 recording with Celia Cruz, entitled "Only They Could Have Made This Album," is a superb example of salsa's African roots. The songs from "Pun Pun Catalu," "Rinkinkalla," and "Burundanga" make use of African linguistic and musical references. "Burundanga" is an outgrowth of the music of *santeria*, the Afro-Caribbean religious cult.

El Gran Combo (de Puerto Rico) has had great success, probably owing to the optimism and enthusiasm present in their songs. They have great musical talent, an admirable sense of humor, and a massive popular fol-

singers to choose this theme for a starting point.

Colón and Blades further delineate the salsa ethic in the song "Plastico."

aprende, estudia, pues nos falta andar bastante, marcha siempre hacía adelante para juntos acabar con la ignorancia . . . recuerda se ven las caras, y jamás el corazón.

Their lesson continues in "Siembra."

Left, Friday night disco; and right, Festival San Sebastián.

lowing in Puerto Rico. Anyone interested in being immediately indoctrinated into the League of Salsa Fanatics had best go out and buy one of their albums right now.

The road to a better future (like Puerto Rican Spanish) is not always easy to follow, and the song "Resignación" suggests an amusing relief for the "estress" of making a fulfilling life for one's self:

Digame señor siquiatraci qué debo hacer? He perdido mis amigos y a mi mujer. Yo te voy a recetar jarabe de "me resbala." Junto con una pomada y un unguento de "a mi que." Y si tu sabes Inglés y la cosa sigue fea Te tomas cinco pastillas de "I don't care."

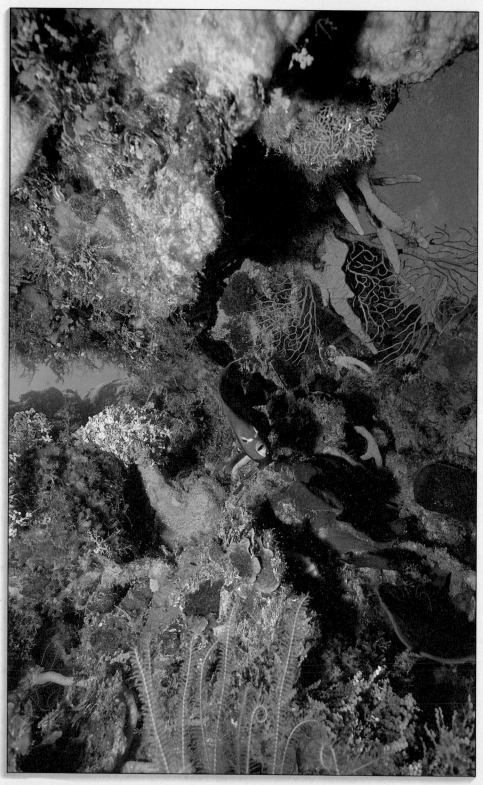

BURIED TREASURES: DIVING IN PUERTO RICO

Divers plunge into waters all over the world, but nowhere is it done with such pleasure as in Caribbean waters. The waters off Puerto Rican shores are warm, clear, and, as rumor has it, populated with the ghosts of long lost treasure ships.

In the later years of the 16th Century, Spain, Puerto Rico's mother country, supported her colony by shipping an annual stipend of two and one half *marviedes* from Mexico, another colony. This shipment, called the *situado*, was a miserable failure, as privateers repeatedly intercepted the gold. Much gold was stolen. Much more, however, fell to the floor of the ocean.

Modern divers might not stumble upon the lost treasures of the Old World, but there are many chances to drift through skeletal vessels, and who knows what might be found.

More certain pleasures will be found in the natural underwater beauty of the island and its surrounding outcroppings. The Caribbean chain is made up of a series of protruding mountains. Like icebergs, the Caribbean islands show only one-tenth of themselves to the land-locked visitor. Divers — snorkelers to some extent, but particularly those equipped with scuba gear — can explore the fascinating rock surfaces of the islands' downslopping sides. In effect, the diver can swim down the sides of a mountain, exploring terrain she would usually have to climb through above sea level.

The islands themselves are just the most basic of entertainments. There are the ubiquitous coral formations, of course, multicolored and multifaceted. Look for some of the exotic varieties, like fire coral, or brain coral. But the most rewarding of all underwater treats is the abundance of wildlife.

The Caribbean boasts more than 2,000 varieties of fish. The parrot fish carries itself with a quizzical look, its brilliant turquoise and orange colorings more than whimsically reminiscent of its avian namesake; the grouper, with its reddish stripes running lengthwise may be seen as an aquatic zebra; the moray eel is a prehistoric remnant of the deep.

Abundant too are snapper, mullet, jew fish, tuna, dolphin, mackerel, permit, bonefish, barracuda, amberjack, blow fish, sting ray and jelly fish.

Beauty, as so often happens, mingles with potential danger. Barracuda are generally harmless, but provocation will bring trouble. Any jellyfish, as anyone who's spent any time in the water knows, can be painful. Watch out for congregations of the jelly fish. Streams of the fish half a mile wide and miles long have been spotted flowing through Caribbean waters.

Culebra and Vieques, two islands isolated off the island's northeast corner, provide the best opportunities for diving. Culebra is ac-

cessible by a short flight from Isla Grande Airport, while the magical island of Vieques can be reached either by air or by an hour and a half long ferry trip from Fajardo. The latter is preferable. Good snorkeling is to be had just about anywhere along the Puerto Rican coast, but particularly around Borinquen Point near Aguadilla.

As mentioned above, the waters are warm and wet suits are generally superfluous. However, proper training and equipment is essential. Contact any of the following for lessons and information: Caribbean School of Aquatics, Inc., Ocean Park, 723-4740; Caribbean Divers, Fajardo, 724-3292; Caribe Aquatic Adventure, Caribe Hilton Hotel, Puerta de Tierra, 721-0303.

Preceding pages: diver inspects spider crab; a school of grunts. Left, reef scenic and right, black coral. Following pages: butterfly fish; fire coral; puffer fish; inside El Morro.

GETTING THERE

BY AIR

San Juan's **Luis Muñoz Marín International Airport**, just west of the city center in Isla Verde, is one of the largest airports in the Americas, serving not only as Puerto Rico's main port of tourist entry but also as a stopping point for most American and European flights to the Virgin Islands and other points in the Caribbean. Some of the international carriers serving the airport include Air Canada, Air France, Air Jamaica, American Airlines, Avianca, Bahamas Air, British Caledonian, BWIA, Delta Airlines, Eastern Airlines, Iberia, LIAT, Lufthansa, Mexicana, Pan American, PRINAIR, Sabena, TWA, United and Varig Brazilian Airlines.

Sometimes known as Isla Verde, the airport terminal is a sunny and florid two-level structure, with departures on the upper deck and arrivals on the lower. Free buses run to all the car rental agencies not in the airport, and those operated by the Metropolitan Bus Authority run to various parts of the city for only $.25. A taxi to Old San Juan should run you about $15. Fares are determined on a per-mile basis, with $.80 initial charge and an additional charge of $.10 for every .125 miles (.2 km). Suitcases are carried for a charge of $.50 a piece. The Airport Limousine Service carries passengers to Old San Juan for $1.75 and to the Condado for $1.50.

AIRLINES

ALM
Tel: 791-2150.

Aero Virgin Islands
Tel: 791-1215.

Aerolineas Dominicanas
Tel: 724-7100.

Air BVI
Tel: 791-2117.

Air France
Tel: 791-8282.

Air Jamaica
Tel: 724-2555.

American
Tel: 721-1747.

Avianca
Tel: 723-2500.

British Airways
Tel: 800-247-9297.

BWIA
Tel: 724-2555.

Capitol Air
Tel: 791-1740.

Crown Air
Tel: 723-1212.

Delta
Tel: 721-1011.

Eastern
Tel: 728-3131.

Flamenco Airways
Tel: 724-7110.

LACSA
Tel: 724-3330.

Iberia
Tel: 721-5630.

Lufthansa
Tel: 723-9553.

Mexicana de Aviacion
Tel: 721-2323.

PanAm
Tel: 753-6018.

VIASA
Tel: 721-3340.

Vieques Air Link
Tel: 722-3736

BY SEA

While regular passenger service to Puerto Rico is rare, cruise ships are commonplace. San Juan is the most popular cruise port in the Caribbean, receiving over 500 vessels and 400,000 visitors yearly. Several modern "tourism piers" have been constructed at the harborside in Old San Juan, with the result that most cruise companies plying the South Atlantic make at least an afternoon stop in San Juan.

TRAVEL ESSENTIALS

VISAS & PASSPORTS

No visa or passport is required for U.S. citizens entering Puerto Rico from the United States. Foreign nationals are required to present the same documentation required for entry into the continental U.S.

MONEY MATTERS

All business in Puerto Rico is transacted in American dollars. Owing to its isolation from main supply lines, Puerto Rico is slightly more expensive than the mainland. Inflation is not presently a problem, and hovers under 5 percent.

Puerto Rico has no sales tax. There are taxes on alcohol and cigarettes, thought these are figured into marked prices and do not appear as surcharges.

CREDIT CARDS

Most restaurants and hotels in well-traveled areas honor American Express, Master Card and Visa. Carte Blanche, Diner's Club, Enroute and Ideal are accepted at a smaller number of establishments. The Lufthansa card and the Hilton International card pass muster at a handful of the larger resorts.

There are two American Express Travel Services on the island:

Agencias Soler
1035 Ashford Ave., Condado
Tel: (809) 725-0960.

Agencias Soler
8 W. Méndez Vigo St., Mayagüez
Tel: (809) 834-3300.

WHAT TO WEAR

Puerto Rican dressing is extremely casual. Jeans and knit trousers are common legwear. So are shorts, though primarily only among tourists, as locals tend to shun them. Only in a very small number of clubs are jackets and ties required, and businessmen often remove their jackets in the course of the workday. Men frequently wear *guayaberas* – long-sleeve shirts, often cotton, with intricate lace work on the front – as formal wear. Colorful, medium-length dresses are versatile evening wear for women.

Anything more than a light sweater is seldom necessary, even on winter nights in the Cordillera. However, some kind of sunscreen will be necessary for those who plan to spend even a minimal amount of time outdoors. An umbrella will come in useful, especially in late summer on the island's northern coast.

CUSTOMS

Customs regulations resemble those of the United States, and are carried out with similar thoroughness. It is illegal to transport perishable foods, plants or animals into or out of Puerto Rico except with prior permission. This stipulation applies to those traveling to and from the United States as well. Duty-free shops are open for all international flights, and for flights to the United States and U.S. possessions in the Caribbean.

Getting Acquainted

Commonwealth motto: *Joannes est nomen ejus* (John is his Name)
Commonnnwealth song: *La Borinqueña*
Commonwealth flower: *Maga*

Puerto Rico stands in relation to the United States as an *Estado Libre Asociada*, or "Free Associated State." It is most commonly referred to as the "Commonwealth of Puerto Rico." Under an agreement which dates from 1950, Puerto Ricans are American citizens, with almost all the economic and personal rights and responsibilities pertaining thereto. At the head of the island's government is an elected governor; Puerto Rico has an elected Senate and House of Representatives, which work very much like the American system.

While Puerto Rico has presidential primaries, Puerto Ricans are not permitted to vote in national elections. However, they are represented in the U.S. Congress by a resident commissioner who can sit on committes but cannot vote. Puerto Rican residents pay no Federal income tax. Certain sections of the Federal tax code, such as Section 936, the Caribbean Basin Initiative, provide economic incentives for Puerto Rican businesses.

Manufacturing is still the largest sector of the local economy. Puerto Rico is the world's largest producer of pharmaceuticals. Petrochemicals are another strong industry, as is tourism. Puerto Rico remains the banking center for most of the Caribbean.

The island's per capita income is $3,865 per annum, lower than that of any of the United States. Twenty-three percent of the work force is employed by the government, and another 23 percent is unemployed. Transfer payments from the United States to Puerto Rican citizens average about $2.5 billion yearly, about a quarter of the island's gross domestic product.

GEOGRAPHY

Puerto Rico is an island of 3,421 square miles (8,895 sq. km) facing the Atlantic on the north and the Caribbean on the south. It is the smallest of the Greater Antilles, running 100 miles (165 km) east-to-west and 35 miles (58 km) north-to-south. Three off-shore islands of significant size complete its territory: Vieques and Culebra, geologically and geographically part of the Virgin Islands; and Mona, an uninhabited islet halfway between Puerto Rico and the Dominican Republic in the Mona Passage. The Puerto Rico trench, which runs 30,000 feet (10,000 m) deep just north of the island, is the deepest part of the Atlantic.

The island itself has been described as "a mountain range surrounded by sugar cane." While this is not exactly fair, it is true that very little of the island is flat. The Cordillear Central ("central spine"), a mountain range whose peaks reach to well over 3,000 feet (1,000 m.), takes up most of the island's area and is surrounded on all sides by foothills. To the northeast, odd, haystack-shaped limestone formations make up the Karst Country, a unique and fascinating landscape of rock cones and caves.

Puerto Rico is ringed by palm-lined, white-sand beaches and by coral reefs, and is veined with rivers and streams of all sizes. The island has no natural lakes.

TIME ZONES

Puerto Rico is on Atlantic Time, an hour ahead of Eastern Standard Time, and changes to Daylight Savings Time in the American system. On the last Sunday in April, the clock is moved ahead one hour for Daylight Savings Time and on the last Sunday in October the clock is moved back one hour to return to Standard Time.

Thus, barring time adjustments in other countries, when it is 12 noon in Puerto Rico it is:

6 a.m. in Hawaii
8 a.m. in California
10 a.m. in Chicago
11 a.m. in New York, Boston and Montreal
4 p.m. in London
5 p.m. in Bonn, Madrid, Paris and Rome
7 p.m. in Athens and Cairo
8 p.m. in Moscow

9:30 p.m. in Bombay
11 p.m. in Bangkok
midnight in Singapore, Taiwan and Hong Kong
1 a.m. (the next day) in Tokyo
2 a.m. (the next day) in Sydney

CLIMATE

Puerto Rico has one of the most pleasant and unvarying climates in the world, with daily highs almost invariably at 70-85°F (21-29°C). The island is at its wettest and hottest in August, with seven inches (18 cm) the average monthly rainfall and 81°F (27°C) the average daily high. Especially during the rainy season, sudden late-afternoon squalls are not infrequent. Regional variations are noticeable: Ponce and the southern coast are generally warmer and drier than San Juan and the north. Weather is coldest in the higher altitudes of the Cordillera, where the lowest temperature in the history of the island was recorded near Barranquitas: 39°F (4°C). Some average daily high temperatures for San Juan are:

January (75°F/24°C)
February (75°F/24°C)
March (76°F/24°C)
April (78°F/26°C)
May (79°F/26°C)
June (81°F/27°C)
July (81°F/27°C)
August (81°F/27°C)
September (81°F/27°C)
October (81°F/27°C)
November (79°F/26°C)
December (77°F/25°C)

TIPPING

Puerto Rico has a service economy resembling that of the United States, and this means tipping for most services received. Follow the American rules of thumb: 15 percent in restaurants, including *fondas* and *colmados* but not including fast-food joints; 10 percent in bars; 10 -15 percent for cab-drivers, hairdressers and other services. Fifty cents per bag is a good rule for hotel porters, and a few bucks should keep the person who cleans your room happy.

WEIGHTS & MEASURES

While Puerto Rico is norminally in accord with the United States' use of English measures, most weights and measures tend to be metric. Most conspicuously, road distances are in kilometers, gasoline is sold by the liter and meats sold in kilograms. An exception is fluids. Beer is sold in unsatiating 10-ounce bottles.

BUSINESS HOURS

BANKING

Puerto Rico is the banking center of the Caribbean Basin and as such has almost all of the leading North American banks, as well as many European and native Puerto Rican ones. It's harder than one might expect in this much-touristed island to change money, especially outside of the major cities; it's probably best for foreigners to buy their traveler's checks in U.S. dollars.

Most banks are open Monday through Friday from 9 a.m. to 2:30 p.m., with some remaining open Saturday mornings.

FESTIVALS

Almost every holiday is the occasion for a festival in Puerto Rico, many of them legislated, others informal. Every town has its patron saint, and every saint his festival. These, known as *padronales*, are the biggest events of the year in their respective towns. A complete list of these would be impossible to compile, but the most famous is probably Loíza's **Fiesta de Santiago Apostol** in July. The largest is certainly San Juan's wild festival in late June.

A not-very-authentic, but somewhat interesting, year-long festival has been established by the Puerto Rican Tourism Company. The "**Le Lo Lai Festival**" is for those who happen to arrive in a bad season for real festivals, and happen to stay in hotels which participate in the Le Lo Lai program. Le Lo Lai generally involves nightly shows of Puerto Rican music and dance programs staged in hotels. Consult the Tourism Company for details.

COMMUNICATIONS

MEDIA

Puerto Ricans are avid readers of periodical literature, and the national dailies, published in San Juan, cover the entire spectrum of political opinion. Of the Spanish papers, *El Nuevo Día* is probably the most popular, a meaty tabloid with special features and book excerpts well worth the quarter. *El Reportero* is a new paper with a slap-dash look about it which nonetheless boasts some of the island's best journalists.

El Mundo competes with the *Día*. *El Vocero* is a slim paper with more local news. *Claridad*, the Communist newspaper, is provocative reading and popular among the youth of the left. *The San Juan Star*, in English, concentrates heavily on North American news and serves as a sort of Caribbean *International Herald Tribune*.

The best business magazine in this part of the world is the *Caribbean Business Review*, published in San Juan.

A host of local papers rounds off the island's periodicals. Puerto Rico produces few good magazines, but gets most of the weeklies from the United States and Spain. American newspapers are available here on the day of publication: in Spanish, *El Diario de las Americas*, published in Miami; in English, *The New York Times*, *The New York Post*, *The Washington Post* and *The Miami Herald*.

POSTAL SERVICES

Puerto Rican postal services are administered by the United States Post Office. Regulations and tariffs are the same as those on the mainland. The 1986 postage rates are as follows:

(a) letters inside the United States, or to Mexico or Canada, are 25 cents for the first ounce and 20 cents for each additional ounce;

(b) postcards inside the United States, or to Mexico or Canada, are 15 cents;

(c) surface letters to other countries are 40 cents for each of the first 2 ounces, and 13 cents for each additional ounce;

(d) airmail letters to other foreign countries are 45 cents for each half-ounce;

(e) postcards to other foreign countries are 45 cents for each half-ounce and

(f) postcards to foreign destinations are 36 cents and aerograms require 39 cents postage.

Stamps may be purchased at any post office; most are open from 8 a.m. to 5 p.m., Monday through Friday and from 8 a.m. to noon on Saturdays. Stamps may also be purchased from vending machines located in hotels, stores and airports.

The U.S. Post Office-Authorized Abbreviation for Puerto Rico is *PR*.

TELEPHONE & TELEX

Coin-operated telephones are common and cost a dime for local calls. Deposit the coin first. When you hear the dial tone, you may dial the seven-digit number. If the call is long-distance within Puerto Rico and the U.S. Virgin Islands, dial "1" before the number; for other long-distance calls, you must dial "1," then the area code, then the number. An operator will tell you how much to deposit. If you wish to place a call through an operator, simply dial "0." Directions are usually printed on the phone, and are always printed in the first pages of the phone directory.

The phone directories in Puerto Rico are in Spanish, with a special section of blue pages in English providing commercial and government telephone numbers and giving translations of the Spanish headings under which information can be found.

Telegraph facilities are available through Western Union or Telex. Western Union telegraphs and cash transfers arrive at food stores of the Pueblo chain, which is open until 11 p.m.

C A R I B B E A N

Tropical dream destinations.
The Lesser Antilles, a chain of 20 major
islands and countless smaller isles, extend
south from the Virgin Islands to
Trinidad.
They have more to offer
than beaches,
palms and island-
hopping cruises,
including Indian, African
and European ingredients,
a remarkable heritage and
cultural creativity.
Is it really better in the
Bahamas? Where do you
find the beautiful pink
beaches of Bermuda or
the epitome of island magic in Jamaica —
an inn serving rum punch, among scented
jasmine above secluded sands?
Insight Guides *provide the answers.*

WE'LL BE SEEING YOU AGAIN!

Bahamas
Barbados
Bermuda
Caribbean
Jamaica
Puerto Rico
Trinidad & Tobago

A P A
INSIGHT
GUIDES

EMERGENCIES

SECURITY & CRIME

Puerto Rico is not as crime-ridden as other Caribbean islands, nor as dangerous as certain areas of the United States. Nonetheless, it is a place with a high unemployment rate and a tourist population which is often gullible and vulnerable. Travelers would be wise to take certain precautions.

Petty theft and confidence scams are more prevalent in Puerto Rico than violent crimes. Always lock your rooms, especially in smaller lodgings. Never leave luggage unattended or out of sight. Most hotels will store bags at the front desk, as will many restaurants and shops. Never leave valuables in your room. If possible, leave your room key at the front desk when you leave your hotel or guest house for any length of time.

Always lock automobiles, regardless of whether you have left any valuables inside, as the car radios which come with most rentals are extremely valuable, easily saleable and much coveted by thieves.

As traveler's checks are accepted all over Puerto Rico, there is no reason to carry more than the cash you need.

MEDICAL SERVICES

Puerto Rico's health care resembles that of the United States in that is has no *de jure* national health service, and in that the sick are cared for on a pay-as-you-go basis. In practice, however, Puerto Rico's health care is administered on a far more lenient basis than in the United States. Fees are in general much cheaper, and the fact that many Puerto Ricans receive treatment under insurance policies means that being hospitalized for injury is far less of a financial nightmare than it is in the continental U.S.

Certain minor emergency hospitalizations (cuts, bruises, fatigue, sunburn, etc.) can cost as little as $10. Ambulances are always under $100. Most hospitals have 24-hour emergency rooms, but, if possible, check the yellow pages under *Servicio Emergencia de Hospitales*.

Puerto Rico is full of competent medical professionals. If you could choose where to fall ill, you'd doubtless choose San Juan, as the number of universities and clinics there make it full of doctors and medical personnel. Still, facilities in other areas of the island, though often old and disheartening, are generally run by physicians as capable and concerned as any in the Caribbean.

Below are listed some of the larger hospitals with emergency rooms and some of the more popular (not necessarily 24-hour) drugstores in San Juan. For listings in provincial cities, check the yellow pages.

HOSPITALS

Ashford Memorial Community Hospital
Tel: 721-2160.

De Diego Hospital
310 De Diego Ave., Stop 22, Santurce
Tel: 721-8181.

Hospital Nuestra Senora de Guadelupe
435 Ponce de Leon, Hato Rey
Tel: 754-0909.

Metropolitan Hospital
1785 Carr. 21, Las Lomas, P.V., Río Piedras
Tel: 783-6200.

Ophthalmic Institute of Puerto Rico, Inc.
160 Ponce de Leon, Old San Juan
Tel: 724-3164.

San Martin Hospital
371 De Diego, Río Piedras
Tel: 767-5100.

PHARMACIES

Farmacías El Amal
617 Europa, Santurce
Tel: 728-1760.

Farmacías Moscoso
Arzuaga Fte Plaza Street, Ri Piedras
Tel: 753-1394.

Walgreens

1130 Ashford Ave., Condado
Tel: 725-1510.

Mayagüez

Walgreens
Mayagüez Mall
Tel: 832-2072.

Ponce

Seedman's
Centro del Sur Shopping Center
Tel: 840-7878.

Special Considerations: Puerto Rico has few of the dangerous bacteria and diseases that plague other semi-tropical areas, but one deserves special mention. Almost all of the island's rivers are infected with the bacteria "*chisto*," which can cause severe damage to internal organs over the years. Some say that river water is safe to drink and swim in on the upper altitudes of mountains, provided it is running swiftly, but this guide does not recommend it. Drinking water is safe.

USEFUL TELEPHONE NUMBERS

San Juan

Police
Tel: 724-0935.

Fire
Tel: 722-1120.

Ambulance
Tel: 751-6868.

Medical Center of Puerto Rico
Tel: 754-3535.

Assist (for medical emergencies)
Tel: 343-2222.

Coast Guard
Tel: 729-6870.

Rape Hotline
Tel: 765-2285.

Poison Treatment Center
Tel: 754-8536.

American Red Cross
Tel: 758-8150.

GETTING AROUND

DOMESTIC TRAVEL

By Air: Puerto Rico is dotted with airports. While most international and many domestic flights to San Juan use **Muñoz Marín Airport** in Isla Verde, many others use San Juan's second airport, **Isla Grande**, just across an estuary south of Puerta de Tierra. Ponce and Mayaguex have modern, if small airports which give residents 20-minute access to the capital. Also, part of Ramey Air Force Base near Aguadilla has been converted to a civilian airport which serves domestic flights as well as charters and some international flights from Canada. Dorado, only a 45-minute drive west of San Juan, has an airport which services its resorts. Vieques has a fine airport, and the Vieques Air Link, which leaves Isla Grande and costs only $25 each way, is a pleasurable means of getting to and from that charming island.

Small planes can be chartered at Isla Grande Airport.

By Bus: Bus service, both local and long-distance, is extensive in Puerto Rico. Among the cheapest ways to travel is by Puerto Rico Motor Coach, with its $6 bus service from San Juan to Mayagüez. Buses leave every two hours between 6 a.m. and 6 p.m. More information at Tel: 725-2460.

Puerto Rico's major cities are linked by *públicos*, small modern vans which assemble at informal stands all over San Juan and in pre-established locations in the smaller cities. *Públicos* are very cheap and comfortable, probably the best alternative to having one's own car. San Juan, Ponce and Mayagüez have very efficient local bus services. In San Juan, fares for all rides are $.25. Buses can be hailed at signs reading "*Parada de Guaguas*."

TOUR COMPANIES

Borínquen Tours
Tel: 725-4990, 725-2460.

Fuentes Bus Line
Tel: 780-7070.

Gray Line Sightseeing Tours
Tel: 727-8080.

United Tour Guides
Tel: 721-3000 ext 2597.

WATER TRANSPORT

As Puerto Rico is fairly rectangular in shape, with few awkward peninsulas and bays, it lacks the extensive water transportation networks of other islands in the Caribbean. There are some exceptions: the ferry from the tourist piers of San Juan to Catano, a mile across San Juan Bay, is a time-saver and, at a $.10 a ride, a real bargain. Ferries leave the docks at Fajardo twice daily (9:15 a.m. and 4:30 p.m.) for Vieques; fare $2 each way. Ferries from Fajardo to Culebra leave 4 p.m. Monday through Saturday with a 9 a.m. boat Sundays, Saturdays and holidays; fare $2.25. Boats can be chartered in Mayagüez for the arduous 45-mile trip to the Isle of Mona.

PRIVATE TRANSPORT

CAR RENTAL

Puerto Rico has one of the highest per capita rates of car ownership in the Americas, and an automobile is a necessity for anyone who wants to see the island extensively. Puerto Rico therefore has an inordinately high concentration of car rental dealerships. A complete listing can be found by looking in the local yellow pages under *Automóvilesl Alquiler*. Avis, Budget, Hertz and National rental offices are located in the arrival terminal at Muñoz Marín Airport; others are a short shuttle-bus trip away. Basic charges range from $25 to $55 per day, usually with unlimited mileage. Smaller companies often have excellent automobiles and are less ex-

pensive. Insurance is usually an extra $6-7 per day for full coverage; be sure to get it, and check the terms of the coverage before signing anything.

Most rental agencies require that you be at least 21 years old and carry a major credit card. Some will take a large cash deposit in lieu of the card. Foreign drivers may need to produce an international driver's license or license from their home country. U.S. licenses are valid in Puerto Rico.

AAA
Isla Verde
Tel: 791-1465.

Atlantic
Santurce, Tel: 721-3811;
Aguadilla, Tel: 890-8181.

Avis
Tel: (800) 331-1212.
Isla Verde (airport), Tel: 791-2500;
Mayagüez, Tel: 833-7070;
Ponce, Tel: 848-4188.

Bargain
San Juan
Tel: 725-5350.

Budget
Condado, Tel: 725-1182;
Hato Rey, Tel: 751-4330;
Dorado, Tel: 796-6404.

Hertz
Tel: (800) 654-3131;
Condado, Tel: 725-2027;
Isla Verde (airport), Tel: 791-0840;
Puerta de Tierra, Tel: 721-0303;
Ponce (airport), Tel: 842-7377;
Mayagüez (airport), Tel: 832-3314.

Thrifty
Isla Verde (airport)
Tel: 791-4241.

National
San Juan
Tel: 791-1805.

Motoring Advisories: Speed limits are not often posted in Puerto Rico. They're listed in miles, paradoxically – distance signs are in kilometers. The speed limit on the San

Juan-Ponce *autopista* is 70 m.p.h. (115 k.p.h.). Limits elsewhere are far lower, especially in residential areas, where speed-bumps (*lomos*), provide a natural barrier to excess.

Puerto Rico's older coastal highways take efficient routes but can be slow going, due to never-ending traffic lights. Roads in the interior are narrow, tortuous, ill-paved, and always dangerous. Often, they run along dizzying cliffsides. Frequent landslides mean that roads often wash out. Slow down if you see a sign reading *Desprendimiento* ("Landslide"). *Desvio* means "detour" and *Carretera Cerrada* means "Road Closed." You'll see plenty of these signs on a trip through the beautiful country roads of the Cordillera. Neither hitchhiking nor picking up hitchhikers is advised.

WHERE TO STAY

Puerto Rico has a range of accommodations unusual for a Caribbean island which draws droves of tourists. As one would expect, big resorts set the tone. Still, guest houses, beach houses, grand hotels, flophouses and camping grounds, as well as a host of less conventional settings round out an encouraging, if expensive lodging situation.

Puerto Rico's big resorts are of two types. The first comprises richly accourted, beautifully landscaped beachfront resorts, probably best typified by the **Caribe Hilton**, grandaddy of the tropical Hiltons, in Puerta de Tierra; the **Hyatt Regency Cerromar**, a Rockefeller financed resort just west of San Juan in Dorado; the lavish **Mayagüez Hilton**; and Humacao's famous **Palmas del Mar**. These tend to have casinos and several bars. Except for the Carbie Hilton, all have beautifully groomed golf courses. Each is characterized by big swimming pools, excellent facilities for tennis and exercise and long stretches of lovely beachfront. Another thing these places have in common is that you won't be able to get into them for less than $100 per night.

The second tier of resort hotels are somewhat less lavish, may lack casinos and tend to be about half as expensive as the others. These are typified by the big, white high-rises of San Juan's Condado and Isla Verde areas. They tend to cater less exclusively to holiday-makers and draw a more diverse crowd of guests. Many of these are businessmen, and the Condado hotels in particular have made great efforts over the past several years to draw conventions, especially since the completion of the multi-million-dollar **San Juan Convention Center**.

Guest houses are perhaps the most pleasant lodging option. These tend to be smaller and more intimate than the resorts, averaging around a dozen rooms. Many of them are on beaches and offer the guest the opportunity to walk across the patio, not a check-out lobby, to his morning swim. About half of these have bars; almost all of them have pools.

There are a certain number of run-down, sleazy hotels, most of them in major cities, which have gone to seed and tend to be full of bugs and dirt. They don't have bars. They're not air-conditioned. They tend to stay in business by boarding illegal immigrants and state-supported residents. They're extremely cheap, however, some of them as low as $10 per night, and the real budget tourist may be persuaded to brave the bugs.

The one unique lodging option Puerto Rico offers is the *parador*. These state-run country farmhouses, often an old coffee or sugar *haciendas*, offer the authentic ambience of Puerto Rican rural life. Beautiful old furniture, elegant dining facilities and the opportunity – at some – to pick one's own food for dessert make these well worth trying for those who prefer to see a Puerto Rico that won't remind one of Nice or Miami Beach. These run between $25-$50, about the same as guest houses.

SAN JUAN

Old San Juan

El Convento
100 Cristo St.
Tel: 723-9020.
Elegant, old-world grand hotel with spacious,

tasteful rooms and picturesque location. Big central patio. 100 rooms. $85-$125.

Puerta de Tierra

Caribe Hilton
Fort San Gerónimo
Tel: 721-0303.
Oldest and most venerable of the Caribe hotels. A luxury ensemble of restaurants bars and pools with a lovely sweep bayfront beach. And even a 17th-Century fort. 707 rooms. $150-$225.

Condado and Ocean Park

Atlantic Beach Hotel
1 Vendig St., Condado
Tel: 721-6900.
38 rooms. $38-$65.

Arcade Inn
8 Taft St., Ocean Park
Tel: 725-0668.
19 rooms. $26-$40.

The Beach House
1957 Italia St., Ocean Park
Tel: 727-4495.
Highly "alternative" clientele. 8 rooms. $40-$70.

Canario
1317 Ashford Ave., Condado
Tel: 722-3861.
Bed and breakfast-style guesthouse with large pool and sun decks. 25 rooms. $50-$60.

Canario By The Sea
4 Condado St., Condado
Tel: 722-8640.
Around the corner from the above establishment, with similar service and a beach instead of a pool. 25 rooms. $50-$60.

La Concha Hotel
Ashford Avenue, Condado
Tel: 721-6090.
Mammoth hotel with tennis courts and excellent restaurant. 234 rooms. $105-$175.

Condado Beach Hotel
Ashford Avenue, Condado
Tel: 721-6090.
Big hotel with casino. 251 rooms. $120-$210.

Condado Lagoon Hotel
6 Clemenceau St., Condado
Tel: 721-0170.
Medium sized hotel with pool. Near Ashford, right in the middle of things. 44 rooms. $85-$110.

Condado Plaza Hotel
999 Ashford Ave., Condado
Tel: 721-1000.
The biggest hotel on the Ashford strip, with facilities and prices to match. Casino. 587 rooms. $170-$215.

Condesa
2071 Cacique St., Condado
Tel: 727-3900.
Small bed and breakfast with pool and sundeck. 15 rooms. $42-$54.

Dutch Inn
55 Condado St., Condado
Tel: 721-0810.
A big, old Condado hotel with the feel of a guest house. 144 rooms. $85-$105.

Hosteria del Mar
5 Cervantes St., Condado
Tel: 724-8203.
A small, 15-room guest house in a big-hotel area. Good vegetarian restaurant. No Pool. $35-$115.

Howard Johnson's
1369 Ashford Ave., Condado
Tel: 721-7300.
What you'd expect from a HoJo's: big, full facilities, on the Condado's main drag. 150 rooms. $112-$132.

Jewel's by the Sea
1125 Seaview, Condado
Tel: 725-5313.
Tiny little guesthouse with sundeck. 8 rooms. $30-$60.

Número Uno
1 Santa Ana St., Ocean Park
Tel: 727-9687.
Small and comfortable, close to the beach, with pool, bar. 7 rooms. $40-$70.

The Portal
76 Condado St., Condado
Tel: 721-9010.

No pool, but a good hotel bargain for the neighborhood. 48 rooms. $65-$85.

El Prado Inn
1350 Luchetti St., Condado
Tel: 728-5925.
Bed and breakfast, convenient to park and beaches. 18 rooms. $40-$55.

Ramada Inn
1045 Ashford Ave., Condado
Tel: 724-5657.
Part of the chain, with gambling and good beach and bar access. 96 rooms. $135-$190.

Tanama Hotel
1 Joffre St., Condado
Tel: 724-4160. Modest hotel, with good pool and sundeck. 95 rooms. $35-$55.

Miramar

Excelsior
801 Ponce de Leon
Tel: 721-7400.
Big hotel in a busy part of town, with pool and cocktail lounge. 140 rooms. $71-$92.

Quality Royale
600 Fernández Juncos
Tel: 721-4100.
Miramar's only hotel with gambling, and perhaps its nicest. 155 rooms. $90-$100.

Santurce

Hotel Pierre
105 De Diego Ave.
Tel: 721-1200.
A big hotel with pool, right by the major highways. Convenient for business stays. 184 rooms. $75-$95.

Isla Verde

Carib Inn
Route 187
Tel: 791-3535.
A big hotel with a pool and a top-notch casino. 225 rooms. $80-$105.

Don Pedro Hotel
4 Rosa St.
Tel: 791-2838.
Pleasant and near the sea. 16 rooms. $32-$36.

Empress Oceanfront
2 Amapola St.
Tel: 791-3080.
Intimate for a luxury hotel. 30 rooms. $110-$160.

ESJ Towers
Route 37
Tel: 791-5151.
A mammoth, well-accoutred hotel, with big pool. 319 rooms. $140-$205.

Greem Isla Inn
1-36, Villmar St.
Tel: 726-4330.
Pleasant guest house with air-conditioned units, pool, laundry facilities, amenities and beach frontage on the pretty western edge of Isla Verde. Bilingual staff. 16 rooms. $41-$55.

International Airport Hotel
Tel: 791-1700.
Not much, but good value if you're stuck at Muñoz Marin. 57 rooms. $45-$51.

Mario's
2 Rosa St.
Tel: 791-3748.
Inexpensive and near the water. 59 rooms. $40-$45.

The Palace
Route 37
Tel: 791-2020.
Queen of the big Isla Verde luxury hotels, with gambling galore. 450 rooms. $115-$210.

Travel Lodge
Route 37
Tel: 728-1300.
Quiet, with pool restaurant and bar. Convenient to both town and airport. 91 rooms. $85-$110.

OUT ON THE ISLAND

The Northeast

Family Guesthouse
Route 987, Fajardo
Tel: 863-1193.
Modest guesthouse with bar. Fairly convenient to marinas. 12 rooms. $27.

Hotel Delícias
Puerto Real, Fajardo
Tel: 863-1818.
A good bet, with a restaurant and bar. 20 rooms. $25-$50.

Parador Martorell
6A Ocean Dr. Luquillo
Tel: 889-2710.
Smallest of the *paradores*, and among the msot popular. 7 rooms. $35-$50.

Culebra

Posada la Hamaca
68 Castelar St.
Tel: 742-3516.
Tiny, basic and decent. 6 rooms. $20-$25.

Seafarer's Inn
6 Pedro Márquez St.
Tel: 742-3171.
Guest house near the water, convenient to rental facilities. 11 rooms. $15-$30.

Vieques

Banana's
Flamboyán, Esperanza
Tel: 741-8700.
A pleasant, open-to-the-elements guesthouse in a nice part of the island.

Casa del Francás
Esperanza
Tel: 741-3751.
Quite simply the best place to stay in all of Puerto Rico. $55-$69.

Ocean View Hotel
Plinio Peterson Street
Tel: 741-3696.
Largest hotel in the offshore islands, with moderate prices. 32 rooms. $17-$32.

Sea Gate Guest Hotel
Barriada Fuerte
Tel: 741-4661.
On the pleasant end of the guest-house scale, with rural prices. 16 rooms. $35-$45.

The Northwest

Hyatt Dorado Beach Hotel
Route 693, km. 10.8, Dorado
Tel: 796-1600.
You don't get much more luxurious than this. Golf, tennis, swimming, gambling in the poshest and most beautiful of natural surroundings. 308 rooms. $263-$550 (sic).

Hyatt Regency Cerromar
Route 693, km. 12, Dorado
Tel: 796-1010.
More incredible luxury in a larger complex a mile down the road from the above listing. 508 rooms. $175-$450.

Parador Guajataca
Route 2, Quebradillas
Tel: 895-3070.
Good country parador, if expensive. Near to the sea, but convenient to mountain and karstic hikes. 38 rooms. $52-$63.

Parador Montemar
Route 107, Aguadilla
Tel: 891-5959.

Parador Vistamar
Route 113, km. 7.9, Quebradillas
Tel: 895-2065.
Less rural than Parador Guajataca, but closer to the sea. 36 rooms. $37-$47.

Villa Antonio
Route 115, km. 12.3, Rincón
Tel: 823-2645.
Pool and tennis, near surfing. 53 rooms. $32-$40.

Villa Cofresí
Route 115, km. 12.3, Rincón
Tel: 823-2450.
Right by the above. A little more upmarket, but no tennis. 59 rooms. $40-$75.

The Cordillera

Parador Baños de Coamo
Route 546, km. 1, Coamo,
Tel: 825-2186.
The best way to see the famed baths. One of the island's nicest paradors. 48 rooms. $35-440.

Parador Hacienda Gripiñas
Route 527, km. 2.5, Jayuya
Tel: 721-2884.
Remote even for a parador, on a plantation in the heart of Puerto Rico's coffee country. 19 rooms. $25-$36.

Parador Hacienda Juanita
Route 105, km. 23.5, Maricao.
One of the best *paradores*. Fresh fruit for dinner. Beautiful, old-fashioned furnishings. 21 rooms. $25-$30.

The South Coast

Caribe Playa
Route 3, km. 112, Patillas.
A real find, convenient to water and other sports at good prices. 36 rooms. $36-$54.

El Coche
Route 14, Ponce
Tel: 842-9607.
Basic.

Holiday Inn
Route 2, km. 255, Ponce
Tel: 844-1200.
Biggest and best hotel in Ponce. Good-size pool. 120 rooms $85-$115.

Hotel Melia
2 Cristina St.
Ponce
Tel: 842-0261.

Palmas del Mar
Route 923, Humacao
Tel: 852-6000.
With the possible exception of the Dorado resorts, the great retreat of the rich in Puerto Rico. Unmatched gambling and golfing. $95-$115.

The Southwest

Boqueron Hotel
Route 101, Cabo Rojo
Tel: 851-2518.
Excellent hotel value. Convenient to beach, with pool. 41 rooms. $31-$50.

El Combate
First, El Combate
Tel: 745-0308.
Very basic guest house. No pool. 17 rooms. $30-$55.

Copamarina Hotel
Route 333, Guanica
Tel: 842-8300.
Fairly large, full-facility (pool, restaurant, bar, etc.) hotel near the site of the first U.S. landing in Puerto Rico. 72 rooms. $44-$52.

Cuestamar
Route 307, km. 7.4, Cabo Rojo
Tel: 851-2819.
Good hotel with small pool. $40-$45.

Mayaguex Hilton
Route 2, km. 153, Mayagüez
Tel: 834-7575.
Tres cher, but the best in the west, with a huge pool and prices to match. 145 rooms. $96-$139.

Palma Hotel
Méndez Vigo Street, Mayagüez
Tel: 834-3800.
The urban Mayagüez experience. 47 rooms. $28-$45.

Parador Oasis
Luna Street, San German
Tel: 892-1175.
Great spot for a parador. 22 rooms. $35-$39.

Parador Villa Parguera
Route 304, Lajas
Tel: 899-3975.

Perichi's Beach Colony
Route 102, Cabo Rojo
Tel: 851-3131.
Small and close to the beach. 15 rooms. $35-$39.

Viento y Vela
Route 304, Lajas
Tel: 899-3030.
Guesthouse with pool. Convenient to Phosphorescent Bay.

FOOD DIGEST

WHAT TO EAT

Aside from having a delectable and historic native cuisine, Puerto Rico benefits from its American and Caribbean connections in having just about all the "ethnic" cuisines you'd find in the largest cities of the United States. Especially in San Juan, Spanish, U.S., Mexican, Chinese, French, Swiss, Brazilian, Japanese and other food is plentiful.

Puerto Rican cuisine differs from that of its Spanish neighbors in the Caribbean almost as much as it differs from that of the mainland U.S. Relying heavily on beans, rice and whatever Puerto Ricans haul out of the sea, it is a mild, filling, well-balanced style of cookery. See the feature on Puerto Rican Cuisine for all the saucy details.

WHERE TO EAT

You can get Puerto Rican food in all manner of spots, ranging from modest urban *fondas*, where a rich *asopao de camarrones* will run you under five bucks; to the rural *colmados* where roast chicken is the order of the day; to the posh restaurants of Old San Juan and the Condado, such as **La Mallorquina**, the Caribbean's oldest continuously operating restaurant. The restaurants of San Juan tend to be concentrated in certain areas.

While fondas are all over town, European cuisine tends to be concentrated in the trendier parts of Old San Juan and in the more expensive areas of the Condado and Santurce, such as Ashford Avenue. American fast food joints are in the Condado and the modern shopping malls in Caroline and Hato Rey. Bars are everywhere.

SAN JUAN

Old San Juan

The Butterfly People
152 Fortaleza St.
Tel: 723-2432
Steaks, omelettes in a quichery atmosphere.

La Chaumiere
367 Tetuán St.
Tel: 722-3330.
Top-notch French place and atmosphere with creperie upstairs.

Friquitín Kruhigger
San José Street
Dominican fast-food, delicious, unusual and cheap. Order the *tiburón* (shark) sandwich.

La Mallorquina
207 San Justo St.
Tel: 722-3261.
Oldest restaurant in the Caribbean. Very old-world, with a first-rate *asopao* and an unsurpassable flan for dessert.

El Méson Vasco
47 Cristo St.
Tel: 725-7819.
Interesting Basque food, with a view of the Plaza San José.

El Patio de Sam
102 San Sebastián St.
Tel: 723-1149.
A San Juan institution, with magnificient steak sandwiches and generous and knowledgeable bartenders.

Tetuán 20
20 Tetuán St.
Tel: 722-5330.
The name might not be too imaginative, but the Puerto Rican specialties are.

La Zaragozana
356 San Francisco St.
Tel: 723-5103.
Spanish and other continental specialties.

Puerta de Tierra

Escambrón Beach Club
Muñoz Rivera Avenue
Tel: 722-4785.
Puerto Rican food.

Tasca
54 Muñoz Rivera Ave.
Tel: 722-2410.
Seafood in a pleasant ambience.

Condado

The Chart House
1214 Ashford Ave.
Tel: 728-0110.
Delectable seafood dinners from all over. Glamarous, if expensive, deck for drinks and food.

Escargot
1106 Magdalena St.
Tel: 722-2436.
Probably the best restaurant in San Juan. French delicacies in an intimate, unpretentious atmosphere.

Lotus Flower
999 Ashford Ave.
721-1000 (ext 1950).
The best Chinese restaurant in San Juan, in the Condado Plaza Hotel.

Maison Bleue
1108 Magdalena St.
Tel: 725-9505.
French.

Mama's Little Italy
1157, Ashford Ave.
Tel: 722-2021.
Oldest Italian restaurant in San Juan. A place for table wine and rollicking good times.

Scotch & Sirloin
1020 Ashford Ave.
Tel: 722-3640.
Great steaks and a formidable wine list. Outdoor patio. As the advertisement says, "The only thing we overlook is the lagoon."

Santurce

Heidelberg Haus
361 De Diego Ave.
Tel: 723-0803.
One of the older San Juan gringo hangouts with a pleasant, if expensive, bar.

Swiss Chalet
105 De Diego Ave.
Tel: 721-2233.
Another oldie, with excellent American-style food.

Isla Verde

Cousin Ho's
Carib-Inn Hotel, Route 187
Tel: 791-3535.
Terrific Chinese food of all descriptions.

OUT ON THE ISLAND

Arecibo

El Gran Café
Route 2
Tel: 879-5151.
Local and international specialties in an unpretentious setting.

Cabo Rojo

El Bonío
Route 102, km. 13.9
Tel: 851-2755.
Some of Cabo Rojo's best seafood.

Catano

Riomar
56 Carmen St.
Tel: 788-2225.
Excellent seafood in an area that is full of the stuff. A ferry trip from Old San Juan.

Humacao

Tulio's Seafood
1 Aduana
Tel: 852-5471.
Acclaimed food *outside* of Palmas del Mar.

Mayagüez

Méson Español
Route 102, km. 5
Tel: 833-5445.
Good Spanish cuisine in the oddest place.

Dug Out
In the Palma Hote, Méndez Vigo Street
Tel: 834-3800.
Puerto Rican food in a homey place right in
the middle of things.

Ponce

Lydia's
Ramal 52, Los Caobos
Tel: 844-3933.
Ponce's best seafood offerings.

Salinas

Greco
25 A St.
Tel: 824-2245.
Capital of a booming city filled with seafood
restaurants.

CULTURE PLUS

MUSEUMS

Casa del Libro
255 Cristo St., Old San Juan
Tel: 723-0354.
A beautiful collection of old manuscripts and
documents dating from the days of San Juan's
founding, as well as some of Puerto Rico's
best modern graphic work, in a charming,
cool old house. Open: 11 a.m. to 4.30 p.m.
Monday to Friday; Admission: free.

Casa del Callejón
Callejon de la Capilla and Fortaleza Street,
Old San Juan
Tel: 721-1689.

Museum of Fine Arts
253 Cristo St., Old San Juan
Tel: 724-5998.
A huge disappointment, with only second-
rate modern exhibits usually on display in
one small room. Open: 9 a.m. to noon and 1
p.m. to 4 p.m. daily except Monday and
Thursday; Admission: free.

Museum of Fine Arts
Las Americas Ave. Ponce
Tel: 848-0505.
An art museum of staggering scope and
beauty, with major works of many of the
great figures of European art. Excellent works
from Rubens, Van Dyck, Gainesborough
and others in a visionary building of hexagonal rooms designed by Edward Durell Stone.
Open: 10 a.m. to noon and 1 p.m. to 4 p.m.
Monday to Friday, 10 a.m. to 4 p.m. Saturday, 10 a.m. to 5 p.m. Sunday; Admission:
Adults $2, children $1.50.

Museum of the Seas
Pier One, Old San Juan
Tel: 725-2532.
Lots of maritime tools and exhibits, as well
as maps, from the Age of Sail: Open: when
cruise ships dock; Admission: free.

Pablo Casals Museum
101 San Sebastián St., Old San Juan
Tel: 723-9185.
A tiny, innovative museum crammed with
memorabilia of the great cellist who made
Puerto Rico his home. Highlights include
manuscripts and mementos of Casals's in-
volvement with the United Nations.
Videotapes of Casals concerts played on
request. Open: 9 a.m. to 5 p.m. Tuesday to
Saturday, 1 p.m. to 4 p.m. Sunday; Admission: free.

Pharmacy Museum
Casa de los Contrafuertes, Old San Juan
Tel: 724-5998.
A 19th-Century pharmacy reassembled in
the oldest house in the city. Open: 9 a.m. to
noon, 1 p.m. to 4.30 p.m. except Monday;
Admission: free.

San Juan Museum of Art and History
Norzagaray Street, Old San Juan
Tel: 724-1875.
At two rooms, tinier than this city deserves,

but a good primer on the relationship between the creative arts and the development of the city. Open: 8 a.m. to noon, 1 p.m. to 4 p.m. Monday to Friday; Admission: free.

Tibes Indian Ceremonial Center
Route 503, Km. 2.7, Tibes
Tel: 840-2255.
A 1,500-year-old Taino village excavated in 1975 remarkably intact, with plazas, *bateyes*, and a rock ring possibly used as an astronomical observatory. Informative guides and museum. Open: 9 a.m. to 4.30 p.m. except Monday; Admission: Adults $1, children $.50.

ART GALLERIES

Almost all of Puerto Ricos' cities and their native crafts, from Aguadillan lace to Loizan vejigante masks, but an art "scene," as understood in New York, exists only in San Juan. Here, the combination of a radiant light and an active network of patronage have worked to draw most of the finest painters of Puerto Rico and many from North America and Europe. Sculpture thrives, as do the crafts of Puerto Rico and other Latin-American nations. Most galleries hare huddled together on a few of Old San Juan's streets, but you'll find plenty of pleasant surprises in San Juan's other neighborhoods and even out on the island. Here are some of the better spots in the metropolitan area:

Art Students League
San José Street, Old San Juan
Tel: 722-4468.
A small, changing display of some of San Juan's up and coming artist, with a tendency towards the vanguard and the experimental. Open: 8 a.m. to 4 p.m. Monday to Saturday.

Casa Candina
14 Candina St., Condado
Tel: 724-2077.
The ceramics capital of the island, with some truly first-rate paintings and sculpture exhibits, in a shady, porch-ringed building remote from the bustle of nearby Ashford Avenue. Offers ceramics classes. Open: 9 a.m. to 5 p.m. Monday to Saturday.

Galería Diego
51 Maria Moczo St., Ocean Park
Tel: 728-1287.
Changing exhibits of local painting and sculpture. Open: 10 a.m. to 6 p.m. Monday to Friday, until 9 p.m. on Thursday, and 10 a.m. to 1 p.m. Saturday.

Galería Labiosa
312 San Franciso St., Old San Juan
Tel: 721-2848.
Paintings and sculpture. Open: 9.30 a.m. to 5 p.m. Monday to Saturday.

Galería Palomas
207 Cristo St., Old San Juan
Tel: 724-8904.
A fine collection of Puerto Rican paintings and graphic design. Open: 10 a.m. to 6 p.m. Monday to Saturday.

Galería San Juan
204-206 Norzagaray St., Old San Juan
Tel: 722-1808.
A sizable changing collection of fine paintings in an elegant, old building. Work has a tendency away from the abstract. Open: 10 a.m. to 5 p.m. Tuesday to Saturday.

Galerías Botello
208 Cristo St., Old San Juan
Tel: 723-9987.
Fine Haitian paintings, among other things, in an artist-operated gallery. Open: 10 a.m. to 6 p.m. Monday to Saturday.

CONCERTS

The San Juan Symphony Orchestra has progressed in a few short years to a position of great respectability. Frequent concerts are held in the Fine Arts Center Festival Hall, known locally as the *"Bellas Artes,"* in Santurce. Chamber music ensembles are numerous at the university and among private concert-givers. The highlight of the classical music year comes in early June, when the San Juan Symphony's performances at Bellas Artes are complemented by guest appearances from musicians from around the world, some of them as renowned as Emmanuel Ax and Maxim Shostakovich.

BALLETS

There are plenty of opportunities to see ballet in San Juan. The Friends of San Juan Ballet periodically host performances with the Symphony Orchestra at Bellas Artes. The San Juan City Ballet are frequent performers at the restored Tapia y Rivera Theater in Old San Juan, and give matinee performances. Rounding out dance offerings are the modern dance shows given at the Julia de Burgos Amphitheater in Río Piedras as part of the UPR Cultural Activities.

LIBRARIES

Puerto Rico is not long on public libraries; most are in universities and private foundations, and much exchange of books rests on person-to-person lending. Here are a few exceptions;

Ateneo Puertorriqueño
Ponce de Leon, Stop 2, Puerta de Tierra
Tel: 722-4839.

Volunteer Library League
250 Ponce de Leon, Santurce
Tel: 725-7672.

MOVIES

Puerto Rico is woefully understocked with movie theaters, even in San Juan. A handful in Santurce show first-runs and oldies, but it's best to look them up in the phone directory under "*Cínemas*" to find out what's playing on the day.

Good films can be seen at unexpected places, however. The Amphitheaters at the University of Puerto Rico show frequent art films, especially in the UPR Cultural Activities series, whose showings are at 5 p.m. and 8 p.m. every Tuesday. For more information, call 764-0000, ext 2563.

NIGHTLIFE

The nightlife of Puerto Rico ranges from the tranquility of coffee and conversation to the steamy, fast-lane excesses of San Juan's clubs. On cool nights in the Cordillera, nightlife resembles what one assumes Puerto Ricans have enjoyed for decades, if not centuries. Townspeople gather round local plazas and sing to the accompaniment of guitars, finding time between tunes for a couple of sips of Corona or Bacardi.

San Juan duplicates much of this rural nightlife – on weekends in the old city, youths of high school and college age mill about the Plaza San José by the hundreds, stopping into bars and restaurants and coffee houses, and trying to get groups together to go dancing.

But in San Juan and other cities, partying is in general taken with more reckless abandon. The whole city is crowded with bars and dancing establishments of all description. In Old San Juan, **El Batey**, **Los Hijos de Borínquen** and **El Patio de Sam** provide good spots for drinking and talk. In Santurce, **Shannon's** is crowded with hard-drinking, hard-rocking *norteamericanos*. **Neon's** in Old San Juan is a loud, video-oriented dance joint, while **Juliana's** in the Caribe Hilton caters to a more suit-and-tie-oriented crowd. Those who wish to opt out of such hedonism would do well to sip a cup of coffee in one of Old San Juan's finer establishments, like the **Café-Bar 1897**, where you can hear jazz and salsa as well.

NIGHTSPOTS

El Batey
Cristo Steet, Old San Juan
Tel: 721-0303.
Best bar on the island. Small, loud, great juke-box. Open until 6 a.m.

Isadora's Discotheque
Holiday Inn, 999 Ashford Ave., Condado
Tel: 721-1000.
Busy, late night, singles scene hangout.

The Jazz Museum
107 San José St., Old San Juan.
Tel: 268-0019.
Drinks, nightly jazz.

Juliana's Disco
Caribe Hilton, Puerta de Tierra
Old San Juan
Tel: 721-0303.
Renowned, if not always hopping, disco.
Bring a tie and money.

Maria's
204 Cristo St., Old San Juan.
Singles' bar.

Neon's
Tanca St., Old San Juan.
Wild, young people's disco. Video. Expensive drinks.

The Palace
Route 187, Isla Verde
Tel: 791-2020.
Variety of lounges and floor-shows.

1919 Lounge
Condado Beach Hotel, Condado
Tel: 725-2302.
Ritzy piano bar. Open until 3 a.m.

The Place
154 Fortaleza St., Old San Juan
Tel: 724-1923.
Jazz sessions nightly after 9 in a big room with streetfront porches.

Shannon's
De Diego and Loíza streets, Santurce.
San Juan's Irish bar, with two pool tables and nightly hard rock live. Air-conditioned ice cold.

Small World
San José Street, Old San Juan.
Expats' drinking hangout.

Zanzibar Lounge
Dupont Plaza, 1309 Ashford Ave., Condado
Tel: 724-5657.
Dancing and music nightly.

GAMBLING

Gambling, illegal in all but two of the United States, is legal in Puerto Rico. Casinos offer blackjack, roulette, poker, slot machines and all manner of games of chance. Casinos are permitted only in hotels, and tend to be open from mid-evening until early morning. Jackets and ties are often mandatory. The following hotels have casinos:

San Juan

Caribe Hilton, Puerta de Tierra.
Caribe Inn, Isla Verde.
Condado Beach, Condado.
Condado Plaza, Condado.
Palace, Isla Verde.
Quality Royale, Miramar.
Ramada, Condado.

Dorado

Hyatt Dorado Beach
Hyatt Regency Cerromar

Humacao

Palmas del Mar

SHOPPING

In San Juan, the more upmarket shopping areas tend to be concentrated in the Old City and the Condado. Old San Juan boasts the more boutiquey atmosphere of the two. It's probably also what one could call more "authentic," with plenty of shops selling tourist baubles, curios, t-shirts and various other items. Among the better stores in the Old City are its jewelry shops, especially numerous along Fortaleza Street, which have signs reading "*Joyería*." Other specialties include leather and various arts and crafts, ancient and modern. Spanish imports can be found at **Espana en Puerto Rico** on Fortaleza Street. Also on Fortaleza, the **Butterfly People** restaurant sells much of its display. Rounding out the bohemian side of things, there's a famous hammock shop at the bottom of Cristo Street. **Gonzalez Padin**, the oldest department store on the island, is located right in the middle of town.

The Condado lures customers with slightly more money to spend, and thus sells more goods of lasting value. Clothing, porcelain, crystal, jewelry – each is represented in at least a handful of shops which are called "Boutique" or "Shoppe." There's less of a marketplace ambience in Condado, and a decidedly touristic tone to the merchandise there.

Hato Rey, Santurce and Isla Verde are more workaday marketplaces for permanent residents, places you'd go to buy a refrigerator or a television or a car.

An exception is **Plaza de las Americas**, the Caribbean's largest shopping mall, in Hato Rey. This is the best place on the island to go for *norteamericano* merchandise. It is rivalled by the **Plaza Carolinas** shopping center in Caroline. Other malls exist on the island, like the **Centro del Sur** in Ponce and the **Mayagüez Mall** in Mayagüez. Cities as small as Caguas and Cayey have malls of good size.

For traditional (barter) shopping in San Juan, the best marketplace is the **Plaza del Mercado**, a bustling outdoor affair in Río Piedras. Primarily a fruit market, the Plaza del Mercado nonetheless trucks in merchandise of all kinds. Prices are often unlisted and haggling can be intense. Miramar has a smaller market on the same model.

BOOKSTORES

The following have a good selection of books in both English and Spanish:

Bell
BF, 102 De Diego Ave., Santurce
Tel: 753-7140.
Also in Plaza Las Americas, Hato Rey, 753-7140.

Bookword
257 San José St., Old San Juan.

Cultural Puertorriqueña
1406 Fernández Juncos, Stop 20, Santurce
Tel: 721-5683.

B. Dalton
Plaza Carolina, Carolina
Tel: 752-1275.

Hermes
Ashford Avenue, Santurce.

Librería La Tertulia
Amalia Marín and Gonzalez, Río Piedras
Tel: 765-1148.

Librería Hispanoamericana
1013 Ponce de Leon, Río Piedras
Tel: 763-3415.

Thekes
Plaza Las Americas, Hato Rey
Tel: 765-1539.

SPORTS

PARTICIPANT

Swimming

Puerto Rico is ringed with sandy beaches, some of them outrageously popular, others secluded and quiet. Many are *balnearios*, public bathing facilities complete with lifeguards, refreshment stands, dressing rooms and parking lots. Of those around San Juan, the most popular are probably those at **Luquillo** and **Vega Baja**. But all of Puerto Rico's beaches are exceptional, and all beachfront – although the resort hotels will probably do their best to obscure this – is public. Swimmers are advised to be careful of strong surf and undertow at certain beaches, especially in the northwest.

Surfing

Puerto Rico has almost ideal conditions for surfing – warm water, brilliant sunshine and heavy but even tubular surf. Many of the most popular spots are convenient to San Juan: **Pine Grove**, off route 187 in Isla Verde is probably the most renowned, and **Aviones**, so named because of the airplanes that fly over from nearby Muñoz Marin Airport, is just a bit farther down the road in Pinones. In the northwest, **Punta Higüero**, off Route 413 in Rincón, is world famous, and hosted surfing's world championships a few years ago. In the southwest, Jobos Beach proves popular among Mayagüez residents.

Scuba and Snorkeling

Ringed by a submarine forest of coral and subject to some of the greatest variations in underwater depth in the world, Puerto Rico is prime scuba territory for those with the expertise. Those who would like to learn scuba in San Juan can get lessons at:

Caribbean School of Aquatics
1 Taft St., Suite 10-F Condado
Tel: 723-4740.

Caribe Aquatic Adventure
Caribe Hilton, Puerta de Tierra
Tel: 724-1307.

OUT ON THE ISLAND

Fajardo

Carlos A. Flores
Puerto Chico Marina
Tel: 863-0834.

Isabela

La Cueva Submarina
Plaza Cooperative
Tel: 872-3903.

Fajardo is probably the island's capital for water sports. For a relaxing sailing and diving adventure and an exploration of some of the smaller cays off Puerto Rico's east coast, contact:

Jack Becker
Villa Marina Yacht Harbor, Fajardo
Tel: 863-1905.

Snorkeling is also popular among diving pikers. Equipment can be rented or purchased at most dive shops and in certain department stores.

Sailing and Windsurfing

Most of Puerto Rico's sailors head to Fajardo for weekends on the water. Boats of all sizes and descriptions are available for rental. For more information, consult:

Villa Marina
Tel: 863-5131.

Puerto Chico
Tel: 863-0834.

Windsurfing is popular all over the island. Boards can be rented at most dive shops, including some of those listed above.

Fishing

Puerto Rico has no fresh-water fishing to speak of, but its deep-sea fishing is excellent, and many cruise boat companies offer reasonable rates for charters. In San Juan, these tend to be concentrated in Miramar. Here is a partial listing:

Benitez Deep-Sea Fishing

Mike Benitez Marine Services
Club Náutico de San Juan, Fernández Juncos, Stop 9½, Miramar
Tel: 723-2292, 724-6265.

San Juan Fishing Charter
Fernández Juncos, Stop 10, Miramar
Tel: 723-0415.

Golf and Tennis

Golf courses and tennis courts are scattered throughout the island, though most of the better ones are in the larger, more expensive resorts. There are certain arrangements, however, which one can make with these resorts to use their courts and courses on a user-fee basis.

Among the resorts with eighteen-hole championship golf courses are:

Hyatt Regency Cerromar Beach, Dorado
Tel: 796-1234, ext 3013.

Hyatt Dorado Beach
Dorado
Tel: 796-1234, ext 3239.

Palmas del Mar
Humacao
Tel: 852-6000, ext. 2525.

SPECTATOR

If Puerto Rico have a national pastime, it is baseball. The island has produced some of the greatest stars ever to play the game, and you can find someone to talk baseball with in almost any bar. The **Caribbean League** season runs from October to March, and there are teams in the largest cities. Many aspiring big-leaguers (and not a few has-beens) play in Puerto Rico. Games are almost daily, and tickets generally run under $10. Those who want to keep abreast of American and National League action will find complete box scores in all the local papers. Also, Atlanta Braves games are televised on certain national stations.

Basketball is another team sport popular on the island; the *Federación Nacional de Baloncesta de Puerto Rico* has teams in almost all the island's larger cities.

Horse racing in San Juan is at **El Comandante Racetrack** in Canovanas, 10 miles (15 km) east of the city. Races are held on Wednesdays, Fridays and Sundays at 2:30 p.m.; admission is $1-$3. For more information on races, dial 724-6060.

For a truly Puerto Rican sporting experience, it's hard to match cockfighting. In this sport, dozens of the proudest local cocks are matched one-on-one in a tiny ring, or *gallera*. The predominantly male crowds at most events are almost as entertaining as the fights themselves. These highly knowledgeable enthusiasts are often familiar with a cock's pedigree through several generations. The shouts are deafening, the drinking is reckless, and the betting is heavy. Betting is done on a gentlemanly system of verbal agreement, and hundreds of dollars can change hands on a single fight. Gallerias are scattered all over, and the fights in even the most rural areas can draw hundreds. Admission can be expensive ($8 in San Juan), but the beer is cheap. For information on cockfighting in the San Juan area, consult:

Club Gallistico de Puerto Rico
Carr. Isla Verde, Isla Verde
Tel: 791-1557.

Club Gallistico Río Piedras
Km 4.2. Carr. 844, Trujillo Alto
Tel: 760-8815.

LANGUAGE

The language of Puerto Rico is Spanish. While it is by no means true that "everyone there speaks English," a majority of Puerto Ricans certainly do, especially in San Juan. Almost everyone in a public service occupation will be able to help in either language.

The Puerto Rican dialect of Spanish resembles that of other Antillean islands, and differs from the Iberian dialect in its rapidity, phoneme quality and elisions. For a more detailed look at this rich tongue, see our feature *"Let's Hablar Boriqua."*

There are many excellent Spanish-English dictionaries, but **Barron's**, edited at the University of Chicago, is particularly recommended for its sensitivity to the vocabulary and syntax of the Latin-American idiom. Cristine Gallo's *The Language of the Puerto Rican Street* is an exhaustive lexicon of the kind of Puerto Rican slang most dictionaries would blanch at printing.

FURTHER READING

GENERAL

Peterson, Mendel L. *The Funnel of Gold*. Boston: Little Brown (1975).

Severin, Timothy. *The Golden Antilles*. New York: Knopf (1970).

Waugh, Alec. *A Family of Islands*. New York: Doubleday (1964).

Gordon, Raoul. *Puerto Rico: An Introduction*. New York: Gordon Books (1982).

Lopez, Adalberto (Editor). *Puerto Ricans: Their History, Culture and Society*. New York: Schenkman Books.

Petras, J. (Editor). *Puerto Rico and The Puerto Ricans: Studies In History And Society*. New York: Halsted (1974).

Puerto Rico In Pictures. Sterling Publishers.

Puerto Rico: The Riviera Of The West. Insular Government Bureau of Information Publications. New York: Gordon (1976).

White, Trumball. *Puerto Rico And Its People*. New York: Ayer and Co (1975).

HISTORY

Carrión, Arturo Morales (Editor). *Puerto Rico: A Political And Cultural History*. New York: W.W. Norton (1982).

Cordasco, Francesco. *Puerto Ricans, 1493-1973: A Chronology And Fact Book*. New York: Oceana (1973).

Gerber, Irving. *Puerto Rico Long Ago*. New York: Booklab (1978).

Maldonado-Denis, Manuel. *Puerto Rico: A Socio-Historic Interpretation*. Random (1972).

Mathews, Thomas. *Puerto Rican Politics And The New Deal*. New York: Da Capo (1976).

Puerto Ricans: A Brief Look At Their History. ADL.

Santana, Arturo F. *Puerto Rico And The United States In The Revolutionary Period Of Europe And America*. New York: Gordon Books (1979).

Woll, Allen. *Puerto Rican Historiography*. New York: Gordon Books (1979).

POLITICS

Carr, Raymond. *Puerto Rico: A Colonial Experiment*. New York: Random (1984).

Clark Victor S. *Puerto Rico And Its Problems*. New York: Ayer and Co (1975).

Friedrich, Carl J. *Puerto Rico: Middle Road To Freedom*. New York: Ayer and Co (1975).

Garcia, J. *Puerto Rico: Equality and Freedom At Issue*. New York: Praeger (1984).

Heine, Joyce and Juan M. Garcia-Passalacqua. *Puerto Rican Question*. New York: Foreign Policy (1983).

Johnson Roberta. *Puerto Rico: Commonwealth Or Colony?* New York: Praeger (1980).

Lewis, Gordon K. *Puerto Rico: Freedom And Power In The Caribbean*. New York: Monthly Review Press (1963).

Maldonado-Denis, Manuel. *The Emigrations Dialectic: Puerto Rico And The USA*. New York: International Publishers (1980).

Perl, Lila. *Puerto Rico: Island Between Two Worlds*. New York: Morrow (1979).

Perkins, Dexter. *The United States And The Caribbean*. Cambridge: Harvard University Press (1966).

Puerto Rico: The Search For A National Policy. Westview (1985).

Wagenheim, Kal. *Puerto Rico: A Profile*. New York: Praeger (1975).

Williams, Byron. *Puerto Rico: Commonwealth, State or Nation?* New York: Parents Magazine Press (1972).

MIGRATION

Garver, Susan and Paula McGuire. *Coming To North America*. New York: Dell (1984).

GEOGRAPHY

Beller, William S. (Editor). *Puerto Rico And The Sea*. Río Piedras: University of Puerto Rico Press (1974).

Masters, Robert V. *Puerto Rico In Pictures*. New York: Sterling Publications (1977).

Robinson, Kathryn. *The Other Puerto Rico*, San Juan (1984).

COOKERY

Cabanillas, Berta and Ginorio. *Puerto Rican Dishes*. 4th Edition. Río Piedras: University of Puerto Rico Press (1971).

Gordon, Raoul (Editor). *Puerto Rican And Caribbean Cookbook*. New York: Gordon Press (1982).

Hamelcourt, Juliette and the Culinary Arts Institute Staff. *The Caribbean Cookbook*. New York: Delair (1980).

Ortíz, Elizabeth L. *The Complete Book of Caribbean Cooking*. New York: M. Evans (1973).

Valldejuli, Carmen. *Puerto Rican Cookery*. 8th Edition. New York: Pelican (1983).

ARTS, CUSTOMS & SOCIAL LIFE

Acosta-Belen, Edna and Eli H. Christensen. *Puerto Rican Woman*. New York: Praeger (1979).

Cordasco, Francesco. *Puerto Rican Experience: A Sociological Sourcebook*. New York: Littlefield (1975).

Elisofon, Eliot. *A Week In Leonora's World*. New York: Crowell-Collier Press (1971).

Gordon, Raoul. *Puerto Rican Culture: An Introduction*. New York: Gordon Press (1982).

Puerto Rican Drama. New York: Gordon Press (1976).

Puerto Rican Folktales. New York: Gordon Books (1982).

Puerto Rican Music. New York: Gordon Books (1976).

Mason, J. Aldon (Editor). *Puerto Rican Folklore*. New York: Gordon Books (1979).

Maus, Cynthia P. *Puerto Rico In Pictures And Poetry*. New York: Gordon Press (1976).

Singer, Julia. *We All Come From Puerto Rico Too*. New York: Atheneum (1977).

FICTION

Rivera, Edward. *Family Installments*. New York: Morrow (1982).

Sánchez, Luiz Rafael. *Macho Camacho's Beat*. New York: Pantheon (1981).

Soto, Pedro Juan. *Spiks*. New York: Monthly Review (1974).

USEFUL ADDRESSES

TOURIST INFORMATION

Puerto Rico's tourism information facilities are unpredictable but generally worth a visit. The Puerto Rico Tourism Company has its main office at 301 San Justo St. in Old San Juan (Tel: (808) 721-2400). The best source of printed information on Puerto Rico tourism is **Qué Pasa**, the free booklet published each month by the Tourism Company. For a copy, write: Qué Pasa, Box 4435, Old San Juan Station, San Juan, PR 00905.

EMBASSIES & CONSULATES

Stop Numbers, where listed, are not part of the embassies' postal addresses. They are included as a convenience for those traveling to embassies by bus or automobile.

Argentina
Ponce de Leon, Stop 27
Hato Rey 00918
Tel: 754-6500.

Austria
1015 Ashford Ave
Condado 00907
Tel: 725-6878

Belgium
1250 Ponce de Leon
Stop 18, Santurce 00907
Tel: 725-3179.

Bolivia
10 Munet Court St.
Caparra Heights 00920
Tel: 759-7678.

Colombia
Mercantil Plaza, Suite 816
Hato Rey 00918
Tel: 754-1675.

Costa Rica
1661 Panasco
Paradise Hill Río Piedras 00926
Tel: 754-6301.

Denmark
400 Comercio, San Juan 00903
Tel: 725-2514.

Dominican Republic
Avianca Building, Seventh Flor
1612 Ponce de Leon
Stop 23, Santurce 00909
Tel: 725-9554.

El Salvador
Parkside Caparra 00907
Tel: 793-7576.

France
Mercantil Plaza, Suite 720
Ponce de Leon, Stop 27½
Hato Rey 00918
Tel: 753-1700.

Guatemala
Baihbosa Ave, Hato Rey 00918
Tel: 760-1001.

Federal Republic of Germany
Santa Bibiana No. 1618
Urb. Sagrado Corazón
Cupey 00926
Tel: 755-8228.

Haiti
Banco de San Juan, Office 909,
654 Muñoz Rivera, Hato Rey 00918
Tel: 753-0825.

Honduras
E' Corrito St., Guayuado 00657
Tel: 720-1263.

Italy
Amatista Ave., San Juan 00907
Tel: 793-5284.

Japan
Banco Popular, Fifth Floor
San Juan 00904
Tel: 721-4667.

Korea
543 Caroline, Hato Rey 00918
Tel: 751-2255

Mexico
Banco Cooperativo, Office 305
Floor C, 623 Ponce de Leon
Hato Rey 00918
Tel: 764-0258.

Monaco
Madrid No. 2, Santurce 00907
Tel: 721-4215.

The Netherlands
Caribe Shipping Muelle 9
San Juan 00904
Tel: 724-2157.

Nicaragua
1476 Las Palmas St.
Santurce, 00909
Tel: 723-7266.

Norway
400 Comercio
San Juan 00903
Tel: 725-2514.

Paraguay
1350 Ashford Ave., Apt. R-1-A
Condado 00907
Tel: 724-3056.

Peru
1700 Jazmin, Urb. San Francisco
Río Piedras 00927
Tel: 763-0679.

Portugal
Apartado S-3746
San Juan 00904
Tel: 721-2061

Spain
Mercantil Plaza, Suite 1101
Ponce de Leon, Stop 27½
Hato Rey 00918
Tel: 758-6090.

Switzerland
105 De Diego, A/C Swiss Chalet
Santurce 00914
Tel: 721-2233.

Uruguay
251 Himalayans
Río Piedras 00926
Tel: 764-7941.

Venezuela
Mercantile Plaza Office 601
Hato Rey 00918
Tel: 766-4250.

ART/PHOTO CREDITS

Photography by

248/249	**APA Photo Agency**
Page 3, 12/13, 16/17, 26, 49, 66, 67,	**Tony Arruza**
68, 69, 70, 71, 74, 80/81, 116/117,	
128, 129, 138/139, 148, 150/151,163,	
172, 200/201, 226/227, 238, 264	
28, 31, 40/41, 42, 57, 61, 267, 271	**Reproduced from *Historia de Puerto* **
	***Rico*, by Salvador Brau**
34/35, 43, 47, 42, 57, 61, 267, 271	**Reproduced from *Our Islands and* **
	***Their People*, by William S. Bryan**
Cover	**Pat Canova**
254/255, 256/257, 258, 259, 260, 261,	**Stephen Frink**
262/263	
242	**Sandra P. Newbury**
232/233	**Courtesy of Rum of Puerto Rico**
6/7, 14/15, 161, 251, 57, 61, 267, 271	**Edmond Van Hoorick**
5, 8/9, 10/11, 18, 20/21, 22, 23, 24,	**Bill Wassman**
25, 27, 29, 30, 32, 33, 36, 37, 38, 44,	
45, 48, 51, 52/53, 54/55, 56/57, 58,	
59, 60, 61, 62, 63, 64, 65, 72/73,	
78/79, 82, 86, 87, 88, 89, 90, 91, 92,	
973, 94, 95, 96, 97, 98, 99,	
100/101, 102/103, 104, 105, 106, 107,	
108, 109, 110, 111, 112, 113, 114,	
115, 118/119, 120/121, 122, 124, 125,	
126, 127, 130, 131, 132, 133, 134,	
135, 136, 137, 140/141, 142, 144, 145,	
146, 147, 149, 152/153, 154, 155, 156,	
157, 158, 159, 160, 162, 164/165,	
166/167, 168, 170, 171, 173, 174,	
175, 176, 177, 178, 179, 180, 181,	
182/183, 184/185, 186, 188, 189, 190,	
191, 192, 193, 195, 196, 197, 198/199,	
202/203, 204, 206, 207, 208, 209, 210,	
211, 212, 213, 214, 215, 216, 217,	
218, 219, 221, 222/223, 224/225,	
228/229, 234, 235, 236/237, 239, 240,	
241, 243, 244, 245, 246, 247, 250,	
252, 253	

Maps	**Berndtson & Berndston**
Illustrations	**Klaus Geisler**
Visual Consulting	**V. Barl**

INDEX

A

B

N – O

P – Q

T

U – V

W – Z